American Government

Second Edition

American Government

Structure and Process

Michael A. Krasner
Queens College, City University of New York

Stephen G. Chaberski

Macmillan Publishing Co., Inc.
New York

Collier Macmillan Publishers
London

To Deborah
M. K.

To Christopher
S.C.

Macmillan Publishing Co., Inc.
866 Third Avenue, New York, New York 10022

Collier Macmillan Canada, Inc.

Library of Congress Cataloging in Publication Data

Krasner, Michael A.
   American government.

   Includes bibliographies and index.
   1. United States—Politics and government.   I. Chaberski, Stephen G.   II. Title.
JK274.K725   1982   320.973   81-5404
ISBN 0-02-366270-0   AACR2

Printing: 1 2 3 4 5 6 7 8   Year: 2 3 4 5 6 7 8 9

Preface

Our second edition retains the general approach of the first. Our purpose is to present the basic structures of American government and to explain their internal processes as well as the ways in which they interact. We intend also to indicate the significance of these basic facts. Thus (we hope), an attentive student will not only learn the "nuts and bolts" of such institutions as the electoral college, the committee system, and the bureaucracy, but also how these details influence the distribution of power and benefits. We leave value judgements on these issues to the reader.

Of course, the book has been updated and expanded to cover recent events and to respond to suggestions from colleagues and students. Our revisions include discussions of the Carter administration and the stunning early events of the Reagan presidency. Further additions are an extended discussion of the constitution, two new case studies, one on foreign affairs and one on domestic politics, and a consideration of the trends and prospects of the 1980s.

The book's organization is essentially unchanged.

In Chapter 1 we discuss the substance of the Constitution—federalism, bases of representation, methods of election, assignments of power, and so forth—as well as traditions, history, and interests that informed and shaped the framing of the Constitution. We have added an extended discussion of constitutional development.

Chapter 2, "The Presidency," covers formal powers, such as the veto and the function of the commander-in-chief, as well as informal roles such as party leader and chief legislator. These are all illustrated by references to recent conflicts over control of foreign policy and the budget. The institution of the modern White House is described in detail, and its workings in relation to other parts of the government are explained. The chapter compares the styles and working methods of different Presidents. Ronald Reagan's early successes are examined in detail.

In Chapter 3 we present the basic facts about Congress, the number of committees and subcommittees, the powers of the committee chairmen, the procedures for passing legislation; but we also discuss congressional norms and the factors that influence the place of Congress in American politics. The chapter includes discussions of recent trends in Congressional elections, the prospects for 1982, and the recent difficulties of the Democratic leadership.

Chapter 4 discusses the Supreme Court's constitutional responsibilities and its procedures and jurisdictions, as well as the selection of its members. The chapter also considers the Court's role in the political system. Another section of this chapter describes the federal court system and discusses two proposed changes in that system.

Chapter 5 begins by defining bureaucracy—both as a kind of organization and as a part of the federal government. The different types of bureaucratic agency are described. The chapter then considers the workings of these organizations as elements in the political system, including the relations of bureaucratic organizations to interest groups and to other parts of the federal government.

After looking at the main institutions of the national government, we turn to some of those extremely significant nongovernmental elements at work in our political system. Chapter 6 views the bases and structures of interest groups and then considers the behavior and influence of these groups in American politics. The topics covered include the idea of an interest, the types of interest groups, the means and styles of applying pressure, and the results of these actions on the system generally.

Chapter 7 deals with public opinion, including the process of political socialization, voting behavior and elections, and political parties. Various party systems are defined, and party organizations are described. The possibilities of realignment are discussed. The chapter concludes with a consideration of the idea of responsible political parties.

Among nongovernmental institutions affecting the political system, the media, we believe, often get less attention than they should.

Because most of us depend on newspapers, journals, television, and radio for our information about politics, and because the media do influence other political actors in important ways, we have devoted Chapter 8 to this subject. We hope this extensive description and analysis of the structures and processes that produce the news will alert readers and viewers to the biases and deficiencies of the media while informing them of the media's actual role in politics.

Chapters 9 and 10 consider, respectively, policymaking and a number of contemporary issues and trends. In chapter 9 we attempt through two extended case studies to show how the institutions previously described in general terms operate in specific situations. We discuss the individuals, ideas, strategies, power resources, and historical circumstances that shaped the processes and results of policymaking on a recent foreign policy issue—relations with China and Taiwan—and a recent domestic issue—the creation of the Department of Education.

Throughout the book, we have stressed description and avoided value judgments. We leave it to the reader to decide what is good or bad. Before that decision can be made, one must have the facts of the matter. These we provide.

Acknowledgments

Many people have made helpful suggestions and comments on our first edition. We would like to thank particularly Solomon Resnik, Rennie Fulco, Patricia Rachal, Martin Bresnick, Jay S. Goodman, Fred Fox, and Laura Abelack. Thanks also to our stalwart editors at Macmillan, Clark Baxter and Dave Novack.

M. A. K.
S. G. C.

Contents

1 Introduction

The Recent Past

During the period 1974–1980 political scientists, reporters, historians and working politicians stated often and vehemently that political fragmentation had seriously undermined the ability to govern America. Congress had become so decentralized that no president could lead effectively. A profusion of single issue groups, lobbying in Washington, made coherent policymaking impossible.

By August of 1981, however, many of these statements seemed as obsolete as a wood-burning stove. Bolstered by his election victory, a well organized White House staff, effective Congressional liaison, a strong set of televised speeches, and skillful old fashioned wheeling and dealing, Ronald Reagan has demonstrated once again that a president can dominate national policymaking.

Reagan's victories on economic issues—budget cuts and tax reductions—were especially impressive because the opposition Democrats controlled the House of Representatives. But these victories do not necessarily mean that Reagan will dominate on other issues. First, he may not even try to lead on controversial social issues such as abortion law or school prayer. Second, he may not succeed if he does try. Similarly, he may not dominate the making of foreign policy. Already members of Congress have criticized his El Salvador policy and his plan to sell AWACs to Saudi Arabia.

The political circumstances of these issues differ from the circumstances of the economic issues. Most Americans, tired of inflation and slow economic growth, were willing to support the President's plan in the hope that things would improve. Large corporations and conservative interest groups gave him powerful backing. Will the same groups work hard to restore prayer in the public schools? Some will, but others may not. Will the majority of the people so readily follow the President on abortion or busing? It seems unlikely.

We raise these questions to indicate the dangers of generalizing from a few recent examples. Just as changes in oil prices brought back the wood-burning stove, so political changes have restored a powerful presidency and may change yet again to make Congress powerful.

In this book we will describe and explain the institutional framework, including the presidency, the Congress, the courts, and the political parties, in which such power shifts occur and in which President Reagan will continue to operate. In order to understand this framework more clearly, we begin by reviewing the historical and constitutional forces that molded today's institutions.

The Colonial Experience

The pattern of America's governmental institutions is rooted in its colonial past. It was there that the American ideology of government was formed. If, to paraphrase Harold Lasswell, politics is the process of determining who gets what among society's scarce resources, and if government is the instrument through which that process is carried out, then a society's institutions will reflect its understanding of how best to make those allocations. America's institutional framework was created at a time when its history as a set of English colonies, three thousand miles and more than two months' traveling time away from the heart of Western civilization, was fresh in the minds of the framers of the Constitution.

A number of characteristics of the colonial period are reflected in the subsequent structure of American government. The ancient European institution of feudalism had not been transplanted from the Old World to the New. Consequently, there was no aristocracy whose membership was determined by birth and that enjoyed separate legal rights. America was "classless" in that sense (aside from that "peculiar institution"—slavery). Every citizen was the equal of any other, at least in legal terms. Whatever social stratification occurred developed mostly from differences in earned wealth or recently acquired family property. This had some legal consequences, such as the right to vote, which in some areas depended on owning a certain small amount of property. But, because no one had superior standing by virtue of noble birth (a detested concept), wealth differentials could be assumed to be, by and large, the product of hard work, skill, and "proper" living. American society could be seen (especially by those who had achieved some success, but even by the many for whom the achievers served as models) as a classless meritocracy, or what Alexander Hamilton conceived of as an aristocracy of talent rather than of birth.

Because many of the immigrants to the New World had been fleeing religious persecution, America developed a strong sense of religious tolerance. Despite Quaker Pennsylvania, Catholic Maryland, and Puritan New England, the colonists generally opposed a state-supported or established church. This feeling was incorporated as one of the fundamental freedoms protected by the Bill of Rights.

Colonial governmental institutions, together with the experiences gained from operating within those institutions, strongly influenced America's development. Widely separated settlements in the early days required a good deal of self-government. The town meeting, especially in the north, became the model of democracy and freedom, an ideal that remains firmly entrenched in this country. Because most of the colonies initially received a "charter" from the king (a document authorizing the existence of the colony as well as its purpose), the founders of the country were accustomed to the concept of an organic superlaw. This paved the way for the desire to create first the Articles of Confederation and, a decade later, the Constitution as the "supreme law of the land."

Popularly elected legislatures were regular features of the colonies. Because they were local in origin, in contrast to the king's appointed governors, the legislatures were seen as the people's representatives, struggling against the tyranny of an executive power that represented not the colonists but a foreign sovereign. Finally, the colonial experience was an expansive and exploratory one. A new country had to be settled; the vast land had to be cleared and planted; and the wilderness had to be tamed. Virtually unlimited resources were out there waiting to be taken, and the taking needed little in the way of government, except to build a few roads and to counter the sporadic opposition of the native Americans whose rights did not count for much.

The Constitutional Framework

One can find a nearly direct line from these colonial experiences to their postcolonial ideological and structural counterparts. Because it was the king's abuse of his power that had led to revolution, power came to be distrusted and concentrated power came to be feared. Consequently, government was to be limited and divided among institutions (in a large part of the country not much was needed anyway), in order to prevent the concentration of power that might be capable of abuse. The supreme document would give only certain delegated powers to the central government, all others to be retained by the noncentral units.

The states, in fact, were the most important unit of government. The constitutional union, born after the brief and unhappy tenure of the Articles of Confederation, was to be a federal one. Although it was recognized that it was necessary for the federal government to be strong enough to carry out the tasks to be assigned to it, the concept of federalism meant that the states were distinct entities, each with its own jurisdiction, surrendering together only limited and specified powers to that federal government. All other governmental powers were left to reside with the states. Although the federal government was to be supreme in those areas in which it was delegated power to act, and although it was entitled to take all the measures "necessary and proper" to carry out its functions, the states were still to be the fundamental units of government. The ex-colonists had not yet forgotten their original colonial attachments.

Even the limited authority given to the federal government accorded it a substantial amount of power. This, too, had to be broken up, with the power dispersed among several institutions. This constitutional scheme is commonly known as the separation of powers. But Richard Neustadt probably describes it more accurately by characterizing it as "separated institutions sharing power."

The legislative, or lawmaking, power was given to a Congress composed of two houses, one elected on the basis of population, the other by equal state representation. The executory, or enforcement, power was vested in a President, elected at four-year intervals by a "college" of outstanding citizens selected by the states. The adjudicatory, or judging, power was granted to "one Supreme Court" and other lesser ones to be created by the Congress at a later time. In many instances, however, the different powers overlap to some extent. For example, if an administrative agency makes rules to guide private conduct in a certain area of subject matter and determines who is violating those rules, is that the exercise of legislative, executive, or judicial power? It is not always clear which branch of government is properly exercising what power. Although the institutions are separated from each other, they all share the power granted to the federal government.

Not only do the powers overlap, but the system popularly known as checks and balances adds to the inaccuracy of the term *separation of powers.* Congress can make laws, but the President can veto and, thereby, undo Congress' work (subject only to being overridden by a two-thirds vote). The Supreme Court can invalidate a law passed by Congress and signed by the President by deciding cases as if the law did not exist, provided it deems the law to be contrary to the Constitution. Although Court Justices serve for life, it is the President who appoints them and a house of Congress that must confirm the appointment. The President can negotiate and sign treaties, but they do not become effective unless the Senate ratifies them. These, and many, many others like them, are instances in which a substantive power, appropriate to be exercised by the central government, is shared by two or three institutions. One institution can "check" the other by refusing to cooperate. In this way a balance among the federal institutions is sought that might prevent the dominance of one institution through the excessive centralization of power.

But if balance and the fear of dominance are one side of the separation-of-powers issue, the other side bears the necessary consequences. If the separated institutions share power and cannot draw clear lines in the gray areas, it is foreseeable, if not inevitable, that the institutions will be in competition for the decisive voice in those gray areas. If there is one theme presented by this book, it is that American national government is characterized by institutional conflict and competition. Indeed, the system is rigged to produce such conflict because of the constitutional ground rules. Those rules pit the institutions against each other by requiring joint effort in many areas, by not clearly defining the appropriate boundaries of each branch, and by not providing a mechanism to enforce cooperation when it is not forthcoming voluntarily or a mechanism that would render cooperation unnecessary. The political skill of the artful compromise is doubly necessary in a system that has no machinery for resolving disputes among those who share power. And, with the passage of time, the boundaries of institutional power will change, as new circumstances give rise to different political alignments and forces.

Institutions in government are centers of power. Three power centers are expressly established in American national government by the Constitution: Congress, the Presidency, and the Supreme Court. But, in the more than two centuries since the Philadelphia convention, several other power centers have evolved through extraconstitutional or nonconstitutional means. These institutions have developed in good part to meet certain needs that the formal, named institutions could not or would not fulfill.

Political parties, which help organize the political and electoral processes, are one such institution. Nowhere are parties mentioned in the Constitution. Indeed, in 1787 they did not exist in any form we might recognize as a political party. They are, nonetheless, one of the significant structural elements of American government.

The federal bureaucracy is another power center. Although the Constitution, in retrospect, seems to hint at this institution by reference to executive departments, its emergence as a center of power together with its vast size are certainly beyond the scope envisioned initially by the framers. Interest groups (or pressure groups) form centers of power around particular issues or economic interests. They, too, were only vaguely envisioned by the framers as part of the structure of American politics. And, although freedom of the press was guaranteed in 1791, the news media were not then a power center, despite the partisan political nature of most eighteenth-century newspapers. The growth of the press over the years has given it a role to play among the institutions of government that make it a vital part of the structure of government.

In the chapters that follow, the structural elements of these American governmental institutions, both constitutional and extra- or nonconstitutional, are described. Descriptions of the characteristic behavior of those institutions also are provided. And, for illustrative purposes, two brief examples of institutional conflict are given. It must be remembered that although each of the institutions is described separately, these institutions are interrelated and share in the governing of America.

The Changing Constitution

Before beginning the description of the American government institutions as they exist today, it is appropriate to consider and discuss briefly how two centuries of constitutional growth and development have structured American government and its processes.

The first organic superlaw of the new republic was the Articles of Confederation. Proposed to the states by the Continental Congress in 1777, the Articles were not fully ratified until 1781, when Congress met for the first time under the Articles. The Articles basically provided for annual meetings of the states "in Congress assembled" to conduct the business of the United States, each state having one vote. In the interim between these meetings, a "Committee of the States" would manage affairs. The Committee was to consist of one delegate from each state, one of their number to preside but to serve no more frequently than one year out of three. No judicial power was provided for. Canada was invited to accede to the union.

Within a few years, however, dissatisfaction arose over the inadequacy of the Articles. Among the primary causes of complaint was the inability of the "confederate" government to raise revenues on its own, having to rely on appropriations from the states that were often slow or even delinquent in submitting the funds. This meant that the credit of the United States was unreliable, which caused consternation among those interests which had lent money to, or had other commerical dealings with, the government. The perceived powerlessness of the Congress to meet the exigencies of government led Congress, spurred on especially by the larger, commercial states, to resolve to call for a convention that would make another attempt at creating "a more perfect Union."

This constitutional convention met in 1787 and produced an eloquent and elegant document that was largely drafted by James Madison. When this document was ratified by New Hampshire in 1788 (the ninth state to do so), it became the Constitution of the United States.

The Constitution (printed at the back of this book) is organized in a straightforward manner. Many of the significant provisions of the Constitution are discussed in later chapters, but structurally it deals with the following: Article One—the legislative power of the United States; Article Two—the executive power; Article Three— the judicial power; Article Four—general provisions primarily concerning relationships among the states; Article Five—procedures for amendment (Anything in the Constitution can be changed except for equal representation of states in the Senate.); Article Six—provisions for payment of preconstitutional debts, supremacy of federal law, and oaths of office (which cannot require a "religious test"); and Article Seven—ratification.

Analysis of the legal implications of the provisions of the Constitution is beyond the scope of this work, but it is worth noting how the document has been altered since its ratification to meet the changing or later-realized needs of society. Although two methods of proposing constitutional amendments are provided by Article Five, there has never been another constitutional "convention." Similarly, although two methods of ratification are provided, all amendments to the Constitution have been ratified by the state legislatures, except for the twenty-first amendment, which repealed Prohibition (probably because Congress feared that elected state legislators would be reluctant to "come out for alcohol").

The first ten amendments were formally proposed promptly after ratification of the original Constitution. These were basically expressions of Thomas Jefferson's concern that the federal government might have geen given too much power and needed to be restricted. The first eight of these amendments are a list of specific things that the federal government is forbidden to do; the ninth and tenth amendments make it clear that the people and the states retain all powers not given to the federal government.

Historians have noted that Jefferson's acquiescence to the new Constitution was conditioned upon prior agreement that the first Congress would propose these amendments. The political battle over the ratification of the Constitution was a virulent one. The documents now known as *The Federalist Papers* (most of which were written by Madison and Alexander Hamilton) were originally a collection of pro-Constitution polemics, many appearing first in local newspapers. They were a response to the strong anticonstitutional feeling that arose from fears about centralized power which stemmed from colonial times. Jefferson, around whom anti-Federalist opinion collected, was persuaded not to oppose the Constitution in substantial part because his political opponents agreed to support what came to be known as the "Bill of Rights," a phrase pirated from an English parliamentary enactment of 1688.

Two more amendments followed shortly thereafter. When individuals began to sue states other than their own (particularly with respect to land claims in the unsettled regions west of the Appalachians) and received a sympathetic ear from federal judges, Congress and the states soon put an end to the practice by proposing and ratifying the eleventh amendment in 1795. This effectively deprived such suitors of any chance of success, leaving them at the mercy of state judges.

In the presidential election of 1800, Jefferson's Republicans were overwhelmingly successful against Hamilton's Federalists. Under the procedures then in effect, each presidential elector cast two ballots; the person receiving the most electoral votes became President and the person receiving the next highest number became Vice President. It happened that each elector who favored the Jeffersonians cast one ballot for Jefferson and one for Aaron Burr, Jefferson's running mate who was intended to be Vice President. Jefferson and Burr therefore each had the same number of votes, causing a deadlock that was broken only when Hamilton, who opposed Jefferson but despised Burr, threw his support to Jefferson.

As a result of this unanticipated electoral problem, Congress proposed and the states ratified the twelfth amendment which provided, among other things, that electors would cast ballots separately for President and Vice President.

The outcome of the Civil War provided the impetus for the next three constitutional amendments. Congress and the legislatures of most states were controlled by Republicans and the victorious states had little trouble with the amendments. (The rebellious states of the Confederacy were required to approve the amendments as a condition of their readmission to the Union in good standing.) The thirteenth amendment abolished slavery, and the fourteenth amendment made the former slaves citizens, provided for "equal protection of the laws" for citizens of each state, and somewhat ambiguously appeared to forbid states from depriving citizens of rights provided for in the Constitution. The fifteenth amendment guaranteed the former slaves the right to vote.

The next constitutional change arose out of Congress's attempt to levy a federal tax on the income earned by individuals and businesses. In 1894 the Supreme Court ruled that the income tax violated Clause 4 of Section 9 of the first Article of the Constitution on the ground that the clause prohibited direct taxation of persons except in proportion to population. Because income taxation had popular support and was an effective method to raise revenue that was desperately needed by the federal government, Congress and the states "overruled" the Supreme Court and in 1913 approved the sixteenth amendment, which specifically gave Congress the power to tax incomes.

The next three amendments arose out of popular outcries from varying sources. The constitutional requirement that Senators be chosen by state legislatures was thought to be antidemocratic, depriving the people of a direct voice in choosing their legislators. The seventeenth amendment, also ratified in 1913, provided that senators from each state would be "elected by the people thereof."

The eighteenth amendment stemmed from a different source of popular discontent. The view that alcoholic beverages were a source of immoral, disreputable, or illegal behavior was widespread and had the support of well organized *ad hoc* groups such as the multitude of

Temperance Societies. The electoral process, or more pointedly the fear of legislators of being defeated for reelection, impelled Congress to propose, and the state legislatures to ratify, the eighteenth amendment as an expression of social concern. By the Volstead Act, Congress implemented the constitutional policy that ushered in the period widely known as Prohibition.

The political ferment around the turn of the century had also given rise to the movement known as "women's suffrage." As early as 1873, Susan B. Anthony had been convicted of the "crime" of voting, although she was legally ineligible to vote, in a trial that was notable for at least two other anomalies: a justice of the Supreme Court sat as trial judge, and there was a directed verdict of guilty. A society in which only men could choose their governors (although two states allowed women to vote) was eventually persuaded to extend the franchise to women by the nineteenth amendment in 1920.

A narrower concern was addressed by the twentieth amendment. At least since 1804, the term of a newly elected President had begun on March 4 of the year following an election. This meant that Congress could meet for several months with a "lame-duck" President, giving rise not only to a period of uncoordinated action but also providing an extended opportunity for the kind of mischief that had culminated in the famous Supreme Court case of Marbury v. Madison (see Chapter 4). In doubt about their ability to change this situation merely by legislation, Congress proposed amending the Constitution to provide that presidential terms would commence on January 20 and the terms of congressmen would begin on January 3 of the year following election.

With the twenty-first amendment, Congress and the states, for the first and only time thus far, admitted a mistake in the politics of amendment. They ended Prohibition by repealing the eighteenth amendment. Apparently the array of political forces had changed sufficiently so that legislators felt safe in voting for "demon rum."

President Franklin D. Roosevelt's four electoral victories spurred the movement for the twenty-second amendment in 1951, which provided (except as to then-incumbent President Truman) for a limit of two terms for a President. This restored the old "tradition" begun by Washington and Jefferson of serving no more than two terms.

The twenty-third, twenty-fourth, and twenty-sixth amendments were all concerned with voting rights. Congress and the states respectively gave the right to vote for President to residents of the District of Columbia in 1961, prohibited a poll tax in 1964, and allowed eighteen-year-olds to vote in 1971. Considered together with the fifteenth, the nineteenth, and (to a lesser extent) the seventeenth amendments, these later amendments evince a steadily evolving and expanding concern with the right to vote and make the franchise the most common subject for amendment of the Constitution.

Finally, the second most persistent concern—selection of the President—gave rise to the twenty-fifth amendment. Responding to the vice-presidential vacancy caused by the assassination of President Kennedy and to the worries engendered by President Eisenhower's bouts with heart trouble, Congress and the states approved in 1967 a procedure for the selection of a Vice President when a vacancy occurs and another procedure to guard against the inability by the President to discharge the duties of his office. It was only six years later that President Nixon exercised the former of these powers by appointing Gerald R. Ford as Vice President upon the resignation of Spiro T. Agnew.

Despite the substantive expansion of the right to vote, the procedural alterations in the selection and succession of the chief executive, and the changes wrought (or perhaps only ratified) by the abolition of slavery, surprisingly little of the formal mechanics of national government have been modified by constitutional change. Congress, the presidency, and the Supreme Court still exist and still have roughly the same guiding principles and restrictions they have had for two centuries. The primary differences between the governmental institutions of the founding fathers and those of today are in the business of governmental institutions and in the birth and growth of extraconstitutional institutions. It is to these modern structures that we now turn.

GLOSSARY

Amendment   A formal change in the constitution.

Articles of Confederation   The first constitution of the United States which created a very weak central government, leaving most power with the states.

Bill of Rights   The name given to the first ten amendments of the present constitution which contain a list of individual rights and freedoms including freedon of speech, religion, and the press.

Checks and Balances The system incorporated into our present constitution by which separate institutions share power, and prevent any particular institution from becoming too powerful.

Constitution The fundamental law of a country which overrides any ordinary law, establishes a plan of government, and defines individual freedoms.

Federalism A system of government in which power is shared among a central government (called the "federal government" in the United States) and constituent governments (called "states").

Political Action Committee (PAC) A group organized to solicit and distribute campaign contributions; created by the 1976 amendments to the 1974 Campaign Finance Reform Act.

SUGGESTIONS FOR FURTHER READING

Bailyn, Bernard. *The Ideological Origins of the American Revolution.* Cambridge, Mass.: Harvard University Press, 1967.

Beard, Charles A. *An Economic Interpretation of the Constitution.* New York: Macmillan, 1913.

Becker, Carl L. *The Declaration of Independence.* New York: Vintage Books, 1942.

Corwin, Edward S. *The Constitution and What It Means Today,* 14th ed. Rev. by Harold W. Chase and Craig R. Ducat. Princeton, N.Y.: Princeton University Press, 1978.

Farrand, Max. *The Framing of the Constitution of the United States.* New Haven, Comm.: Yale University Press, 1913.

Federalist Papers. By Alexander Hamilton, James Madison, and John Jay. New York: New American Library, 1961.

McDonald, Forrest. *We The People.* Chicago: University of Chicago Press, 1958.

Wills, Garry. *Inventing America.* Garden City, N.Y.: Doubleday, 1978.

———. *Explaining America.* Garden City, N.Y.: Doubleday, 1981.

2 The Presidency

Introduction—President and Presidency

We begin with the **presidency** because of its prominence and because of the common perception that it has become the most powerful part of the federal government. People often think of the President and the Presidency as being the same. They visualize the President and recall his appearance, speech, manner, and actions. People know a great deal about the President—his family, hobbies, even his eating habits. Attention to the President's personal life distracts from the institution of which he is a part—the presidency.

The **presidency** is an institution in the sense of being a set of powers, procedures, and expectations, some of which are derived from the Constitution, others from laws, and still others from precedent and custom. Divided by subject or function, the presidency becomes a set of **roles**—the President as **party leader,** as **chief legislator,** as **chief foreign policy maker.** Presidents are strengthened and sometimes limited by their roles. Each President must decide which of these roles to emphasize and how to play them. These decisions make the presidency the most personal office in the federal government.

The **presidency** is also an institution in the sense of being a group of people—the White House staff and the executive office of the President—who work directly for the President. Although most people think of the White House as the place where the President lives, most of the rooms are offices where several hundred staffers work. The White House is thus mainly an office building where the President and a part of the presidency both work. In this chapter, we discuss the origins, development, and present shape of this institution.

The Constitutional Framework

In Philadelphia in the summer of 1787 debate over the proper form and selection process for the executive ranged over many different alternatives. The delegates to the Constitutional Convention—a number of whom had taken prominent roles in the American Revolution—were understandably prejudiced against kings. Alexander Hamilton's plan for establishing a virtual monarchy in the form of a lifetime chief executive gained no support. On the other hand, the six years of the Articles of Confederation had exposed the need for a stronger central government as well as the weaknesses of legislative government without an independent executive. To many of the delegates, strong legislatures appeared to be dangerously radical and inept. Popular government had to be checked by an independent executive who could guarantee the smooth functioning of the nation's economic life and could adequately protect the citizens of the new nation from foreign threats. The question, then, was not whether there should be an executive, but rather how strong (or weak) the executive should be.

The debates in Philadelphia were inconclusive. Not all the delegates favored a strong executive. Some favored a plural executive; others a President chosen by Congress; and there was support for a direct popular election. Some preferred an executive highly dependent on Congress; others felt that the chief executive should be, within limits, autonomous and selfdirecting and relatively independent of the legislative branch.

The Constitution did not resolve all of these controversies. Instead it postponed most of them, leaving the task of defining the Presidency to the future requirements of the nation. Specifically, the Constitution of 1787 provided only that the President be chosen independently of Congress by electors from each state every four years; that the President was eligible for reelection; that the President was to be **commander in chief** of the armed forces of the United States; that he had the power to grant reprieves and pardons for offenses against the nation; that he could make treaties with foreign nations with the consent of two thirds of the Senate; that he would appoint ambassadors and judges of the Supreme Court and lower courts with the consent of the Senate; and that he could approve or veto bills from Congress. He could also require in writing the opinions of the heads of the executive departments, receive foreign ambassadors, and call special sessions of Congress.

The Constitution established the presidency as an independent institution, defined its constituency, and gave the President quite specific, if limited, powers. Yet even these limited grants of authority would become the subjects of future controversy. What does the term *commander in chief* really mean? Did the framers of the Constitution intend that the President could order American forces into conflict situations anywhere? Or did that require congressional assent? Did the power to make treaties with foreign nations upon the consent of the Senate include the power to make agreements that were not specifically treaties? And could the President do so without

congressional consent? Did the power of the President to compel
written opinions from the heads of the departments also require him
to allow Congress to see those documents? If so, in what
circumstances?

The Constitution also gave the President broader and more
vaguely defined powers. Article II, Section 1 provides that "The
executive Power shall be vested in a President of the United States
of America." But what is meant by the term *executive power?* Does
it allow the President, in extraordinary circumstances, to defy
congressional law? Article II, Section 3 further states that "he shall
take care that the laws be faithfully executed . . ." Does the obligation to execute the laws faithfully permit the President to halt the
spending of funds that Congress has appropriated?

These questions, and many others, were not resolved by the
authors of the Constitution. The Constitution thus established little
more than general ground rules that would loosely govern the struggles among the three separate, but overlapping, branches of government. Like the other branches of government, the powers of the presidency would reflect the needs of the times and the expansion of
demands, both foreign and domestic, that would confront the
nation's leaders.

Getting into Office—Presidential Nominations

Presidential elections are discussed in Chapter 7. In this section
we will consider the recent changes in the nomination process and
the consequences of these changes for the political system. The term
nomination means being selected as the candidate of a party. The
description that follows applies to the two major political parties.

The Old System.   From 1824 to 1960 state and city bosses, interest group leaders, and other party notables gathered at a national
convention to decide the party's platform and to choose the national
candidates. As professionals who were concerned with patronage and
other spoils of victory, they sought to unify the party by choosing
candidates and a platform that was acceptable to the party's major
blocs. Compromise was the order of the day.

Convention delegates voted as their party leaders directed them.
Candidates or their representatives bargained in the smoke-filled
rooms, trading cabinet seats, postmasterships, and platform planks

for convention support. One famous story has Abraham Lincoln telegraphing his campaign manager before the 1860 Republican convention, "Make no deals on my behalf." Fortunately, the manager ignored the order and gained Lincoln's nomination by bargaining away every seat in the cabinet. Whatever the specifics may have been in a particular year, attention to the interests of organized groups was always essential. No presidential candidate could depart substantially from the party consensus.

Three elements have transformed this system: the spread of presidential primaries, held in more than thirty states in 1980; the growth of mass media, especially television; and the nationalization of politics. The last factor has reduced the importance of the regional issues, such as race relations in the South, that sustained state parties and regional blocs. Primaries have taken delegate selection away from the party leaders and opened the state political systems to outsiders. Television has complemented primaries by enabling unknown candidates quickly to gain recognition in particular locales and in the country generally.

The New System—The Politics of Self-nomination. Under the new system, candidates nominate themselves by competing for delegates in primaries, local caucuses, and state conventions. A strong personal organization, an effective television image, and an appealing campaign theme that mobilizes volunteers and primary voters are the essential resources.

Thus, in 1972, George McGovern won the Democratic presidential nomination despite the opposition of such party stalwarts as Richard J. Daley, the major of Chicago, and George Meany, the head of the AFL-CIO. The declining city machines and the labor unions could not stop the McGovern candidacy, which drew its main support from the antiwar movement.

No independent movement sustained Jimmy Carter's 1976 campaign. It was a highly personal campaign—so much so that Carter drew support from conservative as well as liberal Democrats. Yet he held his disparate supporters together well enough to be a formidable candidate in the primaries. In Pennsylvania, for example, Carter's superior organization and media campaign defeated the local Democratic leaders on their home ground.

Ronald Reagan campaigned independently for the Republican nomination for years before finally winning it in 1980. As the candidate of a very conservative faction of the party and bolstered by support from antiabortion groups, and others, Reagan had nearly defeated the incumbent, Gerald Ford in 1976. In 1980, Reagan soundly defeated George Bush and other contenders, and went on to the White House (see Chapter 10 for a detailed discussion of the 1980 election).

Consequences. There are some dangers in the new process. Because candidates nominate themselves, they may not be representative of the major interest groups in the party or skilled at bargaining and negotiating. Jimmy Carter exemplifies both problems. He was more conservative than his Democratic colleagues who controlled Congress from 1977–1981. Frequent conflicts occurred between the President and Congress and little legislation was enacted during Carter's term of office.

Besides failing as an ideological leader, President Carter also foundered in practical politics. He was a master of nomination politics but a disaster as a legislative and executive leader. The same traits of character and patterns of behavior that made Carter a formidable candidate for the nomination made him an ineffective President.

The determination and certitude that sustained him through the lonely years of campaigning obscured the need to mend fences, solicit opinions, build support, and compromise. "Going it alone" with the help of a loyal staff and friends was necessary to an unknown outsider. To a president trying to legislate, this strategy is a costly liability. For instance, when the B-1 bomber's future was at issue, Carter kept silent while House Democrats debated and voted to continue the B-1 program. He gave no signals to the leadership. Three days later, having let them climb onto the limb, he sawed it off by announcing his opposition.

Stubborn self-reliance proved even more costly when scandal touched a close friend in high office. The drawn-out Bert Lance affair tarnished Carter's public standing and professional reputation, and preoccupied him and his close advisors for months. Note that Carter and George McGovern, both products of the new system, had enormous difficulty in disassociating themselves from a discredited colleague. As McGovern had done in the Eagleton affair, Carter responded initially by making an unqualified statement of support. When McGovern later had to repudiate his statement and to force Eagleton off the ticket, he looked both foolish and cruel. Carter waited until long after everyone else in Washington knew that Lance had to go before asking him to resign.

Compare these responses with Dwight D. Eisenhower's reaction to the accusations against his running mate in 1952. Responding as the good, self-protective, consensus politician, Eisenhower first waited in silence, consulting his supporters. Then he allowed others to press in private and in the newspapers for Nixon's resignation. Finally, Ike spoke—off the record, of course—and said, "Nixon's got to be as clean as a hound's tooth."

That Nixon redeemed himself with the Checkers speech is beside the point. Eisenhower, with masterful economy, had left Nixon to survive or perish, all on his own. When Nixon triumphed, Eisenhower embraced him. Had Nixon failed, Eisenhower would have been safely removed, far above the fray.

One may attribute the differences between Eisenhower's response and those of the two Democrats to style or personality. The point remains that people likely to behave in this politically self-damaging manner are now more likely to gain major party nominations and the White House. Unswerving determination, faith in one's own rectitude, and personal loyalty are virtues in the new nomination politics. In Washington politics, they are often vices.

The politics of nomination and the politics of policymaking also differ greatly as regards methods of dealing with other political actors. To gain the nomination Carter had to convince a relatively small portion of the Democratic party faithful that he was the best choice. Either the delegates to the local caucuses or the primary voters were the most important targets. To gain their support Carter could rely on his personal appeal—on traits such as sincerity, honesty, friendliness—and on his general message—the country is basically sound and we need new, uplifting leadership. As long as the overall impressions were favorable, differences on specific issues would fade. Thus Carter was able to attract support from both conservative and liberal Democrats.

Sincerity and ideology may play a part in making policy, but they are very much preliminary to the hard business of forging legislative majorities. To gain other politicians' support, Carter had to be prepared to deal in terms of their interests and the interests of important groups. He had to persuade where he could, concede where he must, but above all he had to accept the necessity of being involved in a constant bargaining process. There was little chance that he could charm or convert Senator Russell B. Long.

Social ease and mutual respect can smooth bargaining. In Washington, as in other capitals, ceremonial deference among powerful leaders is a well-established norm. The Carter Administration distinguished itself by an early, compounded, gratuituous affront to the most powerful of the House Democrats, Speaker Thomas P. ("Tip") O'Neill. As reported by Martin Tolchin, the story began when the Speaker received seats in the last two orchestra rows for Carter's inaugural gala.

> He protested to Hamilton Jordan, the president's senior political advisor. "I said to Jordan, 'When a guy is Speaker of the House and gets tickets like this, he figures there's a reason behind it.'" Jordan replied, "If you don't like it, I'll send back the dollars," and the Speaker exploded: "I'll ream you out, you son of a bitch!" From that day on, O'Neill has privately referred to Jordan as "Hannibal Jerkin."

At the most elementary level, bargaining means patronage and pork barrel. Carter attacked both. He first proposed during the campaign to take the several hundred United States attorney jobs out of partisan politics, a suggestion that met with a stern rebuke from Senator James Eastland, the representative of those who consider these positions to be their political property. The idea remained an idea.

In regard to other positions, however, Carter took a more cavalier attitude toward his party fellows, allowing cabinet officers to make their own choices in many cases. This system produced an ambassadorship for the Republican stalwart, Elliot Richardson. A former cabinet member in the Nixon administration, Richardson was at the time a likely Republican candidate for the governorship of Massachusetts, a race that would have pitted him against the son of the already aggrieved "Tip" O'Neill. There followed the appointment of Evan Dobelle, the Republican mayor of Pittsfield, Massachusetts, to be the State Department's chief of protocol. "We won the election," lamented O'Neill, "but you'd never know it."

Carter meanwhile invaded the hitherto sacred precincts of the Army Corps of Engineers and the only slightly less hallowed halls of the Bureau of Reclamation, both temples dear to the hearts of the Congress, to propose the elimination of nineteen water projects. Eventually he compromised and signed a bill that included nine of the disputed items, but only after a protracted struggle that produced bitter comments from Democratic legislators and their constituents.

We see in these examples the consequences of playing a lone hand and ignoring or challenging key interests and customs. In the primaries, candidate Carter could make such pronouncements without cost. He could challenge and defeat the established party organization. In Washington, however, such rhetoric has its costs and there is no functional equivalent to the primary. The president must deal with the Congress and the Congressional Democrats as they are.

On the other hand, Ronald Reagan, who became the Republican nominee through a similar process, has been very successful in dealing with the Congress. Unlike Carter, Reagan expanded his staff to include people with experience in Washington. For instance, his budget director, David Stockman, had been a Congressperson and a member of the House Budget Committee. His knowledge of the Congressional budgetary process helped Reagan to design an effective strategy for passing his proposals in 1981.

We return to these themes when we discuss the resources and methods of presidential power. Before discussing the President in action, however, we outline the general process by which the institution of the presidency has grown.

The Expansion of the Presidency

Shortly after he assumed office in 1845, President James Polk wrote in his diary, "I prefer to supervise the whole operation of the government myself . . . and this makes my duties very great." Given the relatively few demands on the President prior to the twentieth century, Polk's conception of his role was reasonable. By 1937, however, President Franklin D. Roosevelt, in an attempt to take stock of the sprawling governmental apparatus that had mushroomed under his first administration, appointed Louis Brownlow to head the Commission on Administrative Management. The report of the Brownlow commission opened with the simple declaration that "the President needs help." Yet, in 1973, a noted authority on the presidency, Thomas Cronin, could write that the White House "has become a powerful inner sanctum of government, isolated from traditional constitutional checks and balances."

Clearly, the presidency has undergone a great and far reaching transition. President Polk apparently felt that his duties—however great—were still sufficiently limited to permit him, alone, to supervise the presidential office. President Roosevelt, to paraphrase the Brownlow commission, needed help to do so and sought it from a reluctant Congress. And, by 1973, the presidency, to many experts, had amassed such powers that it presented a danger to the constitutional system itself. But why? What could account for the expanded role of the chief executive?

Certainly periods of crisis and the strong personalities of some Presidents have contributed to the expansion of executive power since 1789. George Washington, Andrew Jackson, Abraham Lincoln, Theodore Roosevelt, Woodrow Wilson, and Franklin Roosevelt all have left their mark on the presidency. These were men of forceful personalities who used the presidency to make dramatic changes in the American political system. When an active chief executive takes on new responsibilities and shapes the institution to his liking, the change is likely to endure long after that President has left office.

Presidential power is not solely, however, a result of men and crises. As an institution, the presidency has developed in response to broad historical changes in American society. As the country became more urbanized and industrialized, as the nation involved itself increasingly in world affairs, and as the economy grew to vast proportions, the public demanded solutions to ever more complex problems. The President was (and is) the only public official elected by *all* the voters. As a result, the needs of an expanding, restless society were felt most acutely in his office.

The people and other politicians also look to the presidency because as a unitary office it promises fast action in emergencies, and Americans think that fast action in emergencies is a good thing. Presidents have also gained prestige and trust from their role as **chief of state.** As the ceremonial leader, the person who leads patriotic celebrations such as the Fourth of July, or throws out the first ball of the baseball season, the President becomes a symbol of national unity much like the English monarch. In a time of crisis people and politicians often feel that rallying around the President is the same thing as rallying around the flag. Anyone who questions the President in such a period is considered misguided or even disloyal.

A catalogue of the historical developments that have shaped the modern presidency would require a book in itself. The most important of these developments follow.

Foreign Affairs

When President Kennedy was assassinated in Dallas on November 22, 1963, an army warrant officer picked up a locked briefcase and walked to a small room in Parkland Hospital where President Lyndon Johnson was being guarded by the Secret Service. The black box, as it is called, accompanies the President wherever he goes. In it are the coded orders that the President would have to send to his military commanders to authorize the use of nuclear weapons.

The United States and the Soviet Union each possess sufficient nuclear missiles to destroy each other in a half-hour. Given the time factor, the President, rather than Congress, out of necessity has become the one to decide whether to use these weapons. Partially because of the requirements of the nuclear age, the constitutional power of Congress to declare war has steadily eroded.

Presidential power in foreign affairs has also increased because of the expansion of American influence and interests globally. After World War II, the United States abandoned its isolationist past to counteract what was felt to be the aggressive designs of the Soviet Union and China. During the Truman and Eisenhower administrations the United States promoted a series of alliances with the purpose of "containing" communism. The United States assumed responsibility directly and indirectly for the security of forty-four nations. Although the Nixon administration promised to replace the "era of confrontation" with the Communist powers with "an era of negotiation," the change in no way lessened America's prominence in world affairs. The United States remains one of the two most powerful nations in the world. Inevitably, this makes the American President a world leader as well as a national leader.

The framers of the Constitution gave little consideration to foreign affairs. The American role in the world, the Founding Fathers felt, would be minimal. Foreign policy was seen as a game played by corrupt monarchies. The United States, on the other hand, was an experiment in democratic self-government. If the people ruled—instead of princes and kings—the Republic would have little need to involve itself in foreign troubles. Although the framers probably did expect the President to be dominant in the area of foreign policy, they could not have foreseen the extent of the American role globally. So today we discover that much of the President's importance is derived from American overseas involvement. When, in 1948, President Truman declared that "I make American foreign policy," he was not simply giving his own views of his office. He was also acknowledging that the presidency, as an institution, had to adjust to the burdens of world affairs.

Domestic Affairs

The transformation of the United States from a largely rural society into an industrial society with large numbers of service workers, congested cities, and underprivileged minorities has demanded a growing response from government. As in the area of foreign policy, it has been the President, as the only leader elected on a nationwide basis, who has assumed responsibility for the social welfare of the nation and for the management of its economy.

In the area of social welfare, Theodore Roosevelt was one of the first Presidents to mount an all-out attack on social injustices. He sponsored pure food and drug legislation, government regulation of the large corporations (trusts), and the federal employees liability acts. Franklin Roosevelt's New Deal programs included unemployment insurance, Social Security, laws enabling unions to organize, and regulation of the securities market and the stock exchange. President Truman's Fair Deal included federally assisted housing programs, racial integration of the armed forces, and increased federal aid to education. These programs, which were begun as responses to pressing national needs, endured and were expanded under later presidents. Under Lyndon Johnson, Medicare was established, major civil rights bills were enacted, and open-housing legislation became law. Although President Nixon cut back funding and dismantled some of these social welfare programs in order to stress the role of individual self-help and to slow the spending of funds for programs that he felt were not producing results, the federal budget continued to increase. Indeed, the slice of the federal budget devoted to social welfare programs was larger than in any previous administration.

Similarly, the management of the nation's economy has, to some extent become a presidential responsibility. When, in August 1971, President Nixon announced the first imposition of wage and price controls since the Korean War, he was acting in the tradition of law and precedent. The Great Depression of the 1930s and the enactment of strong governmental controls over the economy during World War II legitimized presidential management of the economy. As a result, Congress institutionalized the presidential function of economic management by passing the Employment Act of 1946. Under that act, the President is required to report annually to Congress on the state of the nation's economic health, and the act specifically recognizes the responsibility of the President to maintain full employment and maximum economic production and to control inflation.

From 1977 to 1980 President Carter struggled unsuccessfully to shape and get through Congress a coherent policy on energy and the economy. Although he failed, Carter's effort illustrates that the responsibility for initiating this sort of broad policy rests with the presidency. In 1981, Ronald Reagan proposed and the Congress passed a sweeping program of domestic spending cuts and tax reductions that he claimed would curb inflation and unemployment while promoting economic growth. Again, the President acted as the interpreter of the national mood and the initiator of policy.

Reagan's success also changed the historical trend we described at the beginning of this section. Before 1981, Democratic and Republican presidents generally accepted the existance and the growth of social programs controlled by the federal government. But Reagan attacked such programs. He proposed eliminating some, reducing others, and consolidating many into "block grants," to be administered by the states, not the federal government. Reducing federal spending and transferring control to the states reversed the policy of federal growth that began with Franklin Roosevelt's New Deal and expanded with Lyndon Johnson's Great Society in the 1960s. Paradoxically, Reagan used his great power as President to reduce the size and power of the federal government, and, in the long run, the power of the presidency.

The Mass Media

In Chapter 8 the relationship of the media to government is explored in depth, but it is noted here that television and the other news media have magnified the person and the institution of the presidency. Correspondents of the major magazines, wire services, and television networks are regularly assigned to cover the White House. Moreover, when a President wants to address the public directly, the networks normally accord him free prime time. Presidential press conferences, although held far less frequently than in the past, are also televised live. Not unnaturally, people tend to identify with a President whom they see so frequently on television. His style and personality help shape the times and the national mood.

To summarize: Changes in American society have been reflected in the growth of the institution of the presidency. As the twentieth century brought on new and complex problems, the public sought governmental solutions to these problems. The presidency has become the focal point for new public demands. In that sense the President could well be considered "Mr. Cure-all." Whenever something goes wrong in the country—whenever unemployment rises, the stock market drops, the cost of living increases, the balance of payments worsens, workers in major industries go on strike, pollution levels of air and water worsen, discontented minorities demonstrate—the country automatically turns to the White House for a reaction, if not a solution. Each President may respond differently according to his personality, style, and view of his office. But the institution of the presidency will feel the pressures of modern American life regardless of who occupies that office.

Presidential Roles and Power Resources

As the twentieth century has placed new burdens on the President, the number of roles that he must play has multiplied. Similarly, the tools of power to fulfill these roles have grown considerably. There is no hint in Article II of the Constitution of cabinets, White House staffs, summit meetings, executive agreements, impounding funds, executive privilege, or throwing out the first baseball each season. The modern presidency represents an accumulation of roles and powers that go beyond the terse phrases of the Constitution.

Presidential Roles

It is customary to explain the power of the modern presidency in terms of the many **roles** and formal and informal duties the President must perform. This is a useful way to understand the complexities of the presidency, but the student should remember that these roles overlap considerably and that some collide. The role of chief diplomat, for example, may sometimes collide with the President's role as chief legislator. As President Nixon attempted to forge a détente with the Soviet Union, influential members of Congress questioned whether he was doing all he could to improve the plight of Soviet minorities. The President, as chief legislator, had to accommodate to the demands of some powerful congressional leaders even though by so doing he may have complicated his role as chief diplomat.

Additionally, it should be remembered that simply carrying out these roles is not the same as wielding power. Whether a President exercises great power will depend in part on his political skill, style, and personality. The President also can be thwarted in his duties by opposition in Congress, by the federal bureaucracy, and by the public and its spokesmen. Still, by viewing the **presidency** as a collection of roles, we discover that the awesome burden has identifiable parts.

The President is first of all **chief of state.** Nothing in the Constitution names him as such. Yet, in playing this informal role, the President may exercise a kind of symbolic power—power derived from the awe and majesty surrounding the institution of the presidency. Wherever he travels, he is met with the full extent of ceremonial pomp: bands play, officers salute him, and dignitaries line up to shake his hand.

The American President, as chief of state, symbolizes more than simply a head of government. In many countries the two roles are distinct: a king, queen, or President plays a ceremonial role as chief of state, but a premier or prime minister exercises real governmental power. The American presidency, however, combines both roles. The President is the symbol of the nation as well as of the government.

The power that a President derives from his role as chief of state is primarily the power of prestige. Usually, when the President decides to do something, he can count on immediate publicity and the approval of a large segment of the population. This approval may not be sufficient to persuade a recalcitrant legislature or a slow-moving bureaucracy to do whatever the President desires, however. President Nixon, for example, often invoked the prestige of the "Office of the President" in support of his policy in Vietnam. Although Congress ultimately enacted laws to restrict the President's warmaking powers, the ability to manipulate the symbolism inherent in the chief-of-state role can prove to be a valuable asset to the President.

The President is also the **chief executive** of the government establishment. In this role he is carrying out the duties given him by the very broad language of Article II of the Constitution: "The executive Power shall be vested in a President of the United States of America," and the mandates of the various laws that created the executive agencies. Under these grants of authority, the President administers the executive branch. His role here might be better termed "chief bureaucrat." In theory, the President supervises the departments and unaffiliated agencies. But in practice no single person could supervise thirteen departments and dozens of agencies with millions of employees and an annual budget of hundreds of billions of dollars. (See Chapter 5 for details.)

Clearly the President cannot take charge of the daily operations of the executive branch. Even if he could renounce his other roles, which he cannot do, the sheer size and complexity of the executive branch would make personal control of these operations impossible. Most Presidents try to confine themselves to the most important matters. Even in this restricted effort, the President must rely on the White House staff, the Office of Management and Budget, and on the people he appoints to the top positions in the executive branch. (See chart, below.) The people in the White House Staff and in OMB work exclusively for the President, who appoints them—everyone on the White House staff—their loyalty is to him personally. Although most of the employees at OMB are career government workers, they pride themselves on being responsive to the President's wishes.

The President also appoints the heads of the departments, who are called secretaries, and the heads of many agencies, all subject to the Senate's approval. Collectively, the thirteen secretaries are called the Cabinet. In addition, the President appoints about two thousand people to the jobs in the departments and agencies. At first glance one would expect these people to be loyal to the President who appointed them. However, their positions prevent simple loyalty to the President. Usually secretaries and other high officials have inter-

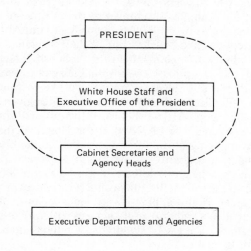

ests that run counter to those of the President's. At the simplest level, the President has general responsibilities such as reducing government spending, whereas the secretaries each have a more narrow responsibility. For instance, the secretary may be in charge of the military, in which case cutting the military budget will likely seem a bad idea to him. It would be far better to cut the agriculture budget, but the Secretary of Agriculture will probably think exactly the opposite, and properly so. We would not expect a secretary to downgrade his own department. Each secretary and agency head must speak for his or her agency; otherwise the people in the agency—the career civil servants—will prevent the secretary or agency head from accomplishing anything. (See Chapter 5 for a more detailed explanation.) Thus institutional responsibility and interest create divided loyalties, and give rise to the oft-quoted statement that "Cabinet members are the President's natural enemies."

Faced with this problem many presidents have tried to govern exclusively through the White House staff as illustrated by the chart on page 30. This approach has its own dangers, including being controlled by the staff (see page 42). At the beginning of his term President Reagan established a strong staff and held frequent Cabinet meetings to emphasize that the newly appointed Secretaries owed their main loyalty to him. He succeeded to a considerable extent. There was very little opposition from cabinet members to the President's budget program even though he cut many of their programs severely. Whether or not this system will work in the long run to overcome the tendency for cabinet members to "go native", that is, to become more representative of their departments than of the President, or the tendency for cabinet members to seek individual access to the President (the dotted lines in the chart on page 30) remains to be seen.

Another, and more controversial, presidential role is that of **commander in chief.** Article II, Section 2 of the Constitution provides that "The President shall be commander in chief of the army and navy of the United States, and of the militia of the several States . . ." Yet the Constitution also declares that "Congress shall have the Power . . . to Declare War." Originally, the draft of the Constitution gave Congress the power to "make" war, the delegates to the Constitutional Convention being determined to prevent the President from beginning a war on his own. The word *declare* was later substituted for *make,* since the writers of the Constitution realized that the President might have to make war in order to repel an attack on the United States without first receiving a congressional declaration of war. The Constitution also gave Congress the power "to raise and support armies," and "to make Rules for the Government and Regulation of the land and naval Forces."

Once again, the framers of the Constitution decided to permit future events and necessities to define more precisely the division of powers between the President and the Congress. Apparently, the intent of the writers of the Constitution was to allow the President, as commander in chief, to order American armed forces into action under certain extraordinary circumstances, such as an attack on the United States itself. In situations short of that, the President would have to seek a congressional declaration of war. If that were granted him, he, as commander in chief, could direct the prosecution of the war. But by retaining the power to raise and support the armed forces, Congress could, presumably, halt the participation of American armed forces in combat by simply refusing to grant funds for the war effort. No money from Congress would mean no weapons for the troops.

Historically, Presidents have interpreted the commander-in-chief clause broadly. Presidents have often ordered American forces into conflict situations without ever asking for a declaration of war. Presidents also have involved the United States in war and only later asked Congress to approve their decisions either by a declaration of war or by a "concurrent resolution," such as the Tonkin Gulf Resolution. President Polk sent troops to repel what he thought to be a Mexican invasion of American territory and President Pierce directed American forces to shell Greyton, Nicaragua. In both instances Congress, after the fact, passed resolutions expressing outrage at being ignored. President Abraham Lincoln is generally credited with giving the commander-in-chief clause its broadest interpretation. During the Civil War, without the consent of Congress, Lincoln added 41,000 men to the armed forces, issued a call for 40,000 volunteers, spent $2 million of public funds for purposes totally unauthorized by Congress, blockaded Southern ports, and issued the Emancipation Proclamation as a means of depleting the work force of the South. Prior to American participation in World War II, President Franklin Roosevelt ordered the American navy to convoy British supply vessels across the North Atlantic. That action resulted in a naval war with Germany in 1940—nearly two years before Congress declared war. Additionally, President Roosevelt, in 1942, permitted the removal from the Pacific Coast of 112,000 persons of Japanese descent—most of them native-born Americans—to concentration camps called relocation centers in the interior of the United States. And in June, 1950 President Truman determined that the North Korean invasion of South Korea constituted aggression in violation of the United Nations Charter. On that basis, he committed American troops to the defense of South Korea without asking Congress for a declaration of war.

In recent years the President's constitutional role as commander-in-chief has become an extremely divisive issue between Congress and the President. The Vietnam War was the source of most of the controversy. In 1964 President Lyndon Johnson asked Congress for a resolution (The Tonkin Gulf Resolution) that would allow the President "to take all necessary measures to repel armed attack against the forces of the United States and to prevent further aggression." The Congress quickly passed the resolution, with only a few dissenting votes.

The Vietnam War continued to escalate for the next three years. As the war escalated so did opposition to the war. As a result, Congress sought to place limitations on the war powers of the President. In 1970 Congress voted to repeal the Tonkin Gulf Resolution. President Nixon, however, continued to conduct the war, citing his role as commander in chief as justification. And in 1970 and 1971 the President ordered American troops into combat or combat-support operations in Laos and Cambodia. Again Congress, through various amendments to Defense Department appropriations bills, sought to halt what was felt to be an unconstitutional use of American forces. Most of these amendments either died in Congress or were vetoed by the President. In the latter case Congress could not muster the two-thirds majority to override the President's veto.

The war continued, but so did congressional opposition to the war. Early in 1973, after the Nixon administration had signed the peace accords ending the American role in the Vietnam War, the President sent B-52 bombers over Cambodia to keep that government in power. Both the House and the Senate voted to cut off the spending of funds for the bombing. That was the first time in the history of the Vietnam war that Congress used its constitutional power to "raise and support Armies" to thwart actions taken by the commander in chief. The President vetoed the bill, but, as a result of congressional anger, he agreed to a compromise bill that ended the bombing of Cambodia on August 15, 1973.

In the wake of the Vietnam War, Congress passed broader legislation that limited the powers of the President to make war. President Nixon vetoed the bill, citing, again, his inherent powers as commander in chief. But Congress overrode the President's veto, and the war powers bill became law. That law now governs the President's ability to make war and modifies the presidential role as commander in chief. It provides that

1. Within forty-eight hours after committing armed forces abroad, the President must report in writing to the Congress, explaining the circumstances and scope of his actions.

2. Use of American forces in combat would have to end in sixty days unless Congress authorizes a longer period. This deadline could be extended another thirty days, if the President certified that the time was necessary for the safe withdrawal of the forces.

3. Within the sixty- or ninety-day period, Congress could order an immediate withdrawal of American forces by adopting a concurrent resolution which is not subject to a Presidential veto.

The 1973 **War Powers Act** does not resolve the constitutional struggle between Congress and the President over the power to make war. Many loopholes still remain. Does "armed forces" include armed forces personnel acting in an "advisory" capacity? Did the Congress, perhaps unwittingly, actually expand the powers of the commander in chief by giving him authorization to conduct "sixty-day wars"?

The War Powers Act does modify the role of commander in chief, but how it will work depends on future contingencies and interpretations. Most likely, we have not seen the end of the constitutional conflict between Congress' power to declare war and the President's role as commander in chief.

Some recent incidents indicate that the Congress will give the President considerable leeway in times of "crisis." When President Ford sent American marines to rescue the crew of the Mayaguez, a commercial ship that had been seized by Cambodia, few congresspeople or senators protested. In April 1980 Jimmy Carter ordered American troops, helicopters, and planes into Iran to rescue the Americans held hostage there. Despite the fact that the rescue force penetrated hundreds of miles into Iran, and despite the fact that they would surely have had to fight to free the hostages, Congress made no serious protests that it had not received prior notice of the rescue attempt. In 1981 President Reagan increased American military aid to El Salvador, sending American soldiers to act as "trainers." Critics predicted an escalation similar to that in Vietnam twenty years earlier. Eventually the Americans would be involved in the fighting, and American forces would enter the war in large numbers. Again Congress made no protest against the involvement of American military personnel in an area of active combat.

Related to the President's role as commander in chief is his role as **chief diplomat** for the nation. Although the Constitution specifically designates the President as commander in chief, it does not confer directly on the President the power to make foreign policy. The Constitution, instead, does so indirectly. It authorizes the President to make treaties with the advice and consent of two thirds of the Senate; to receive foreign ambassadors and ministers; and to appoint ambassadors, ministers, and consuls with the advice and consent of the Senate. The role of chief diplomat is, then, an informal one. The Constitution requires that he share some of his powers with Congress.

As with other presidential roles, the role of chief diplomat has increased as a result of broad historical trends. America's extensive involvement in foreign affairs has led to the proliferation of executive offices and departments, such as the Central Intelligence Agency (CIA), that report directly to the President. The President's access to classified information from these sources is a substantial element of power. Those who presumably lack the information that the President has therefore find it difficult to challenge presidential actions. Still, the Vietnam War demonstrated that powerful senators such as J. William Fulbright of Arkansas could strongly criticize a President's foreign policy and mobilize public sentiment against the President.

The President's power as chief diplomat has expanded in more formal ways. For example, although the Senate must advise and consent by a two-thirds vote to any treaty signed by the President, Presidents have often dodged this requirement by use of the **executive agreement.** Internationally, the executive agreement carries the same binding force as a treaty. But it does not require the approval of Congress. Originally, Presidents used the executive agreement mainly to negotiate trading arrangements with foreign nations. Today, however, executive agreements may cover matters ranging from the stationing of American troops on foreign soil to cultural exchange programs. President Nixon, during his 1972 trip to Moscow, signed an executive agreement to freeze the numbers of intercontinental missles at the level then in existence or under construction. Technically, this agreement did not have to be submitted to the Senate, despite its obvious importance. But because of its very importance, the President did submit the agreement to Congress and won the approval of both houses.

The President's constitutional power to receive foreign ambassadors and ministers also implies the power to recognize foreign governments. Since the time of Woodrow Wilson, Presidents have used this power to further the nation's political objectives. Thus, President Wilson refused to recognize certain revolutionary governments in Latin America and for seventeen years the United States did not recognize the Soviet government, which had been established by revolution in 1917. In recent years Presidents have, for various periods of time, withheld recognition from governments that they deemed inimical to American interests. These have included the People's Republic of China, Albania, North Vietnam, North Korea, Bangladesh, Cuba, and Chile. On the other hand, President Truman's rapid recognition of Israel in 1948 was a sign of approval.

These more or less formal powers of the president as chief diplomat hardly do justice to the prominence that is given to the President as the chief representative of the nation abroad. In 1972 President Nixon demonstrated this awesome power by holding summit conferences in China and the Soviet Union and signing accords on "principles of conduct" between the United States and those two nations. In so doing he altered a pattern of American policy that had been dominant for almost three decades. It was the President, as chief diplomat, and his advisors who had initiated and implemented this dramatic policy reversal. There was no need for formal approval from the Congress or, for that matter, from the American public. (For a detailed look at subsequent events on the making of policy toward China, see Chapter 9.)

In 1959 President Eisenhower observed, "The Constitution puts the President right square into the legislative business." Eisenhower's comment illustrates yet another role that the modern President plays. He has become the **chief legislator** for the nation. Formally, the Constitution grants the President the power to **veto** bills passed by Congress, call Congress into special session, report to the Senate and House on the State of the Union, and "recommend to their consideration such measures as he shall deem necessary and expedient." These powers are, however, quite limited, and it is only in the twentieth century that the President has taken an active role in legislative affairs.

The legislative role of the President begins with his State of the Union message, a duty imposed by the constitutional requirement that "He [the President] shall from time to time give to the Congress information of the State of the Union." Today, Presidents use the State of the Union address, delivered to a joint session of Congress in early January, as a public platform for revealing the legislation they want to see passed by the Congress in the coming year. Later on, the President will send to the Congress messages that fill out the proposals he wants enacted into law.

The State of the Union address gives the President the opportunity to set the agenda for the coming congressional session. By and large it will be his proposals that Congress will debate, pass, or reject. Regardless of how Congress disposes of the President's legislative program, he has, informally, set the priorities for the nation. He has defined the terms of debate concerning national needs. The President, thus, has the initiative in the legislative process; Congress must then react to his proposals.

As chief legislator, the President has another powerful weapon, the **veto power.** If a President approves a bill, he will sign it and the bill becomes law. But, if he disapproves, he can veto the bill and return it with his objections to either the House or Senate, depending on where the bill originated. If, however, each house of Congress votes by a two-thirds majority to override the veto, the bill automatically becomes law without the signature of the President. Alternatively, if the President chooses neither to sign nor veto the bill within ten working days after he receives it, the bill becomes law anyway. If Congress adjourns during the ten-day period after the President receives a bill, the President can kill the bill by simply taking no action at all (this is the "pocket" veto). Occasionally, Congress, either on its own or at the urging of the President, will pass joint or concurrent resolutions, such as the Gulf of Tonkin Resolution. These require no action on the part of the President because they are expressions of sentiment, not of law. Finally, the presidential veto power is qualified by the fact that he cannot simply veto one part of a bill while allowing the remaining portions of the bill to become law. He must accept the entire bill as it emerges from Congress or veto the entire bill. In other words, he has no *item veto* power.

The veto power is a major weapon of the President as chief legislator. It is extremely difficult to override a presidential veto, given the two-thirds vote by the Congress required to do so. Sometimes, simply the threat of a President's veto will cause Congress to tailor a bill to the President's wishes. Indeed, only about 3 per cent of presidential vetoes have been overriden by Congress.

The veto represents a strictly constitutional power granted to the President. However, as the role of chief legislator became more important in the twentieth century, Presidents fashioned new weapons in their conflicts with Congress—weapons and powers not specifically given to the President by the Constitution. Chief among these are the doctrine of **executive privilege** and the withholding of funds appropriated by Congress by means of **impoundment.**

The doctrine of executive privilege is nowhere mentioned in the Constitution. Yet, from the time of President Washington, Presidents periodically have refused to give Congress or the judiciary information that they believed would damage the national interest. Presidents have given several arguments to buttress their refusal to provide information that Congress or the judiciary felt was needed to carry out their duties. President Washington refused to give the Senate Foreign Relations Committee information relevant to the negotiation of the Jay Treaty on the grounds that to give such information would jeopardize confidential negotiations that a foreign government expected would be kept private. Another argument has been that if the President turned over communications between himself and his advisors, no presidential advisor would henceforth give advice freely because he would know that his remarks would later be scrutinized by Congress and the public. Finally, Presidents have argued that their role as commander in chief forbids them to reveal information that might injure the security of the nation. Thus, President Roosevelt, in 1939, refused to divulge to Congress the details of his program to aid the British on the grounds that such information would aid the cause of the Axis powers.

The notion of executive privilege became the center of controversy between the President and Congress as the Watergate incident began to engulf the Nixon presidency in 1973. When former presidential counsel John Dean accused President Nixon of participating in a plot to cover up the burglary of the Democratic headquarters in June 1972, the Senate committee investigating the matter sought tape recordings from the White House that would either prove or disprove Dean's testimony. At first, the President refused to hand over the tapes, citing executive privilege. "No President could ever agree to allow the counsel to the President to go down and testify before a committee," he said. The President went even further. He forbade any present or former members of his staff from testifying before a congressional committee. Then, Attorney General Richard Kleindienst invoked the doctrine of executive privilege even further than the President had. The President, he said, could compel anyone in the executive branch not to testify before Congress.

After the special Watergate prosecutor, Archibald Cox, and his successor, Leon Jaworski, went into federal court in an effort to force the President to turn over the tapes, the President reversed his stand and agreed to turn over some of the tapes requested. He subsequently had to turn over all of them when, in 1974, the Supreme Court ruled that executive privilege did not extend to material required by a grand jury investigating a crime.

Undoubtedly, in the future, Presidents, as chief legislators, will invoke executive privilege in their battles with Congress. However, the President's right to withhold confidential information from the courts and from Congress is in question, as it always has been.

Since the 1920s Presidents have occasionally employed another weapon in their role as chief legislator: the **impoundment of funds.** The Constitution provides that Congress shall appropriate funds for the continued operation of the government, but nothing in the Constitution says that the President must spend those funds. Periodically, Presidents have refused to spend money for programs they opposed. In essence, this informal exercise of power has allowed the President to veto parts of legislation of which he disapproved while signing the entire bill. In other words, the President has exercised a kind of item veto. Thus, the President could sign the appropriations bill to fund the Department of Defense but simply withhold the funds designated for a particular weapons development program he felt was nonessential. This issue came to light during the Nixon years when the administration disclosed that it had impounded—that is, refused to spend—$8.7 billion in monies that Congress had appropriated. However, in a series of decisions, the federal courts curtailed the President's power to defer spending and to impound congressionally mandated appropriations. In 1974, Congress passed the Budget Reform Act described in detail in Chapter 3. The Act provided that either House could block a presidential impoundment.

In the end the success of a President as chief legislator depends on his relations with Congress and on his persuasive powers. If a Republican President confronts a Congress dominated by Democrats (as in the case of Nixon and Ford), or if, in the reverse, a Democratic President confronts a coalition of Republicans and Southern Democrats (as in Kennedy's case), the role of chief legislator is indeed a frustrating one. At that point only the persuasive skills of the President and his assistants can rescue the President's legislative program from collapse. If not handled skilfully, even the White House "lobbying" of Congress may not be enough. One example came to light in the Nixon administration. Charles Colson, an aide to President Nixon, was in charge of persuading various members of Congress to vote in favor of a bill that would have provided funds for an American supersonic transport jet (SST). Senator William Proxmire of Wisconsin was the chief opponent of the bill. According to Proxmire:

> I saw this man sitting in my outer office for two weeks. He never approached me. I didn't know who he was—I didn't even know he was from the White House.

Apparently, Colson's technique (or lack of it) did not persuade Proxmire to vote for the SST, which was subsequently defeated.

Still, any senator or representative knows that if he wants a new federal building or public works project in his district, the price may well be his vote on a bill. Often, the President himself will lobby on an important bill—telephoning members of Congress or inviting them to the White House. In gaining support for his budget program, President Reagan proved himself especially adept at personal persuasion. Congresspeople from both parties commented approvingly on his technique. "It was a very, very soft sell in an extraordinarily gentlemanly manner," said Matthew J. Rinaldo, one of the moderate Republicans who supported the Reagan budget reductions despite initial misgivings. Others called Reagan "charming" and "charismatic."

Finally, the President acts as **chief of party.** Nothing in the Constitution gives him this role. In fact the Constitution is silent on the whole subject of political parties. This is perhaps the presidential role that is most beset by uncertainty. No President has ever been in complete command of his party's organization. Although Presidents select the head of their party's national committee, the committee itself has little power. Because American political parties are marked by little centralized control, the President ordinarily cannot reach local party organizations to influence their choice of nominees for local and state offices. Moreover, because senators and members of the House of Representatives are elected from constituencies that are different from the President's, he cannot necessarily command legislators of his own party to vote the way he wants them to. This was strikingly illustrated when, in 1973, Hugh Scott, the Senate Republican leader, voted for the bill limiting the President's war powers, even though the President threatened to veto it, and did. Earlier in this chapter we described the trends that have further weakened presidential leadership of party.

Because the President has very few formal powers as party leader, he must rely on his personal political skills and on his own popularity. Often the President will build his own informal campaign organization over which he can exercise control more easily than he can over the regular party organization. President Nixon, for example, relied upon the Committee to Re-Elect the President (CREEP) to manage his 1972 campaign. In addition, in his daily contacts with members of his party in Congress, the President will generally rely on his own White House aides to influence votes in Congress rather than on the party machinery.

At times a President's own popularity will enhance his role as party chief. In 1964 President Johnson was elected by a landslide majority. At the same time seventy-one first-term Democratic representatives were elected on the coattails of the President. His name at the head of the ballot helped their election prospects. They were eager to repay President Johnson and did so by supporting him on 80 per cent of all rollcall votes during the next two years. Partially because of this, President Johnson established one of the most impressive legislative records in modern history. A similar mood prevailed in 1981 as Ronald Reagan proposed his legislative program. Every Republican senator and every Republican representative except two supported the President on crucial budget votes. His popularity and the hope that a successful program would make Republicans the majority party helped to produce unusual party loyalty.

Because of the unreliability of party loyalty in Congress, most Presidents have discovered that many, if not most, of their important goals can be achieved only with bipartisan support (support from both parties). As a result, the President may play down his role as party chief in order to gain support from members of the opposition.

Presidential Power Resources

Once, when President Johnson had reviewed the marines in California, and was walking back to a helicopter, he was stopped by a young officer who pointed to another helicopter and said, "That's your helicopter over there, sir." Johnson replied, "Son, they are all my helicopters." When the President travels, he has at his disposal not only helicopters but a fleet of jets. Aboard Air Force One, he can communicate with the White House, his aides, and the military in any part of the world.

The helicopters, the security personnel, the fleets of jets, and the special Pentagon communications unit are the visible trappings of presidential power. What is not so visible is the vast array of offices, staffs, agencies, and other personnel that become attached to the presidency. As the roles the President must fulfill have increased, so have the means to do so. When we speak of the resources of presidential power, we are referring to the immediate White House staff, the Executive Office of the President, and the cabinet. The Constitution makes no specific authorization for the establishment of these advisory bodies. But what one author has called "the political executive" has expanded primarily as the result of the growth of the American system, the increased complexity of the issues, and the position the United States occupies in world affairs.

Where do presidential proposals, orders, directives, speeches, and so on, come from? Certainly not entirely from the head of one man. Given the scope of presidential responsibilites, the President must rely on a network of presidential advisors and assistants. In effect, this network *is* the presidency, or more precisely, the *White House staff*. It is this group that largely plans and carries out the President's program and attempts to devise a strategy for dealing with the other centers of power in the American system—the Congress, the judiciary, the media, the bureaucracy, interest groups, and the public. When one hears such phrases as "Ford's administration" or the

"Reagan team," the commentator is usually referring to that inner circle of close advisors who surround, or surrounded, the President—in other words, the White House staff.

Who, then, are the White House staff? How do they get there? It is very difficult to give general answers to these questions. Each President has organized the operations of the White House differently and has chosen people of differing backgrounds. Yet, one characteristic is common among those who are appointed to high White House positions: they have proved, in one way or another, their loyalty to the President. They are trusted aides, personal confidants of the President. Often, they have served the President in his election campaigns, or they have, through the years, become close friends with the President.

The career of Harry Robbins (Bob) Haldeman, once a close aide to President Nixon, provides one example of how a relatively obscure man could attain a position of considerable influence as a member of the White House staff. In 1960 Haldeman served as an advance man in Nixon's unsuccessful campaign for the presidency. He was in charge of seeing that buses and baggage reached their proper destination on time. When Nixon lost to Kennedy in 1960, Haldeman went to work for the J. Walter Thompson advertising agency in Los Angeles, where he was in charge of Disneyland, 7-Up, and Diaper Sweet accounts. However, during this period, Haldeman maintained close personal ties with Nixon. When Nixon was elected President in 1968, Haldeman moved into the White House as a chief aide on the White House staff. Soon it became apparent that Haldeman exercised greater power than his title as chief aide would indicate. The former advertising man became one of the most powerful men in Washington, and for a simple reason: It was Haldeman who decided who would see the President and who would not.

Haldeman's role was not an invention of the Nixon administration. Wilson had his Colonel House, Franklin Roosevelt his Harry Hopkins, Eisenhower his Sherman Adams, Kennedy his Theodore Sorensen, and Johnson his Bill Moyers. All modern Presidents have come to rely on inner-circle advisers, and some aides emerge more important than others. In the Reagan White House three men, James A. Baker, III, the chief of staff and Edwin Meese, III, whose title is counselor, and Michael K. Deaver, the deputy chief of staff, have emerged as the most powerful. Still, the persons who staff the presidential office have no political power of their own; their survival in their positions depends solely on staying in the President's good graces. But their power is very real—it is not unusual for a cabinet member of great public prestige to wait in line to see a presidential aide.

The President's immediate staff is not, however, made up of only one or two influential aides. Usually four to five hundred people are employed at a cost of several million dollars. But perhaps only a dozen of those occupy positions with access to the President. Among the duties of this staff are lobbying the Congress, maintaining relations with important interest groups, and trying to direct the federal bureaucracy. A Congressional liaison office, headed in the Reagan White House by Max Friedersdorf, organizes small and large favors for Congresspeople, sends staff to Capital Hill to lobby, and dispenses invitations to intimate meetings and state dinners. A press secretary (Reagan's original press secretary, James Brady, suffered severe head wounds in an attempt on the President's life) and his staff issue public statements, answer and evade reporters' questions and look after the presidential image. Other staffers write speeches, do research, and transmit requests and advice from supporters, trying in turn to mobilize them in support of the President's programs.

The White House staff is only a small part of the presidential establishment. Under the **Executive Office of the President,** there were in 1974, fourteen agencies serving the President directly, with a combined budget of $121 million and a total staff of 1,686. Most of these employees occupy offices just west of the White House in the Executive Office Building, a structure that has often been compared to a wedding cake. EOP was established in 1939 by President Roosevelt under an executive order. Since then its offices and duties have proliferated, and each President has added, subtracted, and shifted the offices and duties of the EOP. Some of the most important of the fourteen major offices are the following:

1. National Security Council (NSC). This group was created in 1947 to consider policies and make recommendations to the President in the areas of foreign policy and national security. Although the NSC has been put to various uses by various Presidents, during the Nixon years it emerged as the primary body for coordinating the foreign policy of the United States under the leadership of Henry Kissinger. The members of the NSC include the President, the Vice President, the secretaries of State and Defense, the director of the

Office of Emergency Planning, and the heads of the army, navy, and air force (the Joint Chiefs of Staff). Approximately fifty assistants serve under the head of the NSC, currently William P. Clark Jr., whose official title is special assistant to the President on national security affairs. The NSC is charged with the tasks of planning long-range foreign policy and of coordinating intelligence data from other agencies in the foreign policy establishment.

2. Office of Management and Budget (OMB). As with other offices in the executive establishment, the Office of Management and Budget was designed to bring a vital function of government—the preparation of the federal budget—under closer presidential control. Devised by President Nixon in 1970 as part of his general reorganization of the executive office, the OMB replaced the former Bureau of the Budget.

The OMB was charged with three tasks: (a) to serve, in President Nixon's words, as "the President's principal arm for the exercise of managerial functions," (b) to advise the President on the allocation of funds appropriated by Congress, and (c) to review legislative proposals coming from executive agencies to make sure they are consistent with the President's program. In its managerial function, the OMB attempts to monitor the performance of the cabinet departments and the independent regulatory agencies. In their budgetary function OMB personnel decide the amount of money that a particular bureau, agency, or department will be allocated in the budget that the President annually submits to Congress for its approval. These dual functions give the President formidable powers over the federal bureaucracy. If the OMB decides that a particular program in a particular agency is not achieving its intended result, it can simply lower or eliminate the agency's budget request for the coming year. Or, if the agency is not responsive to the wishes of the President, the OMB can eliminate certain of the agency's powers by simply not funding them. According to Miles W. Kirkpatrick, former chairman of the Federal Trade Commission (FTC), several investigations that his agency was conducting were terminated in precisely this manner.

Under President Reagan the director of OMB, a former Congressperson named David Stockman, became extremely powerful. Stockman and his staff prepared the complex and sweeping budget reductions submitted to Congress in 1981. In consultation with the President's staff they decided which programs to cut and how much.

Later, Stockman defended the program in Congressional hearings, press conferences, and appearances before important groups.

3. Council of Economic Advisers (CEA). Because the President is held responsible for the economic well-being of the nation, and because few Presidents are professional economists, the President has the help of a three-man council of economists. The three members must be confirmed by the Senate. They are expected to give impartial advice on matters of unemployment, taxes, inflation, and federal spending. At the same time they are part of the President's administration.

Informal Tools of Power

We have already noted the informal powers that presidents possess: to persuade, to command media attention, and to give or withhold favors. In 1981 Ronald Reagan used all of these to win Congressional approval for his budget cuts. The President met with dozens of Congresspeople and Senators, singly and in groups. On one memorable morning he had three different breakfasts with Congressional delegations. He also telephoned many key lawmakers, apparently changing one Democrat's vote during a House roll call.

Reagan's media efforts were spectacularly successful. He made three prime time television speeches in support of his program. The first, delivered from the White House on February fifth, outlined the program in general terms. The second was the traditional State of the Union Address to Congress in which he presented a somewhat more detailed version. By appealing to Congress and the people simultaneously, he maximized the pressure on the legislative branch. The third speech, delivered to a joint session of Congress only a month after an assassination attempt, was a personal and political triumph. Greeted by a tumultuous three-minute standing ovation, Reagan used the emotion and drama of his recovery to buttress his appeal. He noted that his health was much improved, but that the health of the economy was not. His speech combined humor, patriotism, and an appeal to rise above party. By contrast, the Democratic party's televised response, watched by a very small audience, consisted of a three-person panel who sometimes disagreed among themselves and never approached the force of the President's message.

When the decisive vote was taken in the House of Representatives, where Democrats held a 52 vote majority, the President and his aides resorted to old-fashioned horsetrading. Southern Democrats, inclined to be conservative anyway, won White House backing for sugar price supports. Since sugar is a major crop in southern states, this concession was worth millions of dollars to the Congressmen's constituents. Altogether 29 Democrats, including 27 from the South, voted with Reagan, and provided his margin of victory. Thus, the new President and his aides demonstrated their skill at the traditional arts of bargaining and personal persuasion *and* the new methods of media campaigning.

We should also note that presidents often rely on past associates and acquaintances, not employed by the federal government, for support and advice. Andrew Jackson had his Kitchen Cabinet of informal advisors who held no official positions. Theodore Roosevelt had his "tennis cabinet;" Warren Harding, his "poker cabinet;" and Herbert Hoover his "medicine ball cabinet." President Johnson often called on personal friends such as Abe Fortas for advice.

President Reagan's "kitchen cabinet," consisting of wealthy California businessmen, had unusually great influence in the early days of his administration. The group maintained an office in the Executive Office Building, a government building next to the White House. From this office they were said to have influenced important appointments. They also organized a national lobbying campaign in support of the Reagan program to reduce domestic spending and taxes. Both the office and its lobbying efforts were stopped abruptly in March 1981 by the White House Staff, which apparently doubted the group's propriety and feared that bad publicity would result.

Personality and Style in the White House

We began this chapter by noting that the President is one person whereas the presidency is an institution. The institution persists; the person changes. So far, we have stressed the powers and duties that confront any occupant of the White House. But each person will meet these duties and exercise these powers according to his own character and habits. This is why it is important to examine the personal styles of Presidents.

President Kennedy, while campaigning for the presidency in 1960, described the presidency as "the vital center of action in our whole scheme of government."

William Howard Taft, impressed with the limitations of his power, declared: "The President can exercise no power which cannot be fairly and reasonably traced to some specific grant of power." These differing views correspond closely to what Louis Koenig has termed "literalist" and "strong" Presidents. Eisenhower, Coolidge, Harding, and Taft would fall into the more restrictive literalist category. Nixon, Johnson, Kennedy, Truman, and Roosevelt, among modern Presidents, would fall into the strong category. The extent to which a President uses his power resources will depend, in part, on his conception of the President's role.

Moreover, a President's personality traits may influence his performance in office. We may think here of Nixon's self-imposed isolation or Johnson's need for approval and public adulation. Nevertheless, it is very difficult to predict how Presidents will perform in office on the basis of personality traits, although attempts have been made to do so. To most of us, Presidents and candidates for the presidency appear only at a distance, and our views of these leaders are influenced by the way they are presented in the media. Still, few would dispute that a President's needs and drives help create an atmosphere in which the President and his subordinates operate. That is an important, if intangible, element of presidential leadership.

The Vice Presidency

John Nance Garner, Vice President for two terms under Franklin Roosevelt, once described the vice-presidency as "not worth a pitcher of warm spit." Indeed, very few people have heard of David Tompkins, Richard Johnson, George Dallas, or Hannibal Hamlin. Yet they were all Vice Presidents of the United States.

Traditionally, the Vice President is selected by the party's nominee for President. Usually the nominee will choose a person who will balance the ticket. For example, John Kennedy from Massachusetts chose Lyndon Johnson, a Texan, to serve as his running mate. Johnson provided both a geographical and ideological contrast to Kennedy. In 1976 Jimmy Carter, a southern moderate, chose Walter Mondale, a northern liberal. Vice Presidents have been chosen for reasons other than ticket balancing. In 1964 Lyndon Johnson chose Hubert Humphrey as his running mate because of Humphrey's strength within the party. Other vice-presidential nominees have been selected because they appealed to a wide variety of opinion within the party and could thus help to heal the wounds that may have developed within the party over the selection of a presidential nominee. President Nixon's choice of Spiro Agnew was an example of one such choice, as was Ford's choice of Nelson Rockefeller.

The formal, constitutional duties and powers of the Vice President are minimal. He is to preside over the Senate, to vote in that body in case of a tie, and (under the Twenty-fifth Amendment) to help determine if the President is disabled, and, if so, to serve as acting President. Informally, Vice Presidents have been delegated chairmanships of various interdepartmental committees, taken goodwill trips abroad, and maintained contact with state and local party officials.

With Jimmy Carter's backing Walter Mondale brought the vice presidency to a new height of activity and influence. Mondale and his staff participated in most major decisions and appeared to have been especially influential in domestic matters. Whether or not George Bush will be as influential in the Reagan administration is unclear. He appears to have gained power from an early victory over Secretary of State Alexander Haig for control of crisis management in the President's absence.

However, the method of selection of the Vice President and his formal duties do not reveal his true importance. In all, twelve Vice Presidents have become Presidents: four were elected after serving their terms and eight assumed office upon the death of the President. When added to the number of Presidents who have been seriously ill, as were Woodrow Wilson and Dwight Eisenhower, or had been the targets of assassination attempts, as were Franklin Roosevelt or Harry Truman—these figures become even more significant.

In the postwar years three of five Presidents previously served as Vice Presidents: Harry Truman, Lyndon Johnson, and Richard Nixon. Thus, despite its seemingly obscure role, the vice presidency has emerged as a training ground for future Presidents and a primary source of candidates for the presidency. John Garner's assessment of the vice presidency may not have been far off the mark, but perhaps John Adams' remark is more appropriate: "I am Vice President," he said. "In this I am nothing, but I may be everything."

Presidential Impeachment

Impeachment is rarely discussed in connection with the presidency. Probably this is because the impeachment power has been employed by Congress only once against a President—Andrew Johnson escaped conviction by one vote in 1868. But as the Watergate scandal unfolded in 1973 and allegations of illegal activities were aired, impeachment was discussed seriously and openly. And the House Judiciary Committee conducted a formal inquiry into the possible impeachment of President Richard Nixon.

Under the Constitution, the President may be impeached by Congress and, if convicted of "Treason, Bribery, or other High Crimes and misdemeanors," he may be removed from office. Impeachment proceedings may be brought only by the House of Representatives, by a majority vote. Should the House pass a bill of impeachment, the Senate then tries the President with the chief justice of the Supreme Court presiding. A two-thirds vote of the Senate is required to convict the President and remove him from office.

Congress has been reluctant to use the impeachment power because of the drastic nature of the act itself and the constitutional ambiguities surrounding impeachment. There has been a natural hesitancy to act against the nation's highest elected official—the only official elected by all the voters. There exists the fear that the frequent use of the impeachment power could turn it into a purely political weapon to be used whenever a President's conduct in office displeases the opposition party or political opponents in his own party.

Moreover, the language of the Constitution is not precise on the subject of impeachment. One controversy concerns whether a President can be indicted for a crime prior to being removed from office through the impeachment process. Most legal scholars lean to the view that the President can be indicted prior to impeachment and conviction, although others have pointed to the difficulty in which the country would find itself with its national leader holding office while under indictment for a criminal offense.

A second constitutional ambiguity involves the issue of precisely what constitutes an impeachable offense. Does the phrase "High Crimes and Misdemeanors" refer only to technical crimes that break specific criminal laws, or should the constitutional language encompass serious abuses of the office of the presidency that may not be indictable crimes. As the House Judiciary Committee in 1974 proceeded in its investigation of the Nixon reelection effort, these controversial issues were hotly debated but not resolved conclusively. (See chapter three, pages 63-65 for further discussion).

Presidential Disability and Succession: The Twenty-fifth Amendment

In September 1919 President Woodrow Wilson suffered a severe stroke from which he never fully recovered. Yet, he stayed in office until his term expired in 1921, during which time Mrs. Wilson, to a considerable extent, exercised the powers of the presidency. President Eisenhower suffered three heart attacks during his two terms in office. The duties of the President were then carried out informally by Special Assistant Sherman Adams, Press Secretary James Hagerty, and Vice President Richard Nixon.

Until the passage of the Twenty-fifth Amendment to the Constitution, the Constitution provided few guidelines in the event of presidential death, resignation, or inability to carry out the duties of office. Article II of the Constitution says only that in such cases, those powers shall "devolve on the Vice President." Nowhere did the Constitution specifically say that the Vice President would become President. Nor did the Constitution clearly define the terms *inability* and *disability*. Moreover, the question of exactly who would decide what constituted "Inability to discharge the Powers and Duties of the [President's] Office" was left unanswered. Finally, Article II was silent on the question of the procedure to be observed in the case of a vacancy in the vice presidency, stating only that Congress may "provide by law" for such a contingency.

The Twenty-fifth Amendment goes some distance in clarifying this gap in the Constitution. It provides specifically that the Vice President will become President in the event of the removal, death, or resignation of the President. Furthermore, in the case of vacancy in the vice presidency, the President must now nominate a Vice President, subject to the approval of a majority of both houses of Congress. It was under this provision that Gerald Ford, in 1973, became the first nonelected Vice President.

The Twenty-fifth Amendment also clarifies the role of the Vice President in the event the President is unable to carry out the duties of his office. It provides that the Vice President becomes *Acting President* if the President informs the Congress that he is unable to perform his duties. Alternatively, the Vice President may become Acting President if he and a majority of the "principal officers of the executive departments" (presumably the Cabinet) or some "other body" created by Congress, decide that the President is "unable to discharge the power and duties of his office." The President may, however, reclaim his office by notifying the Congress that no disability prevents him from resuming his presidential functions. However, should the Vice President and a majority of the principal officers of the executive departments or of the "other body" declare that the President, despite his statement to the contrary, is unable to fulfill his presidential duties, Congress must resolve the conflict. But it would take a two-thirds vote of both houses to uphold the Vice President. Anything less, and the President would resume his office.

If both the President and Vice President are killed or otherwise removed from office, succession takes place according to the Presidential Succession Act of 1947. Next in line are the speaker of the House, the president pro tempore of the Senate (this largely ceremonial office is usually occupied by the senior member of the majority party, currently Strom Thurmond of South Carolina), the secretary of State, the secretary of the Treasury, the secretary of Defense, and the other cabinet members in the order in which their departments were established.

An executive order provides that if succession or the disability procedures of the Twenty-fifth Amendment be delayed, control of the military, including American nuclear weapons, passes to the secretary of defense. On March 30, 1981 a would-be assassin shot President Reagan who underwent extensive surgery to remove the bullet. While Vice President George Bush returned to Washington from Texas, the cabinet gathered at the White House. Ignoring the provisions of the Constitution, the Succession Act, and the executive order, Secretary of State Alexander Haig proclaimed on national television that he was in charge until the vice-president arrived. In private, Secretary of Defense Weinberger disagreed, and a heated argument ensued. Fortunately, no situation arose that required settling the issue.

Summary

The presidency's development and present shape reflect the domestic and international pressures on American society. As the United States became an industrial country and a major international power, the executive branch and especially the presidency have grown in power and size. This does not mean that a particular president will be powerful automatically. We have discussed recent examples of relatively weak presidents such as Jimmy Carter. However, even weak presidents retain considerable authority as Carter showed when he ordered American troops into Iran without consulting Congress. Ronald Reagan's early successes show, on the other hand, that the President can still dominate American politics. Taken together these examples indicate that the power of the presidency depends considerably on the personality, skill, and staff of the incumbent as well as the country's situation.

GLOSSARY

Cabinet A group comprised of the heads (secretaries, in most instances) of all the executive "departments": State; Treasury; Defense; Justice; Interior; Agriculture; Commerce; Labor; Health, Education, and Welfare; Housing and Urban Development; and Transportation.

Commander in chief The President's role, stated in the Constitution, as head of the nation's armed forces.

Chief Diplomat A role associated with the presidency which includes unilateral leadership during international crises, taking the initiative in ordinary times, and the formal powers of making treaties and appointing and receiving ambassadors.

Chief Executive The presidential role, created by the Constitution, of carrying out the laws and the Constitution itself; the President acts as "chief bureaucrat."

Chief Legislator The presidential role as the most important single actor in making laws; this includes initiating most major legislation and the veto power.

Chief of Party The presidential role as the leader of his party.

Chief of State The presidential role as ceremonial leader which includes representing the United States in foreign countries and officiating at national ceremonies.

Executive Agreement An agreement made between the President and a foreign government which has the effect of a treaty, but does not require Senate approval.

Executive Office of the President A group of agencies, such as the Office of Management and Budget, that operate directly under the supervision of the President.

Executive privilege A right claimed by the President and his subordinates to withhold from court (and congressional) view information, documents, or testimony that the President deems confidential and whose exposure to public view would render the proper performance of his job impossible.

Impoundment The refusal by the Executive to spend appropriated funds for reasons other than that the job has already been completed.

Presidency In one sense the roles (including formal and informal powers) associated with the office of the President. In a second sense the people who work directly for the President.

Role The expectations associated with a given office or status. Several sets of expectations are associated with the presidency, giving the President several different roles.

Veto The President's constitutional right to refuse to sign a piece of legislation passed by each House of Congress and to return it within ten days to the house in which it originated, together with his objections to the bill. (The bill then fails to become law, unless each House of Congress, by two-thirds majority, passes the bill again, thus overriding the President's veto.) *Pocket veto* is the President's refusal to sign a bill but where he is prevented from returning the bill to Congress within ten days, as prescribed, because Congress has adjourned. The bill is then killed because the constitutionally prescribed process of return to Congress cannot take place.

War Powers Act A 1973 law that requires the President to report to Congress within sixty days after troops under his command engage in (or are threatened by) hostilities, in order to gain congressional sanction for using the troops; otherwise, he must withdraw the troops after the sixty days unless the President certifies that another thirty days are required to ensure safe withdrawal.

SUGGESTED READINGS

Corwin, Edward S. *The President: Office and Powers,* 4th ed. New York: New York University Press, 1957.

Cronin, Thomas E. *The State of the Presidency.* Boston: Little, Brown, 1975.

Hess, Stephen. *Organizing the Presidency.* Washington, D.C.: Brookings Institution, 1976.

Koenig, Louis *The Chief Executive,* 3rd ed. New York: Harcourt Brace Jovanovich, 1975.

Laski, Harold J. *The American Presidency*. New York: Grosset & Dunlap, Inc., 1940.

McConnell, Grant. *The Modern Presidency*. 2nd ed. New York: St. Martin's Press, 1976.

Neustadt, Richard, *Presidential Power*. New York: John Wiley & Sons, Inc., rev. ed. 1976.

Pious, Richard M. *The American Presidency*. New York: Basic Books, 1979.

Polsby, Nelson, ed. *The Modern Presidency*. New York: Random House, Inc., 1972.

Rossiter, Clinton. *The American Presidency*. New York: Harcourt Brace Jovanovich, 1960.

3 The Congress

Internal Structure: The Parties
   Caucuses and Conferences
Party Leadership: The House
   Party Committees
Party Leadership: The Senate
Norms
Roles of Individuals: Mavericks, Regulars, and Entrepreneurs
   Personal Staffs
   Roles of Individuals: Summary
Functions: What Does Congress Do?
   Legislating: How a Law is Passed, or, More Often, Not Passed
   Appropriations and Authorizations
   Alternate Routes
Other Congressional Functions
   Administrative Oversight
   Casework
   Investigations
   Presidential Appointments
Foreign Policy
   The Ford Administration
   The Carter Administration
Domestic Policy Making
Congress in the Twentieth Century: Summary and Prospects

Historical Background

As indicated in *The Federalist papers,*[1] the men who wrote the Constitution expected Congress to be the most powerful branch of government. Congress would be much more numerous than the President and his staff, which in the early years varied from a few people to none. Therefore, the Congress would have more time and energy to devote to government business. Because they represented specific districts and states, members of Congress would be closer to the people than a President elected by an intermediate group (the electoral college).

The legacy of colonial experience, when governors appointed by the English king frequently overruled the popularly elected legislatures, gave added prestige to the legislative branch. Finally, the framers expected presidential elections to be most often decided in the House of Representatives, according to the provision that provided for a House election in the event there was no majority in the electoral college. A President elected by the House would surely incur large obligations to its members and would likely be "Congress's man." In fact, election by the House has occurred only twice, in 1876 and 1824.

Most people know that the President, not the Congress, now stands at the center of American national government. Some of the reasons for this change will become obvious as the structure and workings of Congress are described. However, the problem of legislative decline is worldwide. In the twentieth century, in all governments that include an elected law-making body, that body's power has declined. The American Congress, more than most national legislatures, has retained at least some of its independence and influence.

Structure[2]

The United States has a **bicameral national legislature.** The Congress is divided into two parts called, collectively, the **Houses of**

[1] Alexander Hamilton, James Madison, and John Jay, *The Federalist Papers,* No. 48 (New York: Mentor Edition, 1963), p. 309.

[2] For a detailed discussion of recent changes in congressional structures and procedures, see Chapter 10.

Congress. Individually, they are called the **Senate,** and the **House of Representatives** (or just the House). Members of the Senate are called **senators:** members of the House of Representatives are called **representatives** or congressmen and congresswomen and, sometimes, congresspeople or congresspersons. The Senate has one hundred members: two from each of the fifty states, who are elected for six-year terms. One third of the senators are elected every two years. There are 435 members of the House of Representatives. This number, set by legislation, is divided among the states in proportion to population, except that each state, no matter how small its population, is entitled to at least one representative. As states gain and lose population (measured every ten years by the census), they gain and lose representatives.

This structure is the result of a compromise that resolved the most important conflict of the Constitutional Convention. The small states feared that if representation in the national legislature were based strictly on population, the large states would overwhelm them and that their interests would be neglected. They therefore insisted that in one house—the Senate—each state be represented equally and that the approval of both houses be required to pass a law.

Constitutional Mandate—Powers and Restrictions

Article I of the Constitution states: "All legislative powers [are] vested in . . . Congress. . . ." Congress is, in other words, the law-making branch. The Constitution also gives Congress specific powers: "to declare war"; "to regulate commerce among the several states and the Indians . . ."; "to raise and maintain an army and a navy"; "to establish courts inferior to the Supreme Court"; and so on.

Lawmaking

A **law** is a binding rule that has the authority of government behind it. Prohibitions against murder and racial discrimination are laws. So are the regulations that set the amount of meat in hotdogs or the safety requirement for airplanes. However, many of the most important laws that Congress makes are not these traditional prohibitions and regulations but are, instead, the **"programs"** featured in newspaper headlines: "Congress cuts education program," or "Congress passes biggest space program." These programs are laws; they are rules that say how the tax money collected by the federal government will be spent. They are the country's priorities: so much for health care, so much for cleaner air, so much for the military.

This kind of lawmaking is based on one of the most important specific powers given to Congress: "No money shall be drawn from the Treasury, but in Consequence of Appropriations made by Law ..." (Article I, Section 9). The government of the United States is not supposed to spend money for any purpose, from buying paper clips to fighting a war, unless Congress has passed a law, called an **appropriation,** that directs the secretary of the treasury to spend the money for that purpose. By using this "power of the purse," Congress could, in theory, seriously limit, or even eliminate, other parts of the government. By refusing to appropriate money for the armed forces or the President's White House staff, Congress could put these organizations out of business. The authority has never been pushed to this extreme, but the threat of serious cuts is a powerful congressional weapon.

Relations to Other Branches: Congress's Place in the System of Checks and Balances

Richard Neustadt said it first, and textbook writers have been happy to quote him since:

> The Constitutional Convention of 1787 is supposed to have created a government of "separated powers." It did nothing of the sort. Rather, it created a government of separated institutions sharing power.[3]

Congress shares its power with the President and with the Supreme Court. Although Congress is designated as the legislative branch, the President is very much part of the lawmaking process. Article I gives the President veto power. If the President dislikes legislation passed by Congress, he can refuse to sign it and return it to Congress, stating his reasons. This is called a **veto.** The fate of the bill is then up to Congress. If Congress passes the bill by a two-thirds vote of each house, it becomes law without the President's signature. This is known as **overriding a veto.** If the vote falls short of two thirds in either house, the bill dies—it has been successfully vetoed.

[3] Richard Neustadt, *Presidential Power* (New York: John Wiley & Sons, 1960), p. 33.

The result of the veto provision is that a combination of the President and one third of one house of Congress can block any legislation. President Nixon demonstrated during his fifth year in office (1973) that this combination can be very powerful. He vetoed nine bills and Congress overrode only one veto. During President Ford's first full year in office (1975), a similar pattern was established. He vetoed fifteen bills. Congress overrode only three vetoes even though President Ford had vetoed popular bills and in spite of the very large Democratic majorities in both houses.

In order to prevent a President from delaying legislation indefinitely, the Constitution provides that unless he acts on a bill within ten days of its reaching him, either by vetoing it or signing it into law, the bill becomes law without his signature. However, if Congress adjourns (stops meeting) before ten days are up, the President may simply leave the bill on his desk and it does *not* become law after ten days. Instead, it dies. As previously defined, this is a **pocket veto.** It can only occur at the end of a session and does not require a two-thirds vote to override it. When Congress reconvenes, it simply takes up the bill again and passes it as if it had never been passed before. Then it goes to the President and he must decide what to do, as he normally would.

The Constitution also divides authority in foreign affairs between the President and Congress. Thus, only Congress can declare war, but the President is commander in chief of the armed forces. The President appoints ambassadors and negotiates treaties, but the Senate must approve both—the appointment of ambassadors by a simple majority, treaties by a two-thirds vote. In spite of this formal division of power, the President now dominates foreign and military policy (as is related in detail in Chapter 2).

Another check on Congress's lawmaking power is the Supreme Court's power of **judicial review,** which means the power of the Court to declare laws passed by Congress (and the President) unconstitutional. Although this authority is not explicitly granted in the Constitution, it is firmly established by custom and precedent.

In addition to its general lawmaking power and its specific powers in military and foreign affairs, Congress has been given certain devices to check the other branches. Congress has the constitutional authority to limit the **appellate jurisdiction** of the Supreme Court. This means that Congress can say what cases can be appealed up to the Supreme Court from the state courts and from the lower federal courts. Because most important cases (such as civil rights cases) reach the Court by this route, this is potentially a very strong power. Congress could pass a law saying that no civil rights cases could be appealed to the Supreme Court. This would have left standing the decisions of state courts and lower federal courts that separate but equal school systems were constitutional. Or, Congress could abolish the Court's appelate jurisdiction completely and leave it with the insignificant jurisdiction granted directly under the Constitution (see Chapter 4). Congress has never used this weapon, although it came close in 1958. The threat remains, and may well have influenced the Court in deciding some issues such as the rights of the accused and released time for religious education.

Congress's ultimate weapon against the President is known as **impeachment.** Most people think that this means removal from office, but impeachment is only the first step in the process by which Congress can remove a President from office. Impeachment means the formal bringing of charges against the President. It is the rough equivalent of an indictment in an ordinary criminal case. The Constitution gives the sole power of impeachment to the House of Representatives. If the House decides there is sufficient evidence against a President, it impeaches—that is, it brings formal charges against—him. The President must then stand trial, with the Senate acting as the jury, and the chief justice of the United States presiding as judge. If two thirds of the Senate find the President guilty, he is convicted and removed from office.

One President has been impeached, but not convicted. Andrew Johnson, who succeeded Abraham Lincoln, was formally charged by the House. The Senate acquitted him by a margin of one vote.

What is an impeachable offense? The Constitution says that a President can be impeached for bribery, treason, and "other High Crimes and Misdemeanors" (Article II, Section 4): In the winter of 1973–1974, the House of Representatives gave its Judiciary Committee the job of investigating President Nixon's conduct to see if he had committed impeachable offenses. From the beginning of the inquiry, there were sharp disagreements over the meaning of "other High Crimes and Misdemeanors."

Some people, notably President Nixon's lawyers and conservative Republicans, felt that only illegal acts—crimes such as obstruction of justice—were impeachable offenses. Others, such as Peter Rodino, the chairman of the committee, and John Doar, the counsel to the committee, felt differently. They argued that a president may be impeached for noncriminal acts such as the abuse of power or the failure to supervise properly his subordinates.

Throughout its hearings, the committee debated the issue. Eventually a majority of the committee, including conservative southern Democrats and some Republicans voted impeachment. The majority passed three articles of impeachment. The first accused the President "personally and through his subordinates" of having participated in the Watergate coverup.

The second said that Nixon had "repeatedly engaged in conduct violating the constitutional rights of citizens . . . impairing . . . the proper administration of justice, or contravening the laws governing agencies of the executive branch. . . ." Specifically, the article referred to attempts to get the Internal Revenue Service (IRS) to audit people the Nixon administration disliked; to attempts to get the FBI to investigate other "enemies," and to the establishment of a secret investigative unit in the White House that carried out illegal acts, including the break-in at the office of Daniel Ellsberg's psychiatrist.

The third article was directed at the President's refusal to comply with subpoenas (legal orders) issued by the Judiciary Committee itself. The committee had asked to see many White House documents and to receive many of the tape recordings made by the White House bugging system Nixon had installed. These orders the President had refused to honor. According to the committee, the President had "[substituted] his judgment as to what materials were necessary for the inquiry, interposed the powers of the Presidency against the lawful subpoenas of the House of Representatives, thereby assuming to himself functions and judgments necessary to the exercise of the sole power of impeachment vested by the Constitution in the House of Representatives." In other words, the committee thought that the President had tried to block the impeachment process.

On the first article, all 21 Democrats voted aye; 6 Republicans out of 17 voted aye. The vote was 27 to 11. Again on the second article, all 21 Democrats vote aye; they were joined by 7 Republicans. The vote was 28 to 10. Nineteen Democrats and 2 Republicans supported the third article. The final vote was 21 to 17.

Shortly after the votes were taken, the President released a long-sought tape recording of his conversations with his advisers. Nearly everyone who heard the tapes thought they proved the President's involvement in the Watergate coverup. Of course, concealing a crime is itself a crime. All the Republicans who had voted against that article announced that they had changed their minds.

Republican leaders in the Senate said that President Nixon's chances of avoiding conviction were slim. They made their opinion known to him in a private meeting and he resigned his office, the first President in American history to do so.

Congressional Self-Rule

Each house of the Congress makes it own rules and determines its own internal structure. These structures and rules are limited only by the Constitution as it is interpreted by the Court. If either house decided tomorrow to abolish committees, or to meet only from 3:00 to 4:00 A.M. on alternate Tuesdays, or to conduct meetings in pig Latin, no other branch could stop them. These examples are deliberately exaggerated and farfetched to emphasize Congress's constitutional autonomy.

The Constitution specifically makes each house "judge of the elections, returns, and qualifications of its own members." This authority has been exercised. At times the House of Representatives has used this authority to deny seats to those having unpopular views, such as the Mormons. Most recently, the House of Representatives voted to deny a seat to Adam Clayton Powell, the black congressman from Harlem, on the grounds that he had misused government funds. In that case, however, the Supreme Court overruled the House, saying that the House had gone beyond its constitutional authority. Once a member was seated, the House could punish him or even expel him. But, the Court argued, to deny a seat to a duly elected representative was unconstitutional [*Powell v. McCormick* 395 U.S. (1969)].

Recruitment: How Do People Become Congresspersons?

At the present time nearly all senators and representatives are members of either the Republican or Democratic party. Over the last thirty years nearly all the people elected to Congress have been members of these two parties. Occasionally, a minor party's candidate has won a House or a Senate seat. The most reliable route, however, is to go through the major parties, to get the nomination, and then to run as the party's candidate in the general election.

The structure of the parties varies considerably from state to state and from congressional district to district. The key to understanding congressional nominations and elections is understanding the difference between a one-party and a two-party system. Many people think that all of American politics is based on competition between two strong parties. The fact is that this kind of competition exists in less than 100 of the 435 congressional district. The other 335 or more are *not* competitive. They are **one-party districts**—areas in which one of the parties is so strong and has the allegiance of so many of the voters that the opposition has no chance of winning.

In most of New York City, for instance, the Democratic candidate will win overwhelmingly unless there is a scandal or some other unusual event. In most rural areas outside the South, Republicans can count on easy victories. In the South most areas still vote solidly Democratic for Congress, a historical carry-over from the Civil War and Reconstruction.

In a one-party district, unless it is a machine area (see Chapter 7), the party structure is weak. Having no opposition, there is no incentive for the party to make itself into a well-disciplined, well-organized operation. Each ambitious individual within the party knows that once he or she gets the party's nomination, he or she will win the election. Therefore, there is no reason to cooperate with others in the party structure. They are only potential rivals; they are not needed as allies. Parties break down into competing factions, which support particular candidates or interest groups. The party leaders do not choose the candidates. *Candidates nominate themselves,* by fighting it out in the primary elections. (The **primary election** is usually held solely for the voters who are members of a particular party. They vote as to whom they want to be their candidate in the regular election.) In a one-party system, winning the primary is as good as winning the regular election. The candidate's personal characteristics become very important. If he or she is a good orator, or well known, he or she has a substantial advantage.

In this highly fragmented, highly competitive situation, the incumbent (the person already holding the office) has even greater advantages than usual. First, the incumbent is known. His or her name appears frequently in the local newspaper and on television and radio news programs. If used wisely, the office itself can become a means for getting still more free publicity. "Congressman Throt-tlebottom pictured at charity ball." "Congressman T. assists at open-ing of new post office." "Congresswoman delivers graduation address to high school class." All of these reflect the congressperson's status as a local celebrity, a status his or her rivals lack. Second, the incum-bent is in a position to his his or her supporters and hurt his or her enemies. If a local interest group needs legislation, he or she may be able to help them get it. If one of his or her constituents is having trouble getting a pension check from the Veterans' Administration, a phone call from the congressperson's office may speed the process. In turn, the incumbent receives votes and other forms of assistance, such as campaign contributions. Third, the incumbent is in a position to take credit for the good things that happen in the district gener-ally. If a new dam or highway is constructed, the congressperson can let it be known that he or she worked hard to bring this new asset to the constituents.

Fourth, all congresspersons are entitled by law to hire a staff at government expense. These employees are not supposed to partici-pate in campaigns, but they almost always do. Furthermore, the activities they carry on as part of their regular jobs—helping con-stituents with problems and drafting and pushing legislation favor-able to important interest groups in the district—have a lot to do with whether the congressperson is reelected or not.

Another privilege of office is the right to free use of the United States Postal Service. Congresspersons (and senators) may send let-ters to their constituents free of charge. This **franking privilege** is supposed to promote communication between people and represen-tative, but it is the rare politician who does not see in it a chance to mention his or her own virtues. In February 1976, Representative Ken Hechler (Democrat of West Virginia), introduced legislation to end the franking privilege. He argued that most of the 317 million pieces of mail sent out in the previous fiscal year at a cost of $34.5 million were "little more than thinly disguised campaign docu-ments." The bill failed.

Just as being a congressperson (or senator) makes one a sought-after celebrity at home, it also provides an opportunity to make points with constituents who visit Washington. Congresspersons and their staffs spend a considerable amount of time catering to the tour-ists from their districts. Having a picture taken with a visiting scout troop on the steps of the Capitol, providing passes to the House Gal-

lery, and arranging for a sight-seeing tour are activities most senators and congresspersons perform energetically.

Given all these advantages, a moderately capable politician, once
elected as a representative in a one-party district, will be difficult to
unseat. A particularly energetic, rich opponent may be troublesome.
The only other threat is some tide of national opinion that goes
against the incumbent's party. In the special elections of 1973 and
1974, and in the regular elections of 1974, Watergate and a recession
enabled the Democratic party to win congressional seats in some districts that had been electing Republicans for thirty years in a row.
Then, in 1980, the tide reversed. Ronald Reagan's popularity, the
growth of conservative groups operating through political action
committees, and the Republican Party's grasp of sophisticated campaign techniques including direct mail fund raising and computer-
ized voting analysis helped to unseat many Democrats (see pages 70-
71 for a detailed discussion).

The basis of a one-party district is, of course, the district's boundaries. Each state legislature draws the lines for the Congressional
districts in that state. Usually the majority party creates districts
that favor its candidates. In 1964 the Supreme Court ruled that all
of a state's congressional districts had to be approximately equal in
population and compact in shape. This decision outlawed the worst
abuses of the old system in which some districts contained ten or
twenty times more people than others, and some were of such complicated shapes as to resemble salamanders (the famous practice of
"gerrymandering," named for a signer of the Declaration of Independence, Elbridge Gerry of Massachusetts).

Still, the majority party can help its candidates. Suppose, for
instance, there is a Democratic city of 200,000 voters, surrounded by
Republican suburbs with 300,000 voters. (See Figure 3.1.) If the
Republicans control the state legislature, the best thing for them is
to make two districts each having 150,000 of the suburban Republicans and 100,000 of the city Democrats (line "A" in Figure 3.1
makes this division). In this way the Republicans get two districts in
which they have a 3-to-2 majority, or two safe seats. For the Democrats, line "B" in Figure 3.1 gives a better outcome by creating one
district with about 175,000 Democrats to 100,000 Republicans and
a second with about 25,000 Democrats and 200,000 Republicans.
Thus there is one safe Democratic seat and one safe Republican seat.

Since the Constitution requires that House seats be apportioned by population as determined by the census, state legislatures are now redrawing districts in accordance with the 1980 census. Even though the Democrats control 27 state legislatures, the Republicans have a great advantage in this process. The Republican National Committee has developed and made available to the state parties a system for analyzing voting and population patterns. Using powerful computers and highly detailed data banks, this system can predict election results from proposed districts and can also generate plans for districts that favor one party or the other. The Democrats do not have this system which requires time and millions of dollars to develop. As a result, the districts drawn for 1982 are likely to favor the Republicans and to enhance their changes of gaining a majority in the House to go with the majority in the Senate won in 1980.

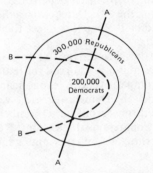

Figure 3.1. *How district boundaries can influence election results.*

In a district with competition between two relatively equal parties, the congressperson's situation is quite different. Here the incumbent must fight not only to win renomination but also to win the election in November against an equally strong opposition party. Thus, he or she is campaigning virtually all the time, both against the rivals within his or her own party and in the opposition party.

Results

The House of Representatives experienced relatively little turnover in the 1950s and 1960s. An increasingly large proportion—from 2.8 per cent of the members in 1911 to 20 per cent in 1970—served twenty years or more. Southern Democrats, who tend to have long careers, controlled a disproportionately large number of committee chairmanships and exercized considerable power.

A variety of factors changed the situation in the 1970s. First, the generation of incumbents elected to the House in the 1930s and 1940s began to age and retire, to be defeated in primaries and elections, or to die. About nineteen Congresspersons retired each year from public life in the 1960s but the average went up to twenty-nine a year in the 1970s. Besides age, the changed political atmosphere brought about by a succession of scandals—Watergate, Koreagate, Abscam—encouraged departure from the House. Representatives complained of constant media scrutiny and public mistrust. Increased pressure from single-issue interest groups was also mentioned by some retirees as a factor in their decision.

Of course, the scandals themselves helped to unseat some incumbents. In 1980 four of the five Democrats indicted in the Abscam affair and the one indicted Republican lost their seats either in primaries or in the regular elections.

The overall result has been a greater turnover caused by more voluntary retirements, and a few forced retirements, but not by any general increase in competitiveness. Republicans have gained more seats in the House since the Democrats held a very large majority as the Watergate scandal turned out large numbers of Republicans in 1974. In the 1980 congressional elections Republicans defeated twenty-seven Democratic incumbents and gained thirty-one seats altogether.

Recruitment: The Senate

At first glance, the situation in the Senate appears rather different from that in the House. At least twenty-five of the fifty states have competitive two-party systems. One would expect that incumbents in these states would have a harder time getting reelected and that there would be greater turnover and, therefore, greater responsiveness to changing moods in the electorate. However, in the period between 1948 and 1970, 76 per cent of the incumbents won reelection in competitive states and 84.1 per cent of the incumbents won overall. Then in the 1970s the situation changed dramatically, following a pattern similar to that of the House elections. Thirty per cent of the incumbent Senators who ran for reelection lost in the years 1972–1980. Between 1976 and 1980 the combination of deaths, retirements, and defeated incumbents produced fifty-four new senators and a Republican majority. Since more Democratic senators are up for reelection in 1982 than Republicans, it seems likely that the Republicans will increase their majority.

Differences in constituencies produce an ideological difference between the House and Senate. Because senators represent *whole* states, and because most states have at least some urban areas within them, senators are likely to be more responsive to the needs of cities and the groups within them—especially minorities—than are those members of the House who come from strictly rural districts where there are few minorities, or where minorities are the victims of heavy discrimination. This difference is reflected in the more liberal stands the Senate has taken on issues such as housing, urban renewal, and Social Security.

Internal Structure: Who's Got the Power

We begin this analysis of the internal power structure by discussing the committee system, and then we discuss party structures. In both sections we note the recent trend toward decentralization, toward dispersion of power among more members of the House and the Senate. This trend is in sharp contrast to the system of the 1950s and 1960s when a few senior members dominated both houses of Congress.

The Committee System

The Constitution states that: "Each House may determine the Rules of its Proceedings . . ." In addition to the rules of parliamentary procedure (when a bill may be debated, which amendment is voted first, and so on), this power extends to the broader questions of how to do business and how to organize. Both the House and the Senate have decided to divide themselves into smaller bodies, called **committees,** that do most of the work.

Part of the reason for this decision is the enormous workload that Congress faces. Every year thousands of **bills** (a bill is a proposed law) are submitted to Congress. From 1979–1980 more than 10,000 bills and resolutions were introduced. Many bills are long and complex and deal with obscure or difficult subjects—the regulation of drug manufacture, advanced missile systems, farm price supports. Trying to consider each bill at a meeting of the whole House or of the whole Senate would be impossible. Instead, the bills are referred to committees. Each committee is given certain subjects to handle. Being much smaller than either the House or Senate, committees can work more quickly. Being specialized, the committee members can become experts.

Congress established the number of committees, the responsibilities of each, and the size of each in the Legislative Reorganization Act of 1946. Separate committee systems, which vary slightly, were set up for the House and the Senate. Only senators serve on Senate

Table 3.1
The Standing Committees of the Congress As of January 1981

House of Representatives	Senate
Agriculture	Agriculture, Nutrition, and Forestry
Appropriations	Appropriations
Armed Services	Armed Services
Banking, Finance, and Urban Affairs	Banking, Housing, and Urban Affairs
Budget	Budget
District of Columbia	Commerce, Science, and Transportation
Education and Labor	Energy and Natural Resources
Energy and Commerce	Environment and Public Works
Foreign Affairs	Finance
Government Operations	Foreign Relations
House Administration	Governmental Affairs
Interior and Insular Affairs	Judiciary
Judiciary	Labor and Human Resources
Merchant Marine and Fisheries	Rules and Administration
Post Office and Civil Service	Small Business
Public Works and Transportation	Veterans' Affairs
Rules	
Science and Technology	
Small Business	
Standards of Official Conduct	
Veterans' Affairs	
Ways and Means	

committees; only members of the House of Representatives serve on House committees. In the House there are twenty-two **standing** (permanent) **committees,** whereas the Senate has fifteen. Three of the House committees are considered the most important—Ways and Means, which deals with taxes; Appropriations; and the Rules Committee (discussed in detail on page 94). A congressman who serves on one of these three committees usually serves on no other committee. If a congressman is not a member of one of these committees, he usually serves on two of the nineteen lesser committees. In the Senate, which has nearly as many committees and less than one quarter the membership of the House senators serve on two major committees and one minor committee.

A committee's responsibilities—the jobs assigned to it under the Reorganization Act—determine its power. The power of the Appropriations committees in both houses is based on the fact that they deal with all money bills. Everything that the government does costs money and most of it is paid by by appropriations. Therefore, the Appropriations committees have a say on nearly everything the government does. Because the Senate and House usually follow the committees' recommendations, the committees really exercise the **power of the purse.**

In addition to the House and Senate committees, there are **joint committees** made up of members from both houses. These may be permanent or temporary. A list of the permanent joint committees is presented in Table 3.2. As their titles suggest, these committees deal with special problems, such as the economy, where Congress felt a particular need for a concentrated effort. Members serve on these committees much as they do on the ordinary committees of the House and Senate. Joint committees are advisory bodies; they cannot report legislation. The chairmanship of joint committees alternates between a senator and a representative.

Table 3.2
Permanent Joint Committees of the Congress

Joint Economic Committee
Joint Committee on Taxation
Joint Committee on the Library
Joint Committee on Printing

Select committees and special committees may be set up by either house, or by both houses of Congress jointly. They are temporary committees formed to look into a special problem. The Senate committee chaired by former Senator Sam Ervin, which held televised hearings in the summer of 1974 on Watergate and related matters, was called the Senate Select Committee on Presidential Campaign Practices. It did its work, wrote a report, and ceased to exist as of July 1974.

One other type of committee, the conference committee which is used to reach a compromise on the differences between House and Senate versions of the same bill, is described elsewhere in detail (p. 97).

The Power of Committees

Many years ago President Woodrow Wilson wrote that Congress is a collection of committees that meet together only for the purpose of approving what each has done separately. Although exaggerated, the statement is still largely true. The committee system itself is based on the assumption that many specialized, small groups can do a better job of legislating than one large, undifferentiated group. In addition, congresspeople follow committee recommendations because of laziness, ignorance, fear that the committee will punish the congressman who votes against them, and fear that if the system of mutual approval breaks down the congressman's own committee will be challenged. Most important, congresspersons follow the committees because of respect for their expertise. The volume of legislation and the complexity of important bills make it impossible for a member to know about each bill. Congresspersons will, therefore, rely on the experts—the committee. They have held hearings, studied the issue, and consulted the experts and the interested parties. Their opinion should be respected.

The Power of Committee Chairpersons

From 1955–1966, the chairman of the House Rules Committee was a man named Smith from rural Virginia. As is explained (p. 94), the Rules Committee is very powerful because all bills except money bills must pass through it before going to the floor for a vote by the full House. When the Rules Committee received legislation that Smith disliked, such as civil rights bills, Smith would simply pocket the bill and drive across the Potomac River to his home, an isolated farmhouse without a telephone. Once inside he would turn loose a pack of wild hunting dogs and defy the world to come and get him and the bill.

This tactic worked, even though the supporters of the bill sometimes included the President and majorities of both houses of Congress. Smith was using, in a particularly dramatic and intractable way, a traditional power of a committee chairman: the right to call meetings of the committee to consider legislation, or, in this case, *not* to call committee meetings.

To understand how one man, representing one rural district in Virginia, had the power to defy Presidents and majorities in Congress, it is necessary to analyze the power of a committee chairman in a more general way.

All committee chairpersons are members of the majority party because that party (provided it is united) has the majority of the votes. Because the Constitution grants Congress internal self-rule, the majority can organize in any way it chooses. Most of the time the majority party does not completely reorganize the system. It simply elects its owm members to most of the positions of power, including all the committee chairmanships. From the end of the nineteenth century until very recently, both parties used **seniority** to pick committee chairmen. The member of the majority party who has served longest on the committee is elected chairman automatically.

Seniority is not a law; it is not a rule of the House or Senate. It is simply a practice both parties have decided to follow. Supporters of the seniority system say that it guarantees experienced leadership, prevents destructive conflicts over who will be chairman, and protects congressional independence. Because the choice of chairmen is made automatically, no outside forces, such as the President or interest groups, can influence the decision. Detractors say the practice is arbitrary: that it puts people into power who are unrepresentative of and unresponsive to majority sentiment in the Congress and the country, and that these people are also sometimes incompetent. The same seniority system that made Smith chairman of the Rules Committee made Emanuel Celler, a liberal from Brooklyn, chairman of the House Judiciary Committee, and made Adam Clayton Powell, the black congressperson from Harlem, chairman of the House Education and Labor Committee. In general, however, seniority has favored men like "Judge" Smith—conservative, rural, and southern.

As explained earlier in this chapter, many southern districts are one-party districts, in which the Democratic party nearly always wins. In one-party districts the incumbent has a great advantage over any challengers. Therefore, southern congresspersons have an excellent chance of being reelected year after year and of building up their seniority.

There are also one-party districts in the liberal areas of the North—the big cities—but one election gave the southern Democrats a decisive edge over their northern brethren. In 1946 many of the northern Democrats were beaten as Republicans capitalized on the extreme unpopularity of the Truman administration. The southern Democrats managed to survive and thereby gained at least two years of seniority over the northerners. In many cases the advantage was much greater because the beaten congressmen chose not to run again, leaving their seats to newcomers who, by definition, were at the bottom of the seniority ladder.

Recently, reform-minded members of Congress, in alliance with groups such as Common Cause and the National Committee for an Effective Congress, have been able to make some substantial changes in the seniority system. Since December 1973 the Democratic party in the House has voted to choose the committee chairpersons. Yet, the results of the elections for committee chairmen followed the seniority rule in 1973. In the same year, the Republicans in the Senate adopted a plan by which the Republican members on a committee would elect the ranking member (the leader of the minority party). This change was also one of form only. The results of the voting were the same as applying the seniority rule. In 1975, however, the Democrats deviated sharply from the seniority rule in choosing chairmen in the House of Representatives.

At the beginning of the 94th Congress the rule had been further modified so that the Democratic Steering and Policy Committee would submit nominees for chairmanships to the caucus that would make the final choice. The Steering and Policy Committee was itself a new organization, created in 1972 to strengthen the party leadership. Some members are appointed by the speaker, who is the chairman of the committee, and others are elected to represent different regions of the country. As a group, this committee is considerably more liberal than the old committee chairmen were as a group.

In January 1975 the Steering and Policy Committee voted to oust two incumbent committee chairmen: Wayne Hays of the House Administration Committee and F. Edward Hébert of the Armed Services Committee. The caucus, in its turn, voted to keep Hays, but defeated Hébert and two other incumbent chairmen, Wright Patman of the Banking and Currency Committee and W. R. Poage of Agriculture. Since this dramatic episode, however, both parties have followed seniority in choosing committee chairpersons, although there have been a few deviations in the selection of subcommittee chairs. Most observers feel that the possibility of being dismissed has made chairpersons less arbitrary and less powerful, and gives more power to subcommittee chairpersons and to individual committee members. See Tables 3.3 and 3.4.

Table 3.3
Chairpersons of the Standing Committees of the House of Representatives 1981

Committee	Chairperson and State	
Agriculture	E(Kika) de la Garza	Texas
Appropriations	Jamie L. Whitten	Miss.
Armed Services	Melvin Price	Ill.
Banking, Finance and Urban Affairs	Fernand J. St. Germain	R.I.
Budget	James R. Jones	Okl.
District of Columbia	Ronald V. Dellums	Cal.
Education and Labor	Carl D. Perkins	Ky.
Energy and Commerce	John D. Dingell	Mich.
Foreign Affairs	Clement J. Zablocki	Wisc.
Government Operations	Jack Brooks	Texas
House Administration	Augustus F. Hawkins	Cal.
Interior and Insular Affairs	Morris K. Udall	Ariz.
Judiciary	Peter W. Rodino, Jr.	N.J.
Merchant Marine and Fisheries	Walter B. Jones	N.C.
Post Office and Civil Service	William D. Ford	Mich.
Public Works and Transportation	James J. Howard	N.J.
Rules	Richard Bolling	Mo.
Science and Technology	Don Fuqua	Fla.
Small Business	Parrin J. Mitchell	Md.
Standards of Official Conduct	Louis Stokes	Ohio
Veterans' Affairs	G. V. (Sonny) Montgomery	Miss.
Ways and Means	Dan Rostenkowski	Ill.

Table 3.4
Chairpersons of the Standing Committees of the Senate, 1981

Committee	Chairperson and State	
Agriculture, Nutrition and Forestry	Jesse Helms	N.C.
Appropriations	Mark O. Hatfield	Ore.
Armed Services	John Tower	Texas
Banking, Housing, and Urban Affairs	Jake Garn	Utah
Budget	Pete V. Domenici	N.M.
Commerce, Science, and Transportation	Bob Packwood	Ore.
Energy and Natural Resources	James A. McClure	Idaho
Environment and Public Works	Robert T. Stafford	Vt.
Finance	Bob Dole	Kan.
Foreign Relations	Charles H. Percy	Ill.
Governmental Affairs	William V. Roth, Jr.	Del.
Judiciary	Strom Thurmond	S.C.
Labor and Human Resources	Orrin G. Hatch	Utah
Rules and Administration	Charles McC. Mathias, Jr.	Md.
Small Business	Lowell P. Weicker, Jr.	Conn.
Veterans' Affairs	Alan K. Simpson	Wyo.

Resources of the Office. The following are some of the most important of the power resources that go along with the office of committee chairperson.

The chairperson hires and directs most of the committee staff, sets the agenda, and selects and schedules the witnesses for public hearings.

As mentioned in the case of "Judge" Smith, the committee chairman decides initially whether a bill will be pigeonholed. If he decides to deal with the bill, it is his choice as to whether the full committee handles the bill, whether one of the subcommittees handles it, or whether a new subcommittee is created to handle the bill.

When a bill from his committee reaches the House floor, the chairman can put himself in charge of the bill during floor debate and voting. He can allot time for speeches to the bill's supporters.

He has the option of opening and closing debate on the bill, and he can move the question at any time (call the bill up for a vote).

Personal Resources. How powerful the committee chairman actually is depends in part on how skilfully he uses the resources of his office and in part on how well he develops other, less formal, resources.

As the senior member, the chairman has the opportunity to become the most experienced and the most knowledgeable member of the committee. A prime example of this resource in action was Arkansas' Wilbur Mills, the former chairman of the House Ways and Means Committee. Until he became involved with an exotic dancer, Mills had the reputation of being the most powerful man in Congress. Following several public escapades with the dancer he was stripped of his chairmanship and began treatment for alcoholism.

Prior to these incidents, Mills had dominated the Ways and Means Committee. "Ways and Means" refers to how to raise money, how to tax. It is this committee that decides who will pay how much, what exemptions will be granted, and so forth. Such considerations have made for extremely complicated tax laws whose volumes are as thick as a New York City phone book. It was said of Mills, who has been a member of the committee for more than twenty years, and was its chairman from 1958–1974, that he knew more about the tax laws than any man alive. Other members of the committee respected that knowledge and deferred to him because of it.

Mills exemplified another way for a chairman to increase his power. During the 1960s and early 1970s, he was a tireless worker, often putting in eighteen hours a day. Thus, he maintained his superior knowledge and his control of the committee's staff and business.

Mills' successor as chairman was Al Ullman, of the Ways and Means Committee, a pleasant, able representative from Oregon who had none of Mills' authoritative drive. Ullman rarely succeeded in leading the committee and never dominated it. On important votes the committee often split almost evenly, diminishing its influence in the House and demonstrating the decline of its chairman's power. The present chairperson, Representative Dan Rostenkowski of Chicago has attempted to reassert the power of the chairperson, especially in his efforts to defeat President Reagan's three-year tax reduction proposal. However, Rostenkowski lost this fight as 48 Democrats, including members of the Ways and Means Committee, broke ranks to vote with the Republicans.

Over the years, the chairman has a chance to establish relations with other people in Washington and around the country who are in positions of power. Knowing whom to telephone in a particular government agency, or being on a first-name basis with the representative of a powerful interest group, is a key resource in American politics.

A skillful chairman will build up support for himself within his committee. He will give subcommittee chairmanships to people who agree with him, thus putting his allies in positions of power. He will help other members to get bills passed, putting them in his debt. He will try, when vacancies occur, to recruit new members who share his ideology or are willing to defer to him.

Perhaps the most important benefit of long service is the chance to build a relationship with the committee's staff (described in detail on p. 83), which does much of the actual work of the committee. Like the chairman, the staff constitutes much of the expertise of the committee, and like him they have the experience and contacts to reinforce their technical expertise. Having worked with them for many years, and being in a position of formal authority over the staff, the chairman is likely to be the person who most influences the staff and, through them, the actions of the committee and its relations to other government agencies and private groups.

From his years in Washington, the chairman gains social contacts and a general sort of knowledge that are helpful in accumulating political debts, especially from newcomers. Helping a freshman congressman find a house or a school for his children may do as much to win his vote as the chairman's knowledge or persuasive abilities.

Finally, the chairman derives power from the divisions among those who might oppose him. A chairman can always be overruled by a majority of the members of the committee, and a committee and its chairman can always be overruled by a majority of the House or the Senate. Both are rare, for good reason. A congressman or senator who is considering whether to vote against his chairman or any chairman must realize that, if he does, he will be paid back. Any bill the congressperson or senator wants passed by that committee is doomed unless he can once again get a majority of the committee or the House to go along with him against the chairman. If he is successful the second time, there is the third time to consider, and so forth. Given the resources most chairmen command, and the ideological, ethnic, religious, regional, and other divisions among members of Congress, the chances of consistently overruling the chairman are slim. Therefore, most committee members learn to go along with the committee chairman.

Committee Assignments

Getting onto a good committee is half the battle for a congressperson or senator. In this section we look at how the process operates through the political parties.

The number of Republicans and Democrats on each committee is determined by the number of Republicans and Democrats in that house of Congress. Suppose there are 235 Democrats and 200 Republicans in the House. If a committee has 43 seats, the Democrats will get 23 or 24 of them. In other words, the proportion of seats each party gets will be roughly the same as the proportion of seats they have in that house. If the Senate is divided 55 Democrats to 45 Republicans, the Democrats will get roughly 55 per cent of the seats on each committee—say seven out of a twelve-member committee. If the Republicans gain five seats in the next election, then each Senate committee would be split fifty-fifty.

The question of *which* Democrats and Republicans sit on a particular committee is decided by special party committees, called **committees on committees.** For the Democrats in the House of Representatives, this committee used to consist of all the Democratic members of the Ways and Means Committee plus the speaker and the floor leader, if they are Democrats. This was changed in December 1974. The Democratic caucus, led by the seventy-five newly elected freshmen, voted to give the power to the Steering and Policy Committee. This was widely interpreted as a shift from a conservative to a liberal group.

For the Republicans, a group composed of the elected representatives of each of the state delegations makes the choices. In the Senate the choices for the Democrats are made by a committee selected by the Democratic floor leader, who is elected by all the Democratic senators. Similarly, for the Republicans, the committee on committees is chosen by the elected leader of the Republican conference.

In the past, seniority considerations dominated this process and junior members were relegated to the Post Office and Government Operations committees. Recently, the pattern has shifted to some extent. Seniority still counts, but younger members, even freshmen, may receive assignments on powerful committees such as Appropriations and Armed Services.

Several other factors influence the choices on assigning members to committees. There is some attempt to balance committees geographically and to assign members to committees that reflect the interests of the member's constituency or the member's own interests and expertise. Thus, most of the people on the agriculture committees come from farming areas; in fact, a study done in 1958 found that nearly all the members of the House Agriculture Committee were on subcommittees that regulated farm products grown in their particular districts.

Once seated on an important committee, such as Ways and Means in the House, or Finance in the Senate, a person is unlikely to give up the position. Ordinarily, seniority prevents a member's being removed from a committee without his request. Of course, if his party loses a large number of seats in an election, its share of the committee's seats will diminish. In this case, if there are too many party members on the committee, those with the least seniority will be moved to a lesser committee.

Subcommittees

At the beginning of the 96th Congress in 1979 there were 263 subcommittees—157 in the House, 101 in the Senate, and 5 subcommittees to joint committees.

Under the traditional seniority system, the chairperson of the full committee often controlled that committee's subcommittees. He decided how many subcommittees there would be, who would be on them, and what their jurisdiction would be. Now that chairpersons are selected, their power over subcommittees has declined. More often, the subcommittees' power and jurisdiction are permanently defined. Seniority, rather than the chairperson's wish decides who will chair the subcommittee.

Usually the full committee will accept the recommendations of its subcommittees. They are the ones who have studied the bill; they are experienced and expert in the subject. A committee member who challenges a subcommittee runs the risk that he and his subcommittee will be similarly challenged and that the subcommittee will punish him when they get the chance. Most of the time reciprocal approval is the watchword, just as it is among the full committees. In this situation subcommittee chairpersons exercise many of the powers over the subcommittee that the chairperson exercises over the full committee: scheduling, control of staff, and setting of the agenda.

Committee Staff

Congress and its committees lack the large numbers of experts and the easy access to information that executive agencies have. To strengthen itself in these respects, Congress has appropriated money so that its committees can hire people to work for them on a regular, full-time basis. Some of these people are experts in their fields. Thus, the Aeronautics and Space Committee might hire an engineer, and Agriculture Committee might hire an agronomist. Other staff members are clerks who take care of the committee's routine business, such as the setting up of hearings. For the most part the professional staff are lawyers who can assist both in research and in the writing of legislation.

In 1970 more than 1,600 people worked for congressional committees. By 1979 the figure had risen to 3,900 reflecting the Congress's desires to increase its ability to deal more knowledgeably with complex issues and to deal more competitively with the executive branch. The most important staff members are highly paid professionals who may earn as much as $50,000 a year. Other staff members are file clerks or typists. A recent survey found seventy-nine staff members of all ranks working for the House Public Works Committee, and about eighty staffers working for the Senate Budget Committee. Usually, the chairperson chooses most of the staff, with some positions reserved for the choices of the minority party made by the ranking member. Other staff may be chosen by senior committee members of subcommittee chairpersons or ranking members of subcommittees.

Staff Influence

Obviously, the importance of the staff and its director varies from committee to committee depending on the committee's work, the quality of the staff, and most important, the staff's relation to the committee chairperson.

When a committee's business is complex, requiring expert assistance, when the staff is energetic and capable, when the chairperson and the other members are willing to give responsibility to the staff—then the staff's influence is at its maximum and can be the equal of any representative's or senator's. For instance, Richard J. Sullivan is the head of the House Public Works staff. He came to Washington in 1957 and has served under four committee chairmen.

Among senators and representatives, he is rated as one of the most effective of the staff chiefs. His influence on the committee has been a strong one. Traditionally, the Public Works Committee had dealt with **pork barrel** legislation—the rivers and harbors bills that congresspersons love to display to their constituents. Sullivan helped to move the committee into an involvement with environmental legislation. His influence stems in part from his long service, which has given him the resources of experience, expertise, and knowledge; in part from his hard work and intelligence; and in part from the relationship of confidence that has developed between him and the committee chairman. His suggestions carry great weight with the chairman, and hence with the committee, and hence with the Congress.

On other committees such as the Rules Committee, less research is needed and hearings are informal matters. The staff is not an important part of the committee's operations.

In addition to doing research, committee staffs serve as links between the committee and the bureaucracy and between the committee and interest groups. In this capacity it is sometimes possible for the staff to go into business for itself. In other words, the staff may tell the bureaucracy that the committee wants something when the committee has no such desire. Because of this tendency and because the staff lawyers tend to generate more work by drafting legislation and getting members to introduce it, many congresspersons and senators are skeptical of the staffs' value. They fear government by the staffs amid the deluge of legislation.

Committee System: Summary

Committees are the most powerful parts of the Congress; as such, they decentralize power. In other words, they create many centers of power. But committees are not as powerful as they were twenty years ago. Weakening the power of the committee chairpersons has weakened the power of the committees. Subcommittees and their chairpersons and staffs have gained power, and individual members and their personal staffs have gained power. Thus, power has been further decentralized, further fragmented by being spread among many more people. Today a majority of the House of Representatives are either committee chairpersons or ranking members; subcommittee chairpersons or ranking members; or members of a crucially important committee such as Appropriations or Budget. Each of them has a good power position; each of them can bargain with other power holders.

This dispersal of power hinders speedy, coordinated policymaking and weakens the House in its competition with other branches. For instance, in 1981 the House rejected the budget made by its own committees in favor of President Reagan's budget.This presidential victory indicates the price of reducing the power of committees and committee chairpeople—outside forces can more easily dominate the House.

Internal Structure: The Parties

As was previously explained, committees are the dominant power centers in Congress. The parties—their caucuses, committees, and elected leaders—are the other main internal structure. To some extent the two systems balance each other. Parties are centralizing and committees are decentralizing. The outcome is clearly weighted, however, toward the committees and decentralization.

Caucuses and Conferences

Caucus and **Conference** are two names for the same thing: a meeting of all the party members in a particular legislative body. If all the Democratic senators meet together, it is the Senate Democratic caucus. The Republicans use the term *conference* for the same kind of meeting. The functions performed by such meetings differ according to the party and the house of Congress. Committee assignments are ratified by the caucuses. They elect some of the party leadership, which in the case of the majority party is also the leadership for the whole House. As explained, the House Democratic caucus votes on who will be the committee chairpersons, when the Democrats have a majority.

The caucuses may take a stand on an issue, and try to encourage all the members to abide by it, but such action is rare. During the first year of the Reagan administration, the influence of the House Democratic caucus declined sharply.

Party Leadership: The House

For the majority party the main leader is the **speaker of the House.** He is usually a senior member of the party who has worked his way up through the lesser party jobs. There has been, in other words, an orderly process of succession to the job, even though the speaker is elected by the majority caucus. The speaker presides over the House, which gives him powers of recognition and the power to rule on points of parliamentary procedure. He has some influence on scheduling, refers bills to committees, and appoints the House members of Conference Committees. One recent change has increased the speaker's power within the Democratic party. He appoints some of the members to the Steering and Policy Committee, which, since 1974, makes committee assignments and recommends chairpersons to the Democratic caucus.

As with the other party posts, the speaker's power depends more on his personal resources than his position. When Sam Rayburn was the speaker, his knowledge of House procedure, his central position, his experience in the House, his personal alliances, his energies, and his skills as a negotiator and as a presiding officer made him a formidable figure. His successor, John McCormick, was not, in part because he lacked Rayburn's personal stature. The incumbent, Thomas P. "Tip" O'Neill, Jr. has enjoyed a comparatively good reputation as a party leader. However, during the 1981 budget struggles some House Democrats criticized him for taking an extended vacation at a crucial time and for conceding to President Reagan instead of fighting. O'Neill's subsequent tougher stand on the tax issue may have restored his standing.

The **majority leader,** who is also elected by the caucus, is primarily responsible for leading his party during floor debates and voting. When the speaker is weak, the power of the majority leader may increase. Some observers gave "Tip" O'Neill, then the majority leader, a large share of the credit for having led the Democratic party in the impeachment struggle.

The **minority leader** is elected in the same fashion as the speaker and the majority leader and acts as a floor leader and strategist. Of course, he represents and is elected by the minority party.

Both party leaders appoint **whips** whose job it is to get their party's members to the floor in time to vote on important bills. They are also the main communications and bargaining links between the party's leadership and the members.

Party Committees

In addition to the committees on committees already described, there are **campaign committees,** which raise and distribute funds for election campaigns, and **policy committees,** which are supposed to set party stands on issues, but rarely do.

There are less formal groupings that do try to coordinate and consolidate their members in support or opposition to legislation. In the House, the **Democratic Study Group,** led by Phillip Burton of California, represents the strongest faction of liberal Democrats.

Party Leadership: The Senate

The **president** *pro tempore* is elected by the majority party to the thankless job of presiding over the Senate in the absence of the Vice President. (The latter is supposed to preside, but regularly shirks his only constitutionally appointed duty, other than succeeding the President.) The position has little power and usually goes to a senior member as an honorary title.

Floor Leaders. For both the majority and the minority parties, the floor leaders elected by the caucus and the conference are most important. The majority leader is the main influence on scheduling and has considerable say on committee assignments. Because of his scheduling activities, he is at the center of his party's and the Senate's communications. He knows more about activities, intentions, and desires of individual senators than anyone else. This information can be a useful power resource.

An energetic, skillful majority leader can wield great influence. Lyndon Johnson is the best example. In his heyday in the early 1950s the legend was that he saw and talked with each of the more than fifty Democratic senators every day that the Senate was in session. He used his influence on the committee on Committees to get each freshman Democrat at least one assignment on an important committee. This departure from the apprenticeship pattern created obligations that he drew on in later years. Johnson used the staff and office granted the majority leader to make himself as much the center of Senate political and social life as possible and, thus, to increase his contacts, information, and alliances. Combined with his extraordinary powers of personal persuasion, these elements made Lyndon Johnson one of the two or three most powerful people in Washington.

The minority leader, the whips, and the policy committees function in the Senate as they do in the House, except that the majority policy committee participates in scheduling decisions.

Norms

A **norm** is a standard of behavior that members of a group or an institution are expected to follow. It need not be a written rule; often the most important norms are not. They are enforced by the members themselves and can change as quickly or as slowly as the members do. Those who follow the norms can usually expect to gain the acceptance of the older and more powerful members; those who violate them can expect to suffer accordingly.

In his standard study published in 1960, Donald Matthews described six folkways or norms operating in the United States Senate: **apprenticeship, hard work, specialization, courtesy, reciprocity,** and **loyalty to the institution.**[4]

Apprenticeship is one norm that has diminished greatly perhaps to the point of extinction. Freshman senators used to behave (or at least were expected to behave) like Victorian children. They were to be seen and not heard, to show respect for their elders, and to learn the ways of the Senate. Nowadays, freshmen and other junior members chair subcommittees, preside at hearings, and challenge their elders on important issues such as energy and the Panama Canal Treaties. This change reflects the large recent turnover in the Senate described previously (p. 71). As a majority, the senators elected between 1976 and 1980 have had enough power to challenge the norm. As energetic, experienced people, they were inclined to do so.

The norm of hard work means that senators respect their fellows who do their share of the routine, dull, necessary work of legislation. Senators who neglect these duties in favor of more glamorous pursuits are criticized as "show horses" instead of "work horses." In addition to working hard, a good senator is expected to concentrate on one or two areas and leave his colleagues to concentrate on theirs. Specialization is particularly hard on senators from large states with varied populations, who feel a need to be involved with many issues and programs.

Courtesy extends from the elaborate compliments senators address to one another on the floor, to the more substantive notion that no personal animosity should attach to political conflicts. In a relatively small body such animosities could cause friction and make

[4] Donald R. Matthews, *U.S. Senators and Their World* (New York: Vintage Books, 1960), pp. 92–118.

work difficult. Reciprocity means that, when a senator can, he should do a favor for another senator and expect to get one back. The most common form of such reciprocity is vote trading. If a senator from an inland state is asked to vote for a harbors bill, he may do it. In turn his coastal colleague might support highway legislation or a farm bill. This practice is also called **log rolling,** and is based on the ancient idea, "You scratch my back and I will scratch yours."

Loyalty to the Senate and its traditions is highly prized by most senators. The good senator should never publicly criticize the institution, nor should he challenge its time-honored rules and customs. Otherwise he may not be trustworthy or eligible for the special status and favor of a patriotic member.

In the House similar norms apply, with perhaps an even greater emphasis on specialization, and hard work. Both because of its smaller size and its tradition of individualism, the Senate has developed a more relaxed and informal atmosphere than the House. With 435 members to organize, the House relies more heavily on hierarchy, formality, and a rigid adherence to the rules.

Roles of Individuals: Mavericks, Regulars, and Entrepreneurs

In the days when a small group of senior members, mostly southern, mostly conservative, ruled the Congress, Sam Rayburn, the speaker of the House, gave freshmen the following advice, "If you want to get along, go along." He meant, if you want a good committee assignment, if you want your bills passed, do what the party leaders tell you and don't rock the boat. Members who did so were called "regulars" whereas those who rebelled were called "mavericks." In the House, mavericks were punished with inferior committee assignments and other penalties, but in the Senate's looser atmosphere, they were generally tolerated.

In the present system, the leadership's ability to discipline has greatly declined. As more and more voters have rejected parties, politicians have learned to establish their own organizations and followings. As interest groups have become more active, congresspersons have learned to make their own alliances with them, bypassing the parties. In short, congresspersons and senators have become independent operators—political **entrepreneurs** who owe little loyalty to the party. In many ways they resemble the mavericks of old except that they have become the rule rather than the exception.

Personal Staffs

The growth of personal staffs has also bolstered the individual member. Since 1960 the number of such staffers has nearly tripled. Representatives may have as many as eighteen people on their staff whereas Senate staff size depends on the size of the state from which the Senator comes and averages around thirty-five people. With more assistants to answer constituents' letters, service interest groups, do research and pursue legislation and work in reelection campaigns,[5] representatives and senators are in positions to rely less and less on parties for electoral support or guidance on issues.

Roles of Individuals: Summary

As parties decline, as politicians learn to use the media to create personal followings, as single-issue interest groups proliferate, and as personal staffs increase, members will act more and more independently, further dispersing power in the Congress.

Functions: What Does Congress Do?

Legislating: How a Law is Passed, or, More Often, Not Passed

As we have discussed, a proposed law is called a **bill.** There are two categories of bills: **public** and **private.** The difference is that a private bill deals with a particular person or persons, and a public bill deals with general categories. Public bills are the sort that receive treatment in the media. Usually a private bill compensates an individual for damages suffered in an accident involving the government, or allows someone, who would not otherwise be eligible, to immigrate to the United States.

Formally a bill must be introduced by a senator or representative. In practice most bills are written by executive agencies or interest

---

[5] Early in 1981 a federal court of appeals ruled that it was legal for a senator's aide to have worked full-time on the senator's reelection campaign while drawing his pay as a government employee.

groups and given to the senator or representative. Congress spends most of its time and energy considering bills from the administration (the President and the executive branch, generally.)

Revenue bills must begin in the House. All others may start in either house. Once introduced the bill is given a number and referred to committee. Most of the time there is no question as to which committee should get the bill—farm price supports go to Agriculture, Social Security to Ways and Means, and so on. Occasionally, more than one committee has a logical claim to a bill. The choice may be important because one committee may favor the bill whereas another opposes it. In these cases the speaker of the House and the majority leader in the Senate—the people who make the decision—have a good deal of power over the fate of the bill.

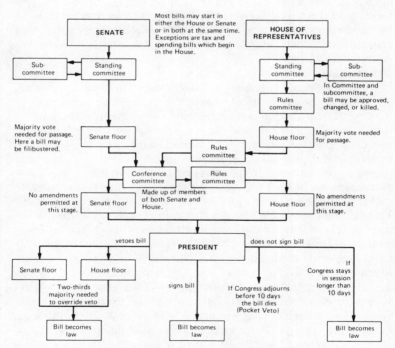

Figure 3.2. The Lawmaking (or unmaking) process.

The 1963 Civil Rights Bill is a good example. Ordinarily, such a bill would go to the Judiciary Committee in both houses of Congress. However, the sponsors wanted to avoid the Senate Judiciary Committee because the chairman, James Eastland of Mississippi, was an ardent opponent of the bill. Because the commerce clause of the Constitution was the bill's legal basis, the Senate leadership had a pretext for sending the bill to the Commerce Committee chaired by the liberal senator from Washington, Warren Magnuson. In the House the pattern was reversed. The bill was referred to the Judiciary Committee headed by the liberal Emanuel Celler from Brooklyn in order to avoid the segregationist chairman of the Interstate and Foreign Commerce Committee, Oren Harris of Arkansas.

Committee Action. In the old system the chairman dominated the committee and could decide the fate of a bill. He could move quickly or slowly, he could kill the bill by refusing to act on it, a technique known as **pigeonholing.** Now the elected chairman must be more responsive to the wishes of the majority of his committee and his party, and is likely to use his formal powers in consultation with them.

Assuming that the chairman is favorably inclined toward the bill, it will be considered either by the full committee or a subcommittee. At this point the subcommittee chairman becomes the key person. If the chairman of the full committee steps out of the picture, the subcommittee chairman takes on the same powers the chairman has on the full committee. The subcommittee chairman can delay a bill or pigeonhole it. If the subcommittee chairman favors the bill, the next step is to get reactions from interested parties. The staff or a committee member will ask the relevant executive agency to give its evaluation of the bill. Interest groups will be asked for their positions. The staff may be directed to do a study of the proposal. If the matter is an important one, or one that members care about, the subcommittee will hold hearings.

A **hearing** is a meeting of the committee or subcommittee at which people give their views on a bill. The people may be other congressmen, or senators, representatives of interest groups—lobbyists—or experts in the field or employees of executive agencies. The chairman decides who will testify, and in what order, although a recent reform gives the minority party the right to schedule one day of the hearings.

Committee members use hearings for a variety of purposes.

Sometimes they are a genuine attempt to get the views of a wide range of people. More often they are an attempt to build up a record in support of the position the chairman or member already holds. Frequently, this effort is combined with an attempt to get some publicity—newspaper or TV coverage—for the cause.

Hearings are frequently a device to get information out of the executive branch. Congressmen find that routine requests often go unanswered or produce vague replies. Getting the secretary of the Department of Health, Education, and Welfare to come before the committee is one way to find out what the guidelines he just issued really mean. This method has its limitations—cabinet officers can talk for long periods without saying anything.

The step after the hearings is called the **markup.** The subcommittee meets in executive session (a meeting closed to the public and press). During the meeting the bill is read and debated, line by line. Amendments are offered and voted up or down. The bill's advocates, usually the chairman and staff, calculate what concessions they have to make in order to keep the majority party united in support of the bill. They also consider what changes might entice a member or two of the opposition party to join the majority. Depending on the lineup of the subcommittee and the nature of the bill, it may change substantially or very little. When the reading is completed, a vote is taken on the complete bill. If it is passed, it goes to the full committee, where the process is repeated. Usually the full committee follows the recommendation of the subcommittee. If the bill is passed by the full committee, the committee then *reports* the bill to the full House. **Reporting** means that the committee makes a report to the House of its findings and recommendations on the bill. A written report is sent along with the final committee version of the bill. If the committee splits, two reports may be filed, one for the majority and one for the minority.

Most bills never get out of committee. They die a quiet death, pigeonholed by the chairman of the full committee, tabled by a majority of the full committee, or pigeonholed by the subcommittee chairman. Perhaps one bill in ten makes it out of committee. From there the problem for its sponsors is getting it to the floor.

The Calendars. After being reported out of the committee the bill is placed on one of three calendars. Private bills go on the **Private Calendar,** to be called up for a vote on the first and third Tuesdays of the month. Usually such bills are passed by unanimous consent.

The presiding officer asks for "unanimous consent." If no one objects, the bill is passed. If two members object, the bill returns, probably permanently, to the committee.

Public bills, dealing with revenue and appropriations, are placed on the **Union Calendar** (the name is the short form of the Calendar of the Whole House on the State of the Union). Public bills other than revenue and appropriations bills are placed on the **House Calendar.** Uncontroversial items may be moved from these two calendars to the floor by means of the **Consent Calendar.** At the request of any congressman, the shift is made. On the first and third Mondays of the month the Consent Calendar is called and bills are brought up for consideration. If any member objects, the bill is passed over. Two successive objections send the bill back to its original calendar.

There are several other ways by which a bill may reach the floor. Certain committees are privileged to bring certain matters directly to the floor. For instance, the Ways and Means Committee may do so with revenue bills. The Public Works Committee may do so on bills affecting rivers and harbors. Usually these committees forego the privilege and instead do as other committees do, they send their bills to the Rules Committee.

The Rules Committee. This committee was originally set up to be a sort of traffic cop for the House. As both the number of bills and of congressmen increased, it was necessary to have some means of regulating debate and procedure. If each of the 435 congressmen spoke for one minute on a bill, it would take more than seven hours to debate that one bill. Add to that the time necessary to debate and vote up or down an unlimited number of amendments and you will see the possibilities of delay and paralysis. To avoid all this, the House gave the **Rules Committee** the authority to set time limits on debate and to limit the number and kinds of amendments, sometimes to eliminate them altogether.

Over the years, however, the Rules Committee has frequently gone beyond this job. Instead of being a neutral traffic cop, it has acted as a highly selective headwaiter. Under a conservative chairman, "Judge" Smith, there formed a coalition of southern Democrats and conservative Republicans that had six votes—one half of the committee. By 6 to 6 tie votes, the conservative coalition denied rules to liberal legislation, especially civil rights bills. Without a rule, the bills could not reach the floor for a vote, so they languished in the Rules Committee.

In 1959 the Rules Committee stopped an aid-to-education bill that had the demonstrated support of the Democratic party leadership and majorities in both houses. Faced with this obstacle to his domestic programs, President Kennedy sought, in 1961, to neutralize the committee by expanding it and adding liberal members. In an epic fight, by a narrow vote, the majority in the House backed the President and Speaker Sam Rayburn.

After the expansion the committee was less troublesome to the leadership. Following Smith's defeat in a 1966 primary election, the committee became quite cooperative. However, its potential for obstruction remains; in 1974 the committee killed a mass transit bill aimed at helping urban areas and a land-use bill backed by environmentalists.

As part of the 1974–75 reforms, the House Democrats gave the speaker the power to nominate the Democratic members of the Rules Committee and the Caucus the power to approve them. Since then, the committee has generally functioned as an arm of the leadership, delaying bills the leadership wanted delayed.

In addition to blocking bills, the committee is in a position to help those bills by giving them a closed rule, which says that the bill cannot be amended on the floor. This is the reason committees such as Ways and Means go to the Rules Committee even though they don't need a rule to get on the floor. It is to their advantage to get a closed rule. Assuming the bill gets a rule, it proceeds to the floor.

Floor Action. The term **floor** refers to a meeting of the full House or Senate in their respective chambers. For a bill that comes to the House floor from the Rules Committee, the first order of business is the adoption of the rules suggested by that committee. For most important legislation, debate on the rule is limited to one hour. Opponents of a bill sometimes use this opportunity to attack the bill indirectly. If the rule is defeated, the bill cannot be considered and will be sent back to committee, usually to stay. Because the Rules Committee is so powerful, this seldom happens.

Most of the rules include a provision that the House resolve itself into the **Committee of the Whole** (a committee consisting of the entire House). This parliamentary procedure permits freer, less formal debate and a smaller quorum than the ordinary procedures. Once the rule is adopted, then the debate on the bill in the Committee of the Whole begins. The first speaker is the bill's **floor manager,** the chairman of the subcommittee or committee that handled the bill or someone designated by the former. The floor leader's job is to devise and execute a plan for getting the bill passed. His speech is followed by a speech from the opposition's floor leader, whose job is to defeat the bill.

Debates in the House are generally brief and do not change many votes.

Amendments. If the bill has a closed rule, permitting no **amendments,** a vote follows immediately after the debate. If the bill has an open rule, amendments are offered and considered. In this process the judgment of the floor manager is crucial. He must decide whether to oppose or accept amendments. He must estimate accurately how much, if any, he has to give up of the original bill in order to muster the votes needed to pass it. He must also be careful not to change the bill so much that its original supporters turn against it.

Debate on amendments is usually limited to five minutes for the person proposing the amendment and five minutes for the floor manager. Voting on amendments is by three methods while the House is in the Committee of the Whole. The voice vote is self-explanatory; a **division** is a standing head count, and a **teller vote** is a more elaborate head count. Members line up and pass before the maker of the amendment and the opposition leader, who do the counting. The Legislative Reform Act of 1970 provided that one fifth of the members could request that the votes of members in a teller vote be recorded. Shortly after this change went into effect, the House voted on financing the SST. Environmental groups opposed the measure, but they had lost every previous vote. This time, on a **recorded teller vote,** the bill was beaten. Members who earlier had been protected by anonymity now feared the wrath of their constituents.

Finally there is a method used only in the House itself. A **roll call vote** means that the list of all the members' names is called; each answers "Yes" or "No" or "abstain." A record is kept of the members votes.

Once all the amendments have been considered, the House changes itself from the Committee of the Whole back into the House and reports the bill to itself from the Committee of the Whole. Amendments adopted in the Committee of the Whole are approved usually without incident.

Before the bill itself is voted up or down, a motion to recommit it to committee is usually offered. These take two forms: a simple motion to recommit the bill and a motion to recommit with instructions to report back forthwith with the following changes. The latter is simply another way of amending the bill.

Assuming that these motions fail, a final vote on passage is taken, and if the bill is passed, it is sent to the Senate.

The procedure in the Senate is quite similar. The bill is referred to committee and to subcommittee, research is done, hearings are held, amendments are offered, and so on. One major difference is that the Rules Committee is much less important. Because the Senate is smaller, because it prides itself on a tradition of debate and oratory, there is a standing rule that provides for unlimited debate unless sixty of those present and voting vote in favor of cutting off debate (this is known as **cloture**). The rule in favor of unlimited debate and the lax enforcement of the rule of germane debate give opponents the opportunity to block majority action.

The Filibuster. The method is simply to hold the floor and talk and talk and talk. The Bible is read aloud in support of the doctrine of the separation of the races, newspapers are read, recipes are given. The opponents are saying, "Unless you drop this bill, we will continue to talk, and you will not be able to do any other business." One way to beat the **filibuster** is to get the sixty votes needed for cloture. Another way is to try to wear out the opposition by holding around-the-clock sessions and forcing them to keep a speaker on the floor twenty-four hours a day. Cloture is sometimes difficult to get because senators feel that they might want to use the filibuster one day, and they don't want to set a bad precedent by breaking someone else's filibuster.

Southern senators used the filibuster to stave off civil rights bills until the 1960s, when enough liberal and moderate votes from both parties combined to invoke cloture and to pass the legislation.

Conference Committee. Let us assume that a bill is passed by the Senate. The chances are very good that the Senate version of the bill differs from the House version. Different amendments will have been offered and accepted, the power relations of the relevant committees will have been different, and so on. To reconcile the differences, each house sends members to a special, temporary committee, called a **conference committee,** that only handles this one bill. The speaker of the House and the majority leader of the Senate appoint the members from their respective houses; they are almost always drawn from the committees that handled the bill. In July 1981 the largest conference committee in history convened to work on the budget bills passed by the House and Senate. Seventy-two senators and 183 representatives, who divided into 58 subconferences, sought compromises on nearly every federal program. Conference committees are supposed to work out a compromise between the two versions. Occasionally they go beyond their mandate and write a bill that is quite different from either of the two.

Whatever the committee produces is returned to the two houses for a floor vote. However, on the way from the House floor to the Conference Committee and on the way back to the House, the bill must pass through the Rules Committee. In 1959 an aid-to-education bill was blocked on the way back from the Conference Committee because a member of the Rules Committee did not like the compromise bill and changed his vote to produce a tie on the committee.

If the bill is passed in both houses, it goes to the President. He may sign it, in which case it becomes law; veto it; or, at the end of the session, exercise a pocket veto. If he vetoes the bill, it returns to the two houses for an immediate vote to see whether the veto will be overridden. If the President uses a pocket veto, the bill must go through the whole process again in the next session.

Appropriations and Authorizations

This is by no means the end of the story. In fact, it is only half the story. Most legislation goes through the entire process *twice*. The reason is that most legislation requires money to be implemented. No law enforces itself. To enforce a civil rights act, investigators must be hired, there must be office staff to type and file reports, and attorneys to prosecute court cases. In addition there must be a building to house all these people and an administrator to organize the office, set policy, and to make sure that the rest of the staff is working properly. There must be a personnel department to recruit all these other people, and a maintenance and cleaning staff, a purchasing department to buy supplies and equipment, and so on.

The money to pay for all of this comes from the United States Treasury Department and ultimately from taxes. In order for the Treasury to give out, or disburse, money to pay a salary or to pay for a government purchase, whether it be a typewriter or a jet fighter plane, Congress must first pass a law saying that the money shall be spent. This is called an **appropriation.** It is the second part of the story.

Most legislation, then, is in two parts. The first bill says that something will be done: trees will be planted, racial discrimination will be prosecuted, hydrogen bombs will be built. Part of this bill *authorizes* a certain amount of money to be spent, but an **authorization** cuts no ice with the Treasury. Unless there is an appropriation, no money will be spent, no trees planted, and no bombs built.

The separate appropriations bill goes through the same process as the authorization bill except that instead of being handled by the subject matter committee, it is handled by the Appropriations Committee and one of its very powerful subcommittees. A second difference is that general appropriations bills are not handled by the House Rules Committee.

What the Appropriations Committees and ultimately the Congress do by passing the appropriations bill is to set aside a certain amount of money for the specified purpose. One way to think about this is to imagine that the Treasury Department is a bank. When the government needs money it goes to the bank and makes a withdrawal. However, it is not reasonable to have different parts of the government simply withdraw and spend money as they please. To ensure an orderly process and to set national priorities, Congress sets up separate accounts.

Each department has an account. Very often Congress goes further and says how much may be spent by a department or agency for a particular purpose. Thus, the army gets so much for salaries and so much for tanks, and the Office of Education gets so much for research and so much for school aid. Money designated for one purpose may not be spent for another.

The amount of money in the account is referred to as **the appropriation.** Thus, we speak of the "military appropriation," meaning the total given to the armed forces, or of the "air force appropriation," or the "pilot-training appropriation."

It is clear from the preceding description and from Figure 3.2 that there are many ways for a bill to fail and only one slow, twisting road to success. Another conclusion is that there are a great many small groups and individuals able to defeat a bill, in addition to majorities of either house.

In the 96th Congress (1979–1980) 14,594 bills and resolutions were introduced: 2,304 were reported out by committees and 613 became law.

Alternate Routes

There are ways of avoiding both subject matter committees and the House Rules Committee. One such method is called a **discharge**

petition. After any committee, including the Rules Committee, has had a bill thirty days, a member may file a petition to discharge the bill from the committee to the floor of the House via the **Discharge Calendar.** The signatures of a majority of the 435 members are required to place the bill on the calendar.

For all the reasons previously cited in the sections on the power of committees and chairmen, members are reluctant to sign such petitions. Anyone who signs it may depend on the committee and its chairman to pay him back many times over. From 1910–1971, 835 discharge petitions were filed, of which 24 were successful. Twenty of the bills passed the House and two were enacted into law.

Other Congressional Functions

Administrative Oversight

Government policy—by which we mean what the government does—is carried out by agencies in the executive branch. The laws that Congress passes are put into effect by bureaucrats. Congress tries to make sure that the agencies are doing what Congress intended, that they are using the money Congress appropriated efficiently, and that they are not abusing their authority. Congress also wants to know whether the program is working.

The President, who is the author, or a least a major contributor to much of the legislation, and who is designated the chief executive by the Constitution, is concerned with the same questions. To some extent he and the Congress compete to influence the agencies. To a great extent, the agencies are able to operate independently of both Congress and the President.

In this section we discuss some of the ways that Congress tries to control the bureaucracy and some of the reasons why these attempts are often unsuccessful.

The greatest obstacle to congressional control is the sheer size of the bureaucracy: As of October 1, 1979, 1.9 million civilians worked for the executive branch. The armed forces employed another 2.2 million people. To even find out what these people are *supposed* to be doing, let alone what they are *actually* doing, is a monumental task for 535 senators and representatives, 3,900 staff aides, and the one investigative agency that works for Congress, the **General Accounting Office (GAO).**

The problem is compounded by the reluctance of the bureaucrats to tell any outside agency what they are doing. Many bureaucrats feel that they know best in their own fields, and that congressmen and Presidents should leave them, the experts, to do the job. A wily bureaucrat knows many ways to avoid releasing facts. He can tell the committee that he is working to get the answers and hope that if he stalls long enough, they will forget or get tired and give up. He can claim the information is unavailable or lost. When forced to report, he can present distorted or misleading information. In cases where military secrets are involved, the bureaucrats, whether civilian or military, can reply that divulging the information, even to a congressional committee, would jeopardize national security. As a last resort, the bureaucrat can simply refuse to give the information. In that case he thinks that he has more political backing than the representative, senator, or committee that is seeking the information. And he may be right. The agency may have strong support from other committees or from powerful interest groups. They may have so much support that Congress will think twice before doing battle.

Expertise is another bureaucratic resource. Many of the subjects in question are complex or highly specialized. Some congressmen may have become experts themselves after dealing with them for many years. Wilbur Mills was a match for any Internal Revenue bureaucrat on the ins and outs of tax laws. On other subjects, however, experience and legal training are not as readily applicable. Few congressmen have the background in nuclear physics or electronics to understand advanced missile systems. The congressperson or senator who challenges the joint chiefs and the civilian scientists on a question of military hardware runs the risk of looking like a presumptuous, ignorant fool.

Faced with an acute shortage of manpower, information, an expertise, congressional committees are hardly in a position to exercise a close, comprehensive watch on the executive branch. This does not mean that Congress never exercises any control, however.

A "Success" Story. The Community Action Program (CAP) of the War on Poverty is a case in which Congress, through its committees, controlled an executive agency very thoroughly. The program began with a broad mandate to promote social change. Congressmen quickly became agitated about the protest and political organization work being carried on by CAP agencies around the country. Many congressmen felt the CAP agencies in their own districts threatened their political interests. Moving quickly, the House

Education and Labor Committee rewrote the legislation, putting severe limits on the kinds of organizing that the CAP agencies were permitted to do. The Appropriations Committee made the limits stick by stating very specifically how all of the CAP appropriation was to be spent. The favored categories were health care and Head Start.

Such examples are relatively rare. Although Congressional Committees spent, by one estimate, 40 percent of their time in oversight during 1979 and 1980, Congress usually defers to the greater expertise, organization, and political power of the bureaucrats.

Casework

One function involving the bureaucracy that some congressmen and their staffs pursue with great energy is called **casework.** Individuals frequently appeal to congressmen for help in dealing with various agencies. Most congressmen try hard to help, seeing this as a good way to build friendly relations with voters. Many congressional staffers, perhaps as many as 2500, do this full time.

The success of such efforts varies from case to case and congressman to congressman, depending on the agency involved, the strength of the individual's claim, the power and persistence of the congressman, the skill of his staff, and so on. Although this activity helps many people, it is a long way from being a systematic surveillance of the executive.

Investigations

One device Congress uses to obtain more general information is the investigation. These may be public, taking the form of committee hearings, or private, in the sense of being done without media attention. Unpublicized investigations may be done by the staff of a committee or by the General Accounting Office. The GAO is one of the six agencies that report directly to Congress. The others include the Library of Congress, whose Legislative Reference Service does academic style research for Congress, and the Government Printing Office.

Headed by the comptroller general of the United States, who is appointed by the President with the advice and consent of the Senate for a fifteen-year term, the GAO has general authority to audit the budgets of most parts of the federal government. Congress may ask the GAO to audit or investigate nearly any program or agency to see that it is being run efficiently and in accordance with Congress's wishes. However, the same bureaucratic resources that thwart congresspersons frequently limit the GAO's investigative powers.

Several public congressional investigations have drawn enormous publicity and produced information of critical importance to American politics. The Senate Select Committee on Presidential Campaign Practices, known by the name of its chairman as the [Sam] Ervin Committee, made the first official inquiry into the events known as Watergate. Their televised hearings helped to alert the country and to create the pressure that ousted President Nixon. As noted, the House Judiciary Committee held hearings and conducted investigations leading to the committee's passage of articles of impeachment that probably decisively shaped public opinion about President Nixon.

In 1975 and 1976 select committees of the House and the Senate investigated the intelligence agencies: the FBI, CIA, Defense Intelligence Agency, and the National Security Agency. At first the hearings produced startling news. The intelligence agencies had defied presidential orders, plotted the assassinations of foreign leaders, deliberately falsified enemy troop levels in Vietnam, and harassed American citizens. Most observers thought that the investigations would lead to increased congressional control of the agencies or to some other reform.

However, the House Committee, headed by Otis Pike, Democrat of New York, became embroiled in a series of disputes with the Ford administration over access to information. At one point the committee threatened to cite Secretary of State Henry Kissinger for contempt. This action created dissension in the House; members felt that the committee had gone too far and thus threatened national security.

Just after this dispute was resolved by a compromise, the CIA's station chief in Athens, Greece was assassinated. Although neither of the committees had revealed the names of any agents, the incident seemed to increase concern about their investigations. Walter Mondale, who at the time was the Senator from Minnesota, later said that the administration had used the murder to foster that impression by orchestrating the funeral and other events to heighten the drama of the situation. The administration denied doing so.[6] In any

---

[6] *New York Times,* 12 May 1976, p. 20.

case, attention seemed to shift from concern about possible abuses by the intelligence agencies to possible abuses by Congress.

After the Pike committee released classified information from a report on the 1973 Arab-Israeli War, the administration refused the committee further access to classified documents. The committee did not challenge this restriction because it could not get backing from the full House of Representatives. When the committee submitted its final report, the House voted 246–124 to keep it secret, thus depriving Congress of the crucial resource of publicity. Daniel Schorr, then a CBS reporter, leaked the report to the *Village Voice,* a weekly newspaper in New York City, which published it. The House moved quickly to investigate itself by directing the Ethics Committee to find the source who had given the report to Schorr. None of the Pike committee's recommendations for reform of the intelligence agencies or strengthening of congressional oversight were passed by the House.

Seeing the Pike committee weakened by controversies about leaked secrets and bound by the presence of conservative senators, Frank Church's Senate committee took pains to preserve secrecy. The committee worked for many months in executive session, out of the public eye, and guarded classified documents zealously. In addition the committee negotiated with the administration for access to information and compromised to avoid confrontations. The Senate adopted the committee's recommendation to create a permanent committee with authority to monitor the CIA and voted to publish the committee's report in two volumes.

These examples make clear the limits and the power of congressional investigations. Neither committee achieved full access to secret documents held by the executive, but both learned more than Congress had ever known. By making public previously secret operations, the committee may have changed the practices of the intelligence agencies. Although the Pike committee eventually lost the support of the House, the Church committee kept the support of the Senate and gained its approval of a proposal to strengthen congressional oversight.

Presidential Appointments

The Senate nearly always approves cabinet appointments, feeling that it is the President's right to pick his own heads of departments. Thus, in 1981 the Senate approved Alexander Haig, President

Reagan's choice to be secretary of State, even though his military career and his association with the Nixon White House during watergate made him a questionable nominee. On appointments to the Supreme Court, the Senate can be more demanding, as President Nixon discovered when two of his nominees—Haynesworth and Carswell—were defeated.

Foreign Policy

At the beginning of this chapter we said that the power of legislatures has declined all over the world. In regard to foreign policy this trend is especially marked. Max Weber, the great German sociologist, explained the reasons for this decline in his *Theory of Social and Economic Organizations:*

> It is impossible for either the internal or the foreign policy of great states to be strongly and consistently carried out on a collegial basis. Collegiality unavoidably obstructs the promptness of decision, the consistency of policy, the clear responsibility of the individual, and ruthlessness to outsiders in combination with the maintenance of discipline within the group. Hence, for these and certain other economic technical reasons in all large states which are involved in world politics, where collegiality has been retained at all, it has been weakened in favor of the prominent position of the political leaders such as the Prime Minister.

The pattern has held true in American politics for most of the twentieth century, especially for the period since 1939. President Nixon's secret air war against Cambodia brought presidential power to new heights and congressional power to new lows. The Congress was eliminated entirely from the warmaking process; it was not even informed after the fact.

Public reaction against the Vietnam War and the presidential abuses of the Watergate scandal gave Congress the political support it needed to reassert its power. By legislation, by oversight, by control of money, by expanding its staff, and by public appeals Congress has attempted to increase its own abilities and to tighten controls over the executive branch.

In Chapter 2 we discussed the passage of legislation to end the war in Indochina and the passage of the War Powers Act. We now survey briefly the effects of these and other congressional efforts during the Ford and Carter administrations. As might be expected, the pattern is mixed, but there is no doubt that congressional activity and influence have risen from their low point in the late 1960s.

The Ford Administration

In the case of American policy toward Southeast Asia in 1974, Congress was both passive and influential. As the Lon Nol government in Cambodia weakened, President Ford and Secretary of State Kissinger tried without success to persuade Congress that further economic and military aid should be given. At the same time, the President and the military went ahead with an airlift conducted by newly painted American Air Force planes, flown in some cases by air force reserve pilots, and leased to an American company reported to have ties to the CIA. Congress made no public effort to stop the airlift, despite having earlier passed laws forbidding direct American involvement.

While the Lon Nol government was falling, the government of Nguyen Van Thieu in South Vietnam lost control of the northern part of the country. The United States had long supported this government. (Some people would go so far as to say that the United States had created it.) The President and the secretary of state made frequent, dramatic appeals to Congress for more aid for Thieu's government. As the defeats continued, Ford and Kissinger took a sharper tone. Ford said that Congress was responsible for the situation in South Vietnam and that only by providing additional aid could Congress assure that the Americans killed in the war had not died in vain. Kissinger said that the question of aid was the question of what kind of country the United States is; whether we were the kind of country that honored our commitments. On April 10, 1975, the President made a televised speech asking for a billion dollars in added military aid. In both Houses of Congress, leaders of the Democratic party (which had won large majorities in the 1974 elections) opposed the aid. At the insistence of freshmen and liberals, the House Democratic caucus convened and voted 189 to 49 against the aid bill. In the Senate many Democrats who had long supported the war and the Thieu government, including Robert Byrd of West Virginia and John Pastore of Rhode Island, now rejected further aid.

Only when it was clear that the South Vietnamese were about to be defeated did Congress approve a plan of mass evacuation. Even then, the Senate barred the use of American troops to guard the operation.

A second instance of strong congressional influence on foreign policy arose in connection with the question of trade with the Soviet Union. The Ford administration was anxious to promote trade as a part of its policy of détente. After certain conditions were written into the trade agreement at the insistence of the Senate (allowance for emigration to Israel of Soviet Jews), the Soviet Union renounced the trade agreement. That was in 1974, and the situation remains unchanged.

In that same year the Congress instituted an embargo on the shipment of arms to Turkey. In the opinion of the majority, the Turks had violated an agreement with the United States by using arms supplied by this country during the Turkish invasion of Cyprus. In July 1975, despite intense personal efforts by President Ford, the House voted 223 to 206 to continue the ban. Later, in October, Congress backed down from this strong stand and allowed some aid to go to Turkey. In spite of this partial retreat, the sum of these three episodes represents a striking change from the old pattern of accepting whatever the President proposed.

The most dramatic example of the new pattern occurred early in 1976 when Congress voted to stop giving aid to one side in the Angolan civil war. Before this vote, the President, the secretary of state, and the CIA had sent substantial amounts of arms and supplies to the "pro-West" faction.

On the other hand, Congress did nothing to stop the airlift to Cambodia. Nor was any opposition offered to the President's aggressive handling of the *Mayaguez* incident in the spring of 1974. In spite of the passage of the War Powers Act, few congressmen or senators objected to the commitment of American marines, planes, and helicopters (and a projected B-52 strike on the mainland). Most senators and congressmen supported the President's unilateral action.

The Carter Administration

The record continued to be a mixture of passivity and assertiveness during the Carter administration. The ratification of the Panama Canal Treaties in 1978 after prolonged debate illustrated the Senate's new assertiveness, power, and decentralization. Several different committees and many senators including very junior members became involved not only in the debate but also in the negotiations with Panama. Under heavy pressure the administration made many concessions. Then the House of Representatives forced further concessions in the laws that implemented the treaties, demonstrating its determination to be involved and influential.

In the making of policy toward the Middle East the Congress had less influence. President Carter gained considerable prestige from his diplomatic triumph at Camp David when he appeared to have singlehandedly persuaded Israel and Egypt to sign a peace treaty. Congress's traditionally pro-Israel stance relaxed sufficiently to permit the Carter administration to make large arms sales to Arab countries. However, Congress used its power on Israel's behalf on many other questions.

On the highly emotional issue of the Americans held hostage in Iran, Congress deferred to the President both when he negotiated and when he used force. No serious sustained objection was raised to his secret use of troops in the failed rescue mission of April 1980. Instead Congress accepted the strained contention that this was a rescue mission and not an act of war governed by the War Powers Act.

Many Americans seem to think that the Iranian hostage crisis proved that American power had declined and that we should act to reestablish our international prestige and power. Ordinarily, such a mood contributes to presidential power, provided that the President leads the effort, as President Reagan has promised to do.

Domestic Policymaking

Congressional influence in domestic matters also declined sharply in the 1960s and early 1970s. The "power of the purse" suffered most. Although this power, like the power to declare war, is plainly stated in the Constitution, a combination of factors has served to whittle it away. The practice of impoundment whereby Presidents refuse to spend money duly appropriated by the Congress expanded enormously under President Nixon. He impounded billions of dollars appropriated for education, housing, agriculture, and water purification. Congress had behaved irresponsibly, Nixon argued, by failing to coordinate spending plans with revenue plans, and he had to correct their errors to protect the economy.

Congress protested, but before the Watergate scandal erupted, it did little of substance. It appeared likely that impoundment, despite its shaky constitutional foundation, would become an accepted practice, established by custom. Congress would have lost a substantial part of its power of the purse. Congressional appropriations, which are laws, would have become mere suggestions to the President.

After Watergate had weakened the presidency, Congress passed the Budget Reform Act of 1974 that gave either house a veto power over **impoundments,** now called, "recisions," and established a House and a Senate Budge Committee and a Congressional Budget Office. The two committees, with the assistance of the CBO, provide the coordination between income and spending that Congress lacked. Each year in the late winter or early spring the President sends his budget to the Congress where it is reviewed by the two committees. By March the standing committees give their budget projects to the Budget committees. By May 1 the committees are supposed to report and each house is supposed to approve a budget that includes guidelines for spending in specific areas and general outlines for raising revenue through taxes and other measures. Differences between House and Senate versions are settled in a conference committee.

The Appropriations Committees and other committees are then supposed to work within these guidelines when making allotments for programs. By September 15 the Budget committees are supposed to propose and the two houses are supposed to approve binding guidelines.

Although some analysts predicted that the system would not work, most now agree that it has worked quite effectively. The Budget committees have gained a respectable share of power. They have won some battles with standing committees and lost others. In September 1975, for instance, the Senate refused to accept the Appropriations Committee's proposal on the military budget because it violated the binding guidelines. On the other hand, in 1977 the Senate Agriculture Committee won a floor fight to amend the guidelines to increase the farm bill by $700,000,000. The Budget committees also suffered a loss of prestige in 1977 from their alliance with the Democratic president. Following the White House's uncertain lead, the Budget Committees twice reversed themselves on budget priorities.

The general trend has been toward strengthening the committees, and therefore strengthening Congress's ability to make coordinated budgetary policy. In the process the Congress has gained an important part in the making of national economic policy since the budget powerfully affects the national economy. In the spring of 1975 the Democrats led Congress to increase the tax cuts requested by President Ford as a way to fight the recession. In 1978, in a reassertion of congressional independence, the chairmen of the Budget committees persuaded President Carter to delay a tax cut in order to curb inflation.

1981—Reagan Takes Control

In 1981 a stunning reversal occurred. The Reagan Administration used the budget process to dominate the Congress. Procedures designed to make Congress powerful made it weak instead. As one observer wrote, "A device originally intended to control the executive was put to use to control the legislature."[7]

Reagan's strategy was based on a provision of the budget process called "reconciliation." Used only once or twice previously at the *end* of the budget process, reconciliation is a set of orders from the full House to the committees which requires them to meet the budget guidelines. When used before, it had been mainly a bookkeeping procedure which insured a final balance. Reagan proposed that reconciliation be done at the *beginning* of the budget process so that the committees would be bound immediately and precisely by the budget resolutions. In the Republican controlled Senate, the President won a relatively easy victory using this strategy.

In the House of Representatives, where Democrats had a majority, the conflict was somewhat harder fought. In May, 1981 the President won the first battle as enough Southern Democrats defected to create *a majority* for the Reagan budget which included the early reconciliation provision. For the next several weeks the Democrats worked in committees to regain lost territory. They shifted cuts among programs to protect the most vulnerable groups. In an effort to increase opposition to the Reagan budget, they proposed eliminating 10,000 small post offices and federal aid to schools near military bases. In response the Reagan administration submitted a complete substitute package, some 4,000 pages long, which cut more deeply into social programs and consolidated many into **block grants.** On June 26, 1981 a coalition of Republicans and conserva-

---

[7] Steven V. Roberts, *New York Times,* 25 June 1981.

tive Democrats passed the President's substitute even though few of them could have read the recently and haphazardly printed gargantuan bill.

By forcing the all-or-nothing, one-vote procedure, the President gained the maximum advantage from his popularity, his televised speeches, his personal lobbying efforts, and from horsetrading and bargaining. Instead of dealing with programs one at a time, the administration dealt with 250 programs in a single blow. Instead of dealing with the particular committees, staffs, interest groups, and agencies associated with a particular program, they virtually eliminated these actors from the process. Instead of the many long separate considerations by the specialized committees, the entire House acted in a few days to change 250 programs. By avoiding the normal legislative and appropriations processes we have described in this chapter, and by constructing a bipartisan coalition of conservatives, Reagan and his aides took power away from the Democrats, away from the committees, and away from the Congress as an institution.

Not only were the committees weakened by reconciliation, but also by the consolidation of many programs into block grants. Under the block grant, programs would be administered by the states, and Congress would have little power to review the states' actions. The committees that had previously specified and enforced goals and standards under which money could be spent would no longer do so.

Opponents charged that the administration had damaged the budget process and upset the balance between the branches. "We are dealing with more than 250 programs with no hearings, no deliberations, no debate," said House Budget Committee member Leon E. Panetta, Democrat of California. Richard Bolling, the chairperson of the House Rules Committee, said, "This is an incipient tyranny. A popular President is attempting to tyrannize a whole Congress, a whole people."

Congress in the Twentieth Century: Summary and Prospects

Congressional power declined in the twentieth century, reaching its nadir during the Nixon administration when the combination of secret war making, executive resolutions, and impoundment threatened to make the Congress into an advisory rather than a policy-making organization. During the later 1970s the Congress reasserted its power on important issues, but it must also be said that Congress had the advantage of competing with weak presidents in Gerald Ford and Jimmy Carter. The aggressive, well organized efforts of the Reagan administration have tipped the balance heavily toward the White House. (See Chapter 10 for further discussion.) Again it must be noted that the opposition was rather weak. The Democratic leadership in the House of Representatives did not mount a consistent or effective campaign to persuade the members or to mobilize interest groups.

Whichever way the balance tips, it remains clear that Congress is primarily a responsive body, capable of modifying or rejecting initiatives from the executive, but not capable of developing its own policy, especially in complex, controversial areas such as energy.

GLOSSARY

Administrative oversight The attempt by Congress to make sure that the executive branch is doing what Congress told it to do and is doing it efficiently.

Amendment A change in a bill.

Appellate jurisdiction The range of cases the Supreme Court can consider on appeal from other courts.

Apprenticeship A norm that includes respect for one's elders, being seen but not heard, and learning one's way around.

Appropriation A law directing the secretary of the Treasury to spend a certain amount of money for a certain purpose.

The appropriation The amount of money appropriated by the Congress for a particular purpose.

Authorization A law that sets the upper limit on the amount of money that can be spent for a particular purpose.

Bicameral legislature A system in which the lawmaking part of government is divided into two parts.

Bill A proposed law.

Block grant Federal money given to the states to spend as the states decide, with little or no restriction or oversight.

Budget Reform Act A law that gives either house of Congress the power to block impoundments and that establishes budget committees in each house and a congressional Budget Office.

Casework The activity of congresspersons and their staffs that involves trying to get help from the bureaucracy for a constituent.

Campaign committees Party committees that raise and distribute campaign funds.

Caucus and conference Both words mean a meeting of all the members of a particular party who are members of a particular house. The Democrats use the term *caucus;* the Republicans use *conference.*

Cloture A vote to end debate.

Committee A smaller part of one of the houses of Congress that is usually assigned to handle a particular subject or subjects.

Committee on committees A committee of a party that decides committee assignments. In other words, this group decides which members of its party will sit on a particular committee.

Committee staff People, sometimes experts in specialized fields, who are hired to work full-time for a congressional committee.

Committee of the Whole A parliamentary device by which the entire House meets as a committee in order to permit freer debate and a smaller quorum.

Conference Committee A temporary committee, consisting of members from both houses of Congress. Its job is to make a compromise between the House and Senate versions of the same bill.

Congressional Budget Office (CBO) an agency, established by the Budget Reform Act of 1974, which provides the Congress with expert assistance on budgetary questions, such as taxes and program costs.

Consent Calendar The legislative schedule for uncontroversial items. To get on this calendar a bill must have the unanimous consent of the House.

Courtesy A norm that includes elaborate compliments, a prohibition against personal animosities, and reciprocity—doing a favor if possible and expecting it to be returned.

Democratic Study Group The largest and most powerful group of liberal democrats in the House of Representatives.

Discharge Calendar The legislative schedule for bills brought out of committee by discharge petitions.

Discharge Petition A device by which any member of the house, after a committee has had a bill thirty days, may petition to have it brought to the floor. If a majority of the members agree, the bill is discharged.

Division Voting by head count.

Entrepreneur   —A senator or representative who operates independently of his or her party.

Filibuster   Attempting to defeat a bill by talking indefinitely, thus preventing the Senate from doing any other work.

Floor   A term used to refer to a meeting of the full House or Senate. Floor action means action by the entire body.

Floor Manager   The person who is in charge of getting a particular bill passed, or, in the case of the opposition, of getting it defeated.

Franking privilege   The right of an incumbent representative or senator to send mail to the people in their district free of charge.

General Accounting Office (GAO)   An independent agency within the legislative branch that carries out audits and investigations at Congress's direction.

Hard work   A norm that emphasizes doing one's share of the routine, dull, unglamorous work.

Hearing   A committee meeting, usually public, at which people give their views on a bill.

House Calendar   The legislative schedule for all public bills other than revenue and appropriations bills.

House of Representatives   One of the two houses of Congress. Members are apportioned to the states by population and are elected for two-year terms. Sometimes called the House.

Houses of Congress   The name for the two parts of the American national legislature.

Impeachment   Formally bringing charges against an officer of the government, such as the President. This term is sometimes used, incorrectly, to mean removal from office.

Impoundment   The practice by which the President ordered the secretary of the treasury not to spend money duly appropriated by Congress.

Joint committee   A committee made up of members of both houses of Congress.

Judicial review   The power of the Supreme Court to declare laws passed by Congress and the President or acts of the President unconstitutional.

Law   A binding rule; a rule enforced by government.

Legislature   The law making part of government.

Log rolling   Trading votes on different subjects: for example, a farm state senator or congressperson supports a mass transit bill and in return gets a vote for a farm bill from an urban representative.

Loyalty   A norm that says that a good member supports the institution, never criticizing it in public, nor challenging its rules and customs.

Majority leader (in the House)   The floor leader of the majority party, elected by all the members.

Majority leader of the Senate   Elected by the majority party to be its chief strategist and floor leader.

Markup   The final committee work on a bill: the bill is read, debated, and written, line by line.

Minority leader (in the House)   Elected by all the members of the minority party; acts as floor leader.

Minority leader (in the Senate)   Elected by the minority party to be its chief strategist and floor leader.

Norm   A standard of behavior that members of a group or institution are expected to follow.

One-party district   An area in which one party is so strong and has the allegiance of so many voters that the other party has no chance of winning an election.

Overriding a veto   The action of Congress in passing a bill by a two-thirds majority after the president has vetoed it.

Pigeonholing   The practice by which a committee kills a bill by never taking any action on it.

Pocket veto   The President blocks a bill by refusing to sign it and leaves it on his desk. If Congress adjourns within ten days of the president's receiving the bill, the bill dies.

Policy committees   Committees of the parties that are supposed to set the official party stands on the issues. Their recommendations are often ignored by the members.

Pork barrel   Legislation that gives tangible benefits, such as new dams, post offices, and highways to a congressperson's or senator's constituents.

Power of the purse   The constitutional authority given to Congress to make appropriations.

President *pro tempore* of the Senate   Elected by the majority party to be the Senate's official presiding officer.

Primary election   An election in which members of a party choose their candidates for regular election.

Private bill   A proposed law that deals with one person.

Private Calendar   The legislative schedule for private bills.

Program   A law that states how tax revenues are to be spent. It specifies the amount of money to be devoted to a particular purpose, such as education or defense, and how the money will be spent.

Public bill   A proposed law that deals with general categories of people or institutions or things.

Reciprocity   The congressional norm that calls for favors to be returned and courtesies exchanged among congresspersons and senators.

Recorded teller vote   Voting by passing in front of a person who counts (the teller), with the names recorded.

Reporting   The action of a committee in presenting a bill to the full house for consideration.

Representative; congressman; congresswoman; congressperson; congresspersons   Titles give to members of the House of Representatives.

Rider   An amendment that is not logically related to the substance of the bill to which it is attached.

Roll call   A vote in which each member's name is called and he or she answers.

The Rules Committee of the House of Representatives   The standing committee that sets the procedure (the rule), including time limit and number of amendments, by which a bill is considered on the floor of the house.

Select and special committees   Temporary committees, usually limited to one house, set up to do a specific job, such as investigating a certain subject or agency.

Senate   One of the two houses of Congress. Two members are elected from each state and serve six-year terms.

Senator   The title given to a member of the Senate.

Seniority   The rule that says that the member of the majority party who has served the longest on a particular committee will be the chairman of that committee.

Speaker of the House   The elected leader and presiding officer of the House of Representatives who is nearly always chosen by the majority party and, therefore, is its leader as well.

Specialization   The norm of working on a few subjects.

Standing committee   A permanent committee.

Teller vote   Voting by passing in front of a person who counts (the teller).

Two-party district   An area in which both parties have a chance of winning an election.

Union Calendar (Calendar of the Whole House on the State of the Union)   The legislative schedule for all revenue and approriations bills.

Veto   The power of the President to block a bill by refusing to sign it and then returning it to Congress.

Whips   These party officers are appointed by the elected leaders of both parties (in both houses of Congress) to perform the communication and coordination jobs within their respective parties.

SUGGESTED READINGS

Crabb, Cecil V., Jr., and Pat M. Holt. *Invitation to Struggle: Congress, The President and Foreign Policy.* Washington: Congressional Quarterly Press, 1980.

Dodd, Lawrence C., and Bruce I. Oppenheimer, eds. *Congress Reconsidered.* New York: Praeger, 1977.

Fenno, Richard C. *Congressmen in Committees.* Boston: Little, Brown, 1973.

————. *Home Style: House Members in Their Districts.* Boston: Little, Brown, 1978.

Fiorina, Morris P. *Congress: Keystone of the Washington Establishment.* New Haven: Yale University Press, 1977.

Harris, Richard. *Decision* New York: E. P. Dutton, 1971.

Hinckley, Barbara. *Stability and Change in Congress.* New York: Harper & Row, 1978.

Matthews, Donald R. *U.S. Senators and Their World.* Chapel Hill: University of North Carolina Press, 1960.

Mayhew, David R. *Congress: The Electoral Connection.* New Haven: Yale University Press, 1974.

Murphy, Walter F. *Congress and the Court.* Chicago: University of Chicago Press, 1962.

Oleszek, Walter J. *Congressional Procedures and the Policy Process.* Washington, D.C.: Congressional Quarterly Press, 1978.

Peabody, Robert L. *Leadership in Congress.* Boston: Little Brown, 1976.

Redman, Eric. *The Dance of Legislation.* New York: Simon & Schuster, 1973.

All of the above are in paperback.

4 The Judiciary

Introduction

The judicial power is the power to decide cases, to adjudicate legal disputes. Normally, that power is exercised in courts, which have the authority to determine facts and apply the law. The parties to the case may be individuals, groups, or organizations, including the government itself.

The Supreme Court

Constitutional Responsibilities

The judicial power of the United States on the national level is given by the Constitution to a Supreme Court. Congress is empowered to create other lower federal courts (called inferior courts) whenever it deems it necessary.

The judicial power of these federal courts extends to a broad range of legal disputes and parties. Conflicts that involve the Constitution are naturally a proper subject for federal courts, as are disputes involving laws made by Congress. Legal questions about treaties made with foreign countries, as well as laws made to comply with those treaties, are brought before federal courts. Admiralty law, which is concerned with the law of the sea, is another component of the work of these courts. It can be seen that the obvious and sensible criterion for inclusion under federal judicial power is subject matter over which states have little control. A subject involving state law rather than federal law would more properly belong in a state court.

The parties involved can also cause a case to be brought before federal courts. Again, the general rule is that the federal courts become involved when it is not appropriate for state courts to make the decision. For example, the Constitution provides that cases where the United States itself is a party would come before a federal court because a state is not more powerful than the federal government. Similarly, controversies between states, between citizens of different states, and those involving a foreign country can be tried in a federal court. Where a representative of a foreign country—a minister or ambassador—is a party, the Constitution declares the proper forum to be the Supreme Court, which is at the pinnacle of this federal court system.

Selection and Composition

Justices of the Supreme Court are appointed in a three-step process. When a vacancy on the Court occurs, the President nominates a person to fill the vacancy. The Senate then votes whether to confirm or reject the nomination. A simple majority of the Senate is necessary. If the nominee is confirmed, the President then formally appoints him to the position.

A Supreme Court justiceship is a lifetime appointment. Until he dies or decides to retire, a supreme court justice cannot be removed except by impeachment. Thus, more often than not, there seem to be "nine old men" on the Court. The selection process by the President is ordinarily, therefore, a careful one, so as not to saddle the country with an inept justice who will sit on the Court for life.

It follows that the confirmation process by the Senate ought to be careful as well, but this is not necessarily the case. Between 1789 and 1900, the Senate rejected more than a third of the President's nominees to the Court; it rejected only one between 1900 and 1968, federal Judge William Parker from North Carolina, nominated by President Herbert Hoover in 1930. Even then it was only the heightened sensitivity of a country in which the Ku Klux Klan had been a violent force through the 1920s that led to Parker's rejection. It became a plausible (whether or not accurate) charge that Judge Parker would be friendly to the Klan, with attendant implications of racism, because of his southern background.

Beginning in 1968 the Senate seemed to be taking its responsibility somewhat more seriously, rejecting three presidential nominations and perhaps reinvigorating its role in the selection process. In 1968, President Lyndon Johnson chose then-Associate Justice Abe Fortas to be chief justice after the retirement of Earl Warren. The Senate rejected Fortas's nomination, largely on the grounds that 1968 was an election year and the new President ought to have the right to make such an appointment.

If that sounds somewhat unreasonable, it has to be remembered that there are no criteria established by the Constitution for confirmation or rejection by the Senate. Prior to 1900 it was quite common for the Senate to make its judgement on purely partisan political grounds that were unrelated to the judicial qualifications of the nominee. After 1900, however, the bywords became *quality* and *competence* and the Senate found it difficult to reject virtually any adequate lawyer until Fortas—except, of course, Parker.

In 1969 and 1970, a Senate in which Democrats were a majority rejected two of Republican President Richard Nixon's nominees to the Court. Clement Haynesworth of South Carolina, a judge of the United States Court of Appeals, was refused confirmation when it became known that he had participated in a decision involving a small corporation in which he held a substantial portion of the stock. Because the worth of the stock was not more than a few thousand dollars, and judges elsewhere had sat on cases in which they held some stockholder interest, the ethical standards of this judgment by the Senate were not too clear. Haynesworth's supporters charged that he was opposed because he was a southerner.

That charge was reiterated when Nixon's next nominee, United States District Judge G. Harrold Carswell of Florida, was rejected. But administration opponents claimed that Carswell's competence was questionable. A group of students at Columbia Law School researched Carswell's record as a federal district judge and discovered that an extraordinarily high percentage of his decisions had been reversed by higher courts, including seventeen civil rights cases in which reversal was unanimous by the judges on the court of appeals. Moreover, Carswell's critics fastened on two incidents in his earlier career that were to haunt him. While running for political office in the 1940s, Carswell had declared that he believed in white supremacy. And, in the 1950s, he had drawn up incorporation papers for a Florida golf course that contained a racially restrictive covenant. Notwithstanding Senator Roman Hruska's (Republican of Nebraska) comment that "mediocrity" ought to be represented on the Court, Carswell was denied confirmation.

After 1970, however, the earlier pattern of almost routine confirmation of presidential nominees has reasserted itself. Although investigation of the nominee's qualifications seems to be thorough, recent nominees to the high Court have been uncontroversial and have been approved by large majorities of the Senate.

If the Senate's standards for approval are not precisely defined, neither are the President's. It is difficult to say who is the best lawyer or judge in the country (even if that were the sole criterion for selection). At any one time, there are probably dozens of persons who would be capable justices. Consequently, a President has a good deal of latitude in making his choice and can conduct an extensive political search for the "right" person. Because so much of the Supreme Court's work consists of interpreting ambiguities in the law, a President will ordinarily try to select someone whose interpretations will generally reflect the President's views of public policy.

Of course, no one makes "deals" about future cases that have not yet arisen. But a President quite naturally hopes that his nominee will decide those future cases the same way he would. He will rarely choose an ideological opponent. For instance, during his campaign in 1968, Richard Nixon pledged to appoint "strict constructionists" to the Supreme Court because, it was thought, such men could be expected to construe constitutional provisions in an ideologically conservative manner. Nixon felt that the Court had been too "liberal" and freewheeling in construing the Constitution, particularly in the areas of criminal law and one-man/one-vote cases.

A generation earlier, President Franklin D. Roosevelt sought similarly to use his power of nomination and appointment to alter the trend of decisions being rendered by the Supreme Court, but he had to wait a good deal longer than Nixon to do it. During Roosevelt's first term, the Supreme Court declared much of his New Deal legislation to be unconstitutional. Because none of the justices died or retired, no vacancies came up until the latter part of 1937, well into his second term. Thereafter, vacancies came rapidly and, before long, the Court took on the color of a "Roosevelt Court," rendering decisions much more to Roosevelt's liking than earlier.

Although President Jimmy Carter was unable to make any Supreme Court appointments during his four years as President, President Ronald Reagan was afforded the opportunity shortly after he took office and he broke new ground in doing so. Justice Potter Stewart submitted his resignation effective at the end of the 1980 term of the Court. Reagan fulfilled a campaign pledge by designating the first woman ever to be nominated for the high Court, Sandra Day O'Connor, an Arizona appellate court judge and former state legislator with impeccable Republican credentials. Moreover, five of the justices are now over seventy years of age and in varying degrees of health, and several of them have indicated that they are contemplating retirement. It appears likely that President Reagan will have ample opportunity in the early 1980s to determine the composition and perhaps the direction of the Court for many years.

Justices of the United States Supreme Court
(In order of seniority: name, year of birth, race, religious affiliation, occupation, party affiliation, home state, position at time of appointment, year of appointment, appointing President)

Warren E. Burger, *Chief Justice*   1907; white; Protestant; attorney; Republican; Minnesota; Judge, United States Court of Appeals, D. C. Cir.; 1969; Nixon.

William J. Brennan   1906; white; Catholic; attorney; Democrat; New Jersey; Judge, New Jersey Supreme Court; 1956; Eisenhower.

Byron R. White   1917; white; Protestant; attorney; Democrat; Colorado; Deputy Attorney General of the United States; 1962; Kennedy.

Thurgood Marshall   1908; black; Protestant; attorney; Democrat; New York; United States Solicitor General; 1967; Johnson.

Harry A. Blackmun   1908; white; Protestant; attorney; Republican; Minnesota; Judge, United States Court of Appeals, 8th Cir.; 1970; Nixon.

Lewis F. Powell   1908; white; Protestant; attorney; Democrat; Virginia; private practice; 1971; Nixon.

William H. Rehnquist   1923; white; Protestant; attorney; Republican; Arizona; Assistant Attorney General of the United States; 1971; Nixon.

John Paul Stevens   1920; white; Protestant; attorney; Republican; Illinois; Judge, United States Court of Appeals, 7th Cir.; 1975; Ford.

Sandra Day O'Connor   1934; white; Protestant; attorney; Republican; Arizona; State Court Judge; 1981; Reagan.

Not all of a President's appointments work out the way he would like. The life tenure of a justice means that he owes no favors to the one who appoints him and will very likely outlast the President in office. Or the President may have misread the appointee's mind, his earlier political career, or his prior decisions. Where an appointee has had an active political life, he may have felt ideologically inhibited or restricted by the political process. Once on the Court he can give free rein, within the limits of the law, to his values and preferences. Thus, he may seem to become an entirely different man as a justice than he was as a public official in another capacity.

President John F. Kennedy, a fairly liberal Democrat, appointed Byron F. White to the Court in 1962. White was a member of the New Frontier team, who had worked for Robert F. Kennedy in the Justice Department during the civil rights crises of the early 1960s. Whatever Kennedy thought then about White's political inclination, few would claim now that White was a member of the liberal wing of the Court.

Republican President Dwight D. Eisenhower's first Court appointment in 1953 was Chief Justice Earl Warren, former governor of California and the Republican candidate for Vice President in 1948. It was the Warren Court whose pattern of decisions Republican Nixon felt had to be changed in 1968. And Eisenhower is known to have bemoaned the choice of Warren as his biggest mistake while in office. Another Eisenhower appointee, William Brennan, was to become a mainstay of the Court's liberal wing.

All of the nation's Supreme Court justices have until now been men and all have been lawyers. Neither characteristic is required for a justice. Although the former reflects a long-standing prejudice, the latter is indicative of a belief that the Court, more than the other branches of government, is the province of those who have been trained in the law. During the 1940s there was some speculation that Edward Corwin, a political scientist who had written extensively and brilliantly about the Court, might be named to it, but this never came to pass. Since then, no nonlawyer has even been publically mentioned in this connection.

Beyond legal training, the experience of justices has been varied. Many have come from major private law firms, especially from Wall Street, and from the corporate structure. Such a business and financial background, although perhaps ideologically conservative, has been useful to a Court that deals so extensively with society's economic arrangements. Many justices have been politicians, holding a variety of elective or appointive positions at various levels of government. A number of U.S. attorneys general, such as Harlan F. Stone, Tom Clark, Robert Jackson, and Frank Murphy have been elevated to the Supreme Court in recent years. Roosevelt's first appointee, Stanley Reed, was the U.S. solicitor general, the government's lawyer before the Supreme Court. Justice Hugo Black was a United States senator and Chief Justice William Howard Taft was a former

President. The great John Marshall was President John Adam's Secretary of State at the time of his appointment. Former Chief Justice Charles Evans Hughes had garnered nearly every political honor available to an American, save the presidency. He had been Governor of New York, an Associate Justice of the Supreme Court, Secretary of State, and presidential nominee of the Republican party in 1916.

Lower courts and state courts have been the source of numerous appointments, such as former Chief Judge of the New York Court of Appeals Benjamin Cardozo and the revered Oliver Wendell Holmes, Jr., of the Massachusetts Supreme Judicial Court. The nation's law schools have yielded professors and deans, such as Felix Frankfurter and Wiley Rutledge, who have brought scholarly distinction to the high Court.

There are no constitutional requirements of age or citizenship for supreme court justices (unlike Presidents and congressmen). But sometimes there are informal requirements that seem to be akin to ticket balancing in electoral politics. For example, for a long time there was thought to be a Jewish "seat" on the Court, held first by Louis D. Brandeis and then, in rough succession, by Felix Frankfurter, Arthur Goldberg, and Abe Fortas. This "tradition" was ended when Fortas resigned in 1969. When Hugo Black of Alabama died in 1971, the Court was without a southerner until Lewis F. Powell of Virginia took his place. Thurgood Marshall's appointment may have established a black seat. And now that the first woman has been appointed to the Court, it is difficult to see how she could be succeeded by a man without causing an enormous political struggle, unless other women had joined her on the Court before then.

At present the Court has nine justices. This is not a constitutional requirement, nor is nine a magic number. There have been as few as five and as many as ten justices. The size of the Court is fixed by law—that is, by Congress—and it can be changed whenever and for whatever reason Congress wishes. For instance, when two justices died during President Andrew Johnson's administration, Congress simply abolished the positions in order to prevent Johnson from filling the seats; however, one position on the Court was restored when Grant became President. The rationale for nine justices seems to be that this number is large enough to handle the case load and encompass a broad knowledge of the law, yet small enough to permit small-group, seminarlike discussions of cases without being too unwieldy.

And, moreover, the number of justices has by now been hallowed by a century of practice. An attempt to change it could all too easily be construed as an overt attempt to exercise "political" control over the Court.

For example, when President Franklin D. Roosevelt proposed in early 1937 to overcome his inability, because of the lack of vacancies, to appoint any justices by increasing the number of justices so that he could appoint one additional justice for each seated justice on the court who was over seventy, the plan was defeated amid cries of "court packing."

The average tenure of a Supreme Court justice is about fifteen and one half years. William O. Douglas had the longest time on the Court (thirty-five years); the shortest tenure was held by James F. Byrnes (slightly more than a year). There have been 101 justices and more than half of them have died on the bench. Some, like Douglas, have retired because of physical infirmity. The ninety-year-old Holmes was asked to retire when it became painfully obvious that he could no longer keep up with the work. Ward Hunt, in the late 1800s, did not sit for the last three years prior to his retirement. Others, such as Byrnes and Goldberg, resigned to accept other government jobs. Fortas resigned under fire, after allegations of corruption, but such incidents have been very rare.

Former Chief Justice Earl Warren maintained an office in the Supreme Court building from which he conducted his affairs until his death. Other former justices, such as Tom Clark and Charles Whittaker, have from time to time been given assignments by the Court, such as a special master or to relieve a temporarily burdensome work load of a lower court.

There is little that can be done to control the activities or decisions of the justices. Supreme Court justices are unassailable while they exhibit "good behavior," although they can be impeached and, upon conviction by the Senate, removed from the Court. What constitutes good behavior, however, is questionable. The only justice to be impeached (Samuel Chase in 1805) was charged with partisan activity and harsh conduct while on the Court, but the Senate acquitted him. When Douglas was attacked in 1970, one of the charges against him was that he had contributed an article to *Playboy* magazine. House Minority Leader Gerald Ford, who spearheaded the effort, said at the time that an impeachable offense was "whatever a majority of the House of Representatives" wanted it to be and he was technically correct. But the proceeding against Douglas never got off the ground.

Court Operations

The Supreme Court sits for most of the year, from October through June. This **term** is fixed by law, but Congress can change it, as they did a few times during the early years of the Republic. The justices take the summer "off" and generally manage to get in a few weeks of vacation. For the rest of that time, they will be reading cases, briefs, and petitions in preparation for the next term. Because the nation's courts do not close up shop over the summer, each justice must still supervise his circuit (see p. 148).

Several thousand cases are appealed each year to the Supreme Court, but the Court takes only a few hundred of what it deems the most important cases, rendering decisions with opinions attached to them. Beginning the first Monday in October, the Court normally sits for two weeks hearing cases and then takes two weeks off. When in session the Court meets in the morning from 10:00 to noon and, after lunch, from 2:00 to about 4:00. Each case to be argued (there are no trials, simply presentations by lawyers) has previously been assigned a specific date and hour. Each case is given one hour for oral argument, one half hour for each side, with occasional extra time allowed if a third party (an *amicus curiae,* or friend of the court, usually the government or another interested group, such as the American Civil Liberties Union) has been granted permission to argue. The justices will have already read the written arguments, or briefs, from each side.

The courtroom where the oral argument takes place is large and impressive. It stands about 25 feet high and is nearly 50 feet wide and about twice as long. Huge dark red drapes hang down on all sides, creating, both acoustically and visually, a hushed, awe-inspiring atmosphere. The rear half of the courtroom contains seats for spectators, who are continually admonished by Court officers to maintain a respectful silence. There are special seats up front and at the sides for attorneys to watch. Inside the well of the Court are tables behind which sit the lawyers in the case. A lectern is set up in the center for the lawyer whose turn it is to argue.

At the front of the courtroom, facing everyone else, is the bench behind which sit the justices. The bench is raised to about eye level. The justices sit in black leather, high-backed chairs that rock and rotate. The bench itself used to be straight across but is now divided into three sections at slight angles to each other, so the sections partially enclose the area around the attorney who is arguing. The change was made to enable the justices at the ends of the bench more easily to hear and to see what is occurring. Microphones have been added in recent years for the same purpose.

The chief justice is seated in the center. On his rights sits the senior associate justice (in length of service) and on his left sits the next senior one. The other justices sit alternately to the right and left of the center in order of their seniority.

Although the issues in a Supreme Court case have been fully briefed in writing, great weight is placed on the oral argument. A justice who, because of illness or otherwise, is not present when the case is argued will not ordinarily participate in the decision. The justices can and often do interrupt a lawyer's presentation in order to ask a question they deem crucial or to inquire about a point not made adequately in the written brief. They might ask hypothetical questions that vary the facts of the case just a bit, in order to see where the logic of an argument runs. It is not always easy to tell which way the justice is leaning from his questions. While he might be probing for weak spots in the lawyer's argument or be raising difficult points, he might also be trying to gain support for his own views by giving the lawyer a chance to present his best arguments. The questions and answers usually count against the lawyer's time limit.

The justices spend almost every Friday in conference, during which they debate among themselves the cases they have heard and, if they are ready, vote on the outcome. During the alternate two weeks when the Court is not in session, they will have read the case briefs thoroughly, done any necessary research on their own, and written tentative and sometimes final opinions. They also read petitions (called writs of certiorari) for new cases to be heard and decide which ones they will hear. (Four justices must ask that a case be heard or else the petition is denied.) In these tasks, the justices are assisted by law clerks—recent graduates of law schools whose tasks include performing legal research and drafting legal memoranda for the justices. Thus, when the justices come to the conferences, they are well prepared to argue the cases among themselves.

The Friday conferences are absolutely secret. Not even trusted law clerks are admitted. Passionate arguments are cloaked with formal civility, such as ritual handshakes and references to "my brother justice." (Beginning with the 1980 term, however, the justices have dropped the phrase "Mr. Justice" from their opinions, apparently in deference to the possibility that a woman would soon be appointed to the Court.) The chief justice summarizes the case and reviews the arguments for each side, but his vote is given no extra weight. He speaks first, then calls on the others for argument in strict order of seniority. When fruitful discussion is concluded, the chief justice then begins the voting by calling on the most junior justice to vote first. Voting then proceeds in inverse order of seniority, with the chief justice voting last. No vote is final until the decision is handed down. A vote is either to affirm or to reverse the decision of the lower court from which the appeal came. A case must be decided by a majority vote. If the vote is a tie (because of an absent justice), there is no decision and the decision of the lower court is affirmed. In such a case, or in other important ones, the justices may decide to put off voting in order to permit deeper consideration and perhaps allow a change of mind.

It is not merely enough for the justices to decide the case. An opinion must be written justifying and explaining the decision. This is vital for both legal and political reasons. A decided case normally stands for or represents some legal principle. There are generally (or will be in the future) similar cases and the legal community (judges, lawyers, legislators, policemen, and litigants) must be informed about what kinds of situations, policies, or activities will be covered by the rule of law announced. In this way everyone can know what the law or legal principle is, as well as how future courts will decide similar cases. In addition, the public needs to know why the Court decided a case the way it did, especially when the question is one of public policy. Then the public, if it disagrees, can take political steps to change the law or amend the Constitution to the extent necessary to overcome the rationale of a disliked decision. A decision for which the reasons are clearly explained and understood is more readily accepted than one that is simply declared or clouded in mystery.

The chief justice, when he is in the majority in a decision, determines who will write the **Opinion of the Court.** (See page 146) He may choose to write it himself or to assign it to another member of the majority. Generally, he will try to assign the opinion to a justice who is an expert in the field or to balance the work load as evenly as possible. If the chief justice is in the minority, the senior associate justice within the majority makes the decision about writing the opinion.

Any member of the minority may write a **dissenting opinion** explaining why he does not agree with the Court's opinion. Several dissenting justices may join in the dissenting opinion, or each dissenter may express his own reasons in a separate opinion.

The judgment of the Court is the decision to affirm or to reverse. On occasion a justice may agree with or concur in the Court's judgment but for reasons different from the others in the majority. In such a case he may write a **concurring opinion** in order to express his reasons for agreeing with the judgment and his differences from the rest of the majority. He may even agree with the Court's opinion but set out an additional reason for concurring.

An extreme example of this is the now famous steel seizure case in 1952 *(Youngstown Sheet and Tube Co., Inc. v Sawyer),* which arose when President Truman seized the steel plants after steelworkers had threatened to strike during the Korean War. The Court, in a 6-to-3 decision, refused to allow the seizure, but there were *seven* different opinions; an opinion of the Court saying little more than "Sorry, Harry," written by Justice Black; five concurring opinions; and a three-man dissent.

A less extreme, but possibly more significant, example is the 1971 *Mitchell v. New York Times* case, where, by a 6-to-3 majority, the Court refused to allow the government to prevent publication of the Pentagon Papers. Three justices (Brennan, Douglas, and Black) said that the government could not censor the press at all; three (Burger, Blackmun, and Harlan) said that the government could do so when national security was in danger; and the crucial three (Stewart, White, and Marshall) said that the government could not do so *in this case,* where there was no evidence of danger to national security.

Similarly, in the 1973 decision declaring capital punishment statutes unconstitutional, four justices joined in the Opinion of the Court holding the laws themselves to be "cruel and unusual punishment" and, therefore, contrary to the constitutional prohibition. Three justices, in a dissenting opinion, thought that the laws did not violate the Constitution. However, the two "swing" justices (Stewart and White) joined the majority but wrote a concurring opinion, stating it to be their belief that these *particular* statutes were unconstitutional because they had been *applied* inconsistently, without any but vague statutory standards to guide the decision makers, and with an apparently discriminatory frequency against blacks. The existence of this concurring opinion has led many states to pass new capital punishment laws. And the Court, with a different majority has subsequently held that capital punishment statutes which provide standards to guide juries can be constitutional. The states hoped that the lack of inconsistency and discriminatory application would convince the two swing justices, when the laws came up again for review, to vote the other way and provide a majority in favor of capital punishment.

After the initial vote among the justices in a case, an Opinion is drafted and circulated among the justices. On occasion a justice who voted one way may change his mind when he sees it in writing, saying in effect, "If these are your reasons, I can no longer agree with your decision." Or, he may only then decide to write a concurring opinion. Opinions may be rewritten, deleting disagreeable passages or justifications in order to gain more support. The more justices aligned behind a particular opinion, the stronger the opinion becomes in the community.

When all the opinions have been written, the Court's decision is handed down. It used to be the pattern that the decisions were announced on "Decision Monday," the first Monday that the Court sat to hear cases after its two weeks of reading and writing. But Chief Justice Burger changed the practice by announcing decisions throughout the two-week period during which the Court is sitting, in order to spread the announcements more evenly over that span.

In the 1979 term of the Court, running from October 1979 through June 1980, the Court issued 140 full opinions. Despite Chief Justice Burger's attempt to spread the decisions throughout the year as evenly as possible, 40 per cent of them were rendered after Memorial Day.

On occasion, in a case deemed especially important, the justice who wrote the Opinion of the Court will read it (or excerpts from it) aloud in open court. More commonly, however, because of the multitude of cases and the time taken by public reading, the written opinion is simply presented to the parties and the public without fanfare.

The Court's decision is final. It is the "court of last resort" in the country; there is no appeal from an adverse decision of the Supreme Court. Dissatisfied parties may file petitions for rehearing or reconsideration, but these are so rarely approved by the Court as to be nearly fruitless. At some point in any decision process, there must be a stopping point, a place where the problem is finally resolved. In the judicial system, the Supreme Court is that place.

Jurisdiction and Procedure

Cases and Controversies

Unlike other institutions of government, which can reach out to grasp issues of public policy in order to resolve them, courts must wait for an issue to be presented in a proper format to them. The Supreme Court has provided a number of guidelines for the federal judiciary concerning this format, many of which are shared by other court systems. The Constitution provides that the Court may rule on "cases [and] controversies," not public issues in general or even issues affecting specifically the judiciary, except under certain circumstances.

A case or controversy means, first of all, a conflict that is sought to be resolved in a court. But, in order to get the court to listen to the problem (that is, in order to be allowed to sue in court), the conflict must have a number of characteristics. The parties to the lawsuit, for example, must have "standing to sue." They must be able to show that significant rights belonging to them are being infringed on, or that they are being (or have been) injured in some respect, through loss of money, property, liberty, or from personal injury.

Although, in most instances where one would think of going to court, this is fairly easy to show, there are marginal cases where there is room for dispute. A taxpayer, for example, cannot ordinarily challenge in court the government's spending habits, no matter how distasteful a certain government program is to the taxpayer. Even though the taxpayer can prove that he is losing money through his having to pay taxes to pay for the program, the Supreme Court has said that the amount of money the taxpayer has lost is so small that he cannot have standing to sue as a result of that loss. But, the Court has added, where the purpose for which the money is spent directly conflicts with a specific constitutional prohibition, such as "an establishment of religion," then the taxpayer may have standing.

Some people may have no standing to sue because the law deems them incapable, for one reason or another. Children and mental incompetents are among these, although a guardian may sue for them. Prisoners may also be deprived of the right to sue in certain circumstances. Only in the last hundred or so years have married women been granted full standing in courts, because formerly such women were considered to be part of a marital unit, of which almost all of the legal rights belonged to the husband.

A case in court must be justiciable—that is, it must be in a form traditionally thought to be able to be decided by a court. There could be a question of fact involved, where a court or jury would have to decide what the truth is, who is being wronged, or how much injury has been done. Or there may be a question of which of two or more laws applies to a particular set of facts. There may be conflicting laws, where the court would have to determine which law predominates. There may be a question of whether any law applies or whether a party to the suit has any legal right to act as he did. In all these instances it has traditionally been the function of courts to resolve the conflicts involved.

But where one of these questions is not clearly presented, or where the case presents a problem that another institution of government ought to resolve, the court may decide that the issue is not justiciable. Many legal issues involving foreign policy have been held to be non-justiciable because they are entrusted to the executive branch. Such an issue presents what the courts call a **political question,** a problem to be decided through the political process, not the judicial one.

For many years, courts regarded the apportionment of legislative districts as a political question, one for the legislature to resolve. But, in 1962, in *Baker* v. *Carr,* the Supreme Court ruled that the deprivation of rights involved in malapportionment was so substantial that, because in the Constitution there was no "textually demonstrable commitment" of the issue to the legislature (among other criteria), the Court would decide the case. Reapportionment then became a justiciable issue.

Similarly, the Court ruled, in 1969, in *Powell v. McCormack* that Congress could not exclude Representative Adam Clayton Powell (Democrat of New York) from his seat in the House. The dissenting opinion urged that it was a political question because the Constitution made each house "the judge of the . . . qualifications of its own members." But the majority held that this was not a "textually demonstrable commitment" of the entire issue to Congress because "qualifications" referred only to age, citizenship, and residence, criteria that Powell concededly met. The Court reversed the decision of the lower court, whose opinion had been written by then-Judge of the United States Court of Appeals Warren Burger.

Courts require that a case must be fought by adversaries; that is, the opposing parties must represent distinct interests, each seeking a different judgment. This is to prevent collusion that might arise when different parties try to gain court approval of an interest they both want to see furthered. Such collusion would not present a real case, for neither side is being injured by the other.

Cases must be real in the sense that they arise from an actual controversy, not a hypothetical one or one that has not yet ripened into an actual dispute. Courts have, for example, declined to hear cases in which a criminal law was challenged as unconstitutional but no one had been prosecuted under the law. In 1961, in *Poe* v. *Ullman,* the Supreme Court rejected a challenge to a Connecticut statute prohibiting the sale of birth control devices because the complaining party had not been prosecuted by the authorities. It was, in effect, a phony case. Four years later, however, the Court did hear a similar case (*Griswold* v. *Connecticut*) because the state finally prosecuted someone under the law, which was then declared unconstitutional.

Although state constitutions may authorize their courts to do so, the Supreme Court refuses to give advisory opinions on the constitutionality or interpretation of laws without a real case being involved. The Court feels that, without the context of an actual controversy, the abstractions of the law will have little content. The facts of a case and the concrete application of the statute give meaning to the law and a clear understanding of its consequences in a way that no hypothetical case can match.

The federal courts will not hear a case unless there is some federal question involved. This means that the issue in the case must concern a point of federal law, an action of some institution or agency of the federal government, a treaty, or the Constitution. Federal courts will not hear a question involving purely state or local laws unless it conflicts with federal law or unless the parties are from different states.

The Supreme Court does not ordinarily sit as a trial court. The Court almost always has only appellate jurisdiction, which means that it hears only appeals from lower courts or state courts in cases that those courts have decided. The Constitution gives the Supreme Court original jurisdiction to try a case only in a few instances, such as where a state is a party or those cases affecting "ambassadors, other public ministers, and consuls."

Case Selection

In most instances the Supreme Court can choose the cases it wants to hear. Unlike trial courts and most intermediate appeals courts, which have to hear all those cases properly brought before them, the Supreme Court can refuse to accept a case if, for some reason, it does not want to hear it.

There are some statutes of the United States that provide for a right of appeal, at the option of the parties, from the trial court directly to the Supreme Court. These provisions occur mostly where the constitutionality of laws is concerned. The decisions of some federal regulatory commissions may also be appealed by right directly to the Court, where a federal statute so authorizes it.

But these circumstances are limited and most of the cases on the Supreme Court's docket get there because the Court has issued a **writ of certiorari** requesting the case. Thousands of petitions for these writs are filed each year, but the Court issues only a few hundred. Most of them come from litigants dissatisfied with the decision of one of the United States courts of appeals or the highest court of a state. When the Court denies a petition for a writ of certiorari, the effect is to affirm, or let stand, the decision of the lower court.

The writ of certiorari, when issued, directs the lower court to forward the record and opinions of the proceedings in the case to the Supreme Court. At least four justices must approve the writ in a decision during a Friday conference, although voting to grant the writ does not mean that the justice disagrees with the decision of the lower court. A docket number is then given to the case, a date and time for oral argument are assigned, and briefs on the points of law to be argued by the parties are requested. Time for reply briefs in response to the opponent's argument is allowed.

A federal statute authorizes the Court to hear *appeals* from the decisions of the highest court in a state when that court (1) has held a federal statute to be invalid or (2) has held a state statute to be valid when challenged on the grounds that it is contrary to the Constitution or laws of the United States. But the Court has concluded that it is not required by the statute to hear all such appeals, and it treats them in much the same manner as petitions for certiorari. Cases on appeal amount to less than 10 per cent of the Court's work load.

There is another, although rarely used, method for a case to get to the Supreme Court. If the court of appeals is uncertain about the controlling point of law in a case, it may *certify* a question to the Supreme Court. The question is posed in such a way that it can be answered affirmatively or negatively. The process of certification means that the lower court wants some guidance, either because prior Supreme Court decisions on the point seem inconsistent with each other (possibly because the trend of law may be changing) or because the point is so new or unique that there seems to be no way to use analogous decisions to reach an answer. The Supreme Court may respond by writing a lengthy opinion, by a simple "Yes" or "No," or by "Yes" or "No" along with a citation to a prior case or line of cases.

When the lower court receives its answer and makes its ruling in the case, the losing party may still petition for a writ of certiorari (or appeal) in order to get the decision reviewed. But such a petition is not likely to be accepted unless the lower court has misapplied or misinterpreted the certified answer.

Several factors may influence the decision of the Supreme Court to accept or reject a case for review. The primary factor is the case load that the Court's schedule permits. Because the justices feel that they have to hear oral argument in order best to be able to decide a case, the number of cases is limited to four or five a day in alternating two-week periods during the year. Therefore, out of the thousands of petitions, they can only accept the 350 or so that they think most require a decision at the highest level. Consequently, many cases that the justices might like to hear cannot be accepted.

Where the courts of appeals in two or more circuits have rendered inconsistent decisions on the same point of law, the Supreme Court generally feels that it must review them in order to make the law clear. When a lower court has made a ruling in an area where the law has not been settled, especially if the case itself is a controversial one, it may come under Court review. If the lower court has ruled contrary to Supreme Court decisions in the past, the Court may accept the case. If there is some overriding public significance to the case, the Court may feel compelled to accept it for review in order to give the matter an authoritative resolution. Should the Court feel that its prior decisions on a particular point of law were wrong or are outdated or that the underlying rationale for them has disappeared, it may look for and accept a case as a vehicle in order to make known its changing view.

Many cases that the Court might feel deserve an opinion from the highest tribunal have been decided, in its view, correctly and for the proper reasons by the lower court. The denial of certiorari may serve then to give the Supreme Court's approval to the lower court's opinion. It is also possible for a lower court's ruling to be reversed virtually without opinion, or with a few sentences often citing the Court's prior decisions in that area. Because four justices must agree to hear it before a case is accepted, it is not often that a trivial case is argued before the Supreme Court.

Varieties of Law

Cases that are argued before the Supreme Court (and other courts as well) deal with several different types of law. At the apex of the legal structure is constitutional law. The Constitution of the United States is the supreme law of the land. No other laws, not even state constitutions, can be in conflict with it. But conflicts frequently develop over the precise meaning of terms and phrases within the Constitution. In many places the Constitution is an ambiguous document and, anyway, it was written nearly two hundred years ago when social, economic, and political conditions were much different. It is in constant need of interpretation and reinterpretation as concrete situations give rise to new contexts in which it must be applied.

Some parts of the Constitution, such as those prescribing two Houses of Congress and the President and Vice President, are so plain as to require no interpretation. But others are vague and ambiguous. Some of these, such as the clause giving the federal government control over interstate commerce, were at one time the causes of many disputes. The commerce clause has now been "interpreted" to such an extent that there are not many significant disputes over its meaning any more. But the questions of "due process of law" or "unreasonable searches and seizures," as examples, have never been conclusively resolved. The content of due process is still a matter of vigorous dispute. What is "unreasonable" tends to vary depending on technology, moral standards and customs, the purposes of governmental activity in the context in which the case arose, and the effects of the actions in general.

A case in which there is alleged a conflict with one or more provisions of the Constitution becomes a constitutional law case. Courts are required then to interpret the Constitution and apply it to the facts in the case. In that way they flesh out the bare bones of the Constitution by giving it concrete meaning, which can then be used to resolve other similar disputes.

The Constitution itself can be changed (as opposed to reinterpreted) only via the amendment process. Amendments can be proposed by a vote ot two-thirds of each house of Congress or by a special convention when two thirds of the states request it. (The president has no formal role here.) But, in order for the amendment to become part of the Constitution, it must be approved by three-fourths of the states. This is ordinarily a lengthy and time-consuming process, most often taking several years.

When Congress or the states object to the Supreme Court's interpretation of the Constitution, they may, in effect, reverse the Court's ruling by amending the constitutional phrase or clause in question. For example, in 1895 the Court ruled in a 5 to 4 decision that a federal tax on personal income was unconstitutional. One justice had switched his vote from an earlier consideration of the tax. In 1913, however, the Sixteenth Amendment, expressly authorizing the income tax, was approved by three quarters of the states. The Court's decision was no longer applicable.

Under consideration today are several constitutional amendments which, if ratified, would reverse the Court's decision permitting abortions in certain circumstances.

Any provision of the Constitution can be altered by amendment except perhaps for the clause in Article I providing that each state is entitled to equal representation in the Senate. Article V expressly provides that no state can be deprived of its "equal suffrage" in the Senate without its consent.

Another variety of law is statutory law. A **statute** is an enactment of a legislative body (such as Congress) with the concurrence of, or by overriding the disapproval of, the executive. Legislatures enact statutes in order to establish public policy, to prohibit certain practices or actions, or to provide money to carry out government programs.

Statutes may not conflict with the Constitution. If a party who is adversely affected by a statute complains that the statute, whether state or federal, is contrary to the Constitution, the Supreme Court (or a lower court) may declare it unconstitutional. The statute, or the offensive part of it, is then void.

But the Court will go out of its way to interpret or construe a statute in such a way so that it is not unconstitutional, if that is at all possible. The Court attaches a "presumption of constitutionality" to legistlative enactments. Sometimes it is only the application by administrators of an otherwise acceptable statute that is offensive. In such cases the Court may rule that the statute is "unconstitutional as applied." The statute may still be valid, although the administrators will subsequently have to apply it in a different manner.

Statutes may be held unconstitutional for vagueness. This would occur when the legislation contains no clear indication of what is lawful and what is not. For example, the Court has struck down numerous loyalty oaths and antisubversive statutes because no one could tell what conduct was prohibited by the laws and what was permissible.

Statutes whose meaning is clear and whose application is fair may be held unconstitutional if their purpose or effect is to contravene a constitutional right. For instance, residence requirements for welfare were perfectly understandable and impartially applied. Yet the Court has ruled that they inhibit the constitutional right to travel and are, therefore, invalid.

Most of the Supreme Court's work with statutes concerns not their constitutionality but their interpretation. The judicial art of statutory interpretation is to determine as precisely as possible the meaning of a statute and the requirements it imposes. Courts try to give effect to the intent of the legislature in passing the law, even though the statute may appear on its face to have two different meanings.

Still another type of law is administrative law. This is a body of law—usually rules and regulations—made by administrators and other government officials in order to carry out a legislative program. The Federal Communications Commission (FCC), the Food and Drug Administration (FDA), and other governmental units publish these regulations. Those persons operating within the field covered by the unit are subject to the rules, which have the effect of law.

Administrative law may not conflict with either the Constitution or statutes that authorized the program or policy involved. Courts are often called on to decide whether a particular administrative regulation, practice, or proceeding is contrary to a statutory mandate or to the Constitution. For example, the Supreme Court has held that a welfare department may not deprive a child of welfare benefits simply because a man (not the child's father) lives in the home with the child's mother. Such a regulation is in conflict with the statute authorizing benefits to needy children who do not have fathers. And, in the same field, the Supreme Court ruled that a welfare department could not stop benefits to a needy family without a prior hearing concerning eligibility because otherwise there would be a violation of the family's constitutional right to due process of law.

Finally, there is **common law.** This is a body of law that has established certain rights and duties by virtue of past judicial decisions. It has been built up over the years by courts in deciding cases where no statutes, administrative rules, or constitutional provisions were determinative. Other forms of law are generally superior to common law and displace it when relevant to a case. But legal relations among people are so complex that governments have not written laws to cover all the contingencies. The common law fills the gaps.

If you are injured by another's carelessness, for example, you have a right under common law to sue to recover a monetary award to compensate you for your injuries (unless that right has been taken away or displaced by something like "no-fault" insurance). Such common law tort actions have been around for centuries. Much of the law of torts is common law, whereas, for example, criminal law is almost entirely statutory. Trial by jury in civil suits is another ancient common law right, preserved from statutory displacement by the Seventh Amendment to the Constitution.

Legislative Control

Congress has the constitutional power to prescribe much of the structure and operations of the Supreme Court and other federal courts. Although it could not abolish the Supreme Court, Congress can, nevertheless, by statute, determine the size of the Court, the salaries of the justices, and the term during which the Court sits. Congress appropriates the money to erect court buildings and it controls, by appropriations, the number of people (clerks, court officers, and so on) who work for the Court.

All of the inferior federal courts are the creatures of Congress. Before permanent federal district courts were established, the Supreme Court justices had to "ride circuit"; they literally had to ride on horseback to reach places within a circuit or area where they would sit individually as a judge in a court of original jurisdiction. It was in this capacity that Chief Justice John Marshall presided over the treason trial of Aaron Burr. Eventually, Congress took pity on the justices and gave this function to newly created lower court judges.

Similarly, when appeals from these district courts became so numerous in the late nineteenth century that they threatened to overwhelm the Court, the Congress established intermediate courts of appeals. These were to screen out cases and provide an appeals framework for federal courts.

The courts of appeals undergo frequent structural revision. In 1980 Congress voted, for example, to divide the old Fifth Circuit Court of Appeals, which covered most of the deep South, into two circuits because the huge territory (from the east coast of Georgia to western Texas) covered by the circuit made it difficult for lawyers and litigants to have their day in court, the court's work load was so large, and the number of circuit court judges (26) was unwieldy.

Congress can add to or subtract from the jurisdiction of the courts. That is, it can determine what kinds of cases the courts can hear and what they cannot. It can provide alternative mechanisms, such as the National Labor Relations Board (NLRB), to resolve disputes in certain specified fields. It can deny a litigant, in specified circumstances, the right to go to court.

Congress, for example, has provided that federal courts of law will not hear civil cases involving a federal question (or a state question where there is diversity of citizenship between the parties) unless there is an amount exceeding $10,000 in controversy. If you sue another person for anything less than that sum, the federal courts will not hear the case. The only exceptions are where another statute expressly allows you to go to federal court to enforce a particular right in disregard of the required amount in controversy. That amount was raised by Congress in 1958 from $3,000 to the present $10,000.

When oil companies attempted in the early 1970s to build an oil pipeline across the frozen wilderness in Alaska, environmentalists sued in federal court, claiming that the construction violated statutes protecting the environment. But congressmen who wanted to see the pipeline built withdrew the case from the court's jurisdiction. They passed a statute depriving anyone of the right to sue to prevent construction.

The extent to which Congress could deprive the Supreme Court of the duty to decide certain constitutional cases is unclear. The Constitution gives the Court power over cases "arising under this Constitution." As long as there are inferior federal courts, individuals can sue if their rights are abridged. In the mid-1950s there was a movement afoot to prohibit the Court from declaring loyalty oaths and similar requirements unconstitutional by an amendment to the

Constitution. This proposed Jenner Amendment (named for its sponsor, Senator Edward Jenner) never passed either house of Congress. Its supporters, however, thought that it was the only way to get around the Courts' jurisdiction in these matters; a simple statute would not work.

Judicial Review

If Congress can exert some control over the Supreme Court, the judiciary has developed a tool of its own against the legislature: **judicial review.** This concept, which was alluded to earlier, enables courts to review laws and declare them unconstitutional. If the Constitution is to be the "supreme law of the land," then it seems clear that congressional actions—statutes—are subordinate to and may not be permitted to stand in conflict with it. But there are two significant problems with this conclusion.

The first is that the Constitution does not say precisely that. Article VI, Section 2 reads: "This Constitution, *and the laws of the United States* which shall be made in pursuance thereof, . . . shall be the supreme law of the land. . . ." (Italics added.) Although there can be little doubt that this section ensures the superiority of federal law over state laws and constitutions, it seems to say that the "laws of the United States"—that is, congressional enactments—are also "supreme."

One might argue that the qualifying phrase, "in pursuance thereof," plainly indicates the appropriate subordination. Therefore, no statute of Congress can be allowed to be in conflict with the Constitution. One might argue further that there would be no point in having a Constitution if Congress could change it simply by passing conflicting legislation. Therefore, a statute may not be in conflict with the constitution.

No matter how persuasive this reasoning may be, it ducks the real question: Who is to determine when a statute is not "in pursuance" of the Constitution? This is the second significant problem.

The Constitution set up three separated, but equal, institutions sharing power (to paraphrase a respected analyst). Although each institution has basically different duties, none is superior to any of the others. (This is popularly, although perhaps inaccurately, called the separation of powers.) All members of the legislature, the executive branch, and the judiciary take the same oath of office to support the Constitution. Why then can the Supreme Court overrule

Congress in the field (legislation) that is specifically the province of Congress? Congress is just as much bound as is the Supreme Court to act constitutionally. Why should the Court be endowed with a superior vision into the soul of the Constitution?

This problem was not unknown to the framers of the Constitution. They had all been schooled in or were familiar with English politics where Parliament was supreme and there was no written constitution. Even today, no English court would strike down an act of Parliament. But the colonial experience was somewhat different. Crown-appointed judges had, on occasion, voided the acts of colonial legislatures. Among the reasons had been that the statutes voided were contrary to the royal or parliamentary charter issued for the colony—in effect, a higher, or supreme, law for the colony. The colonists quite naturally objected to this power, but the principle that courts could invalidate statutes was well rooted in some of the colonies. And the practice continued in a few of the new states after 1776.

The problem of judicial review was debated at the Constitutional Convention in 1787. It was clear to virtually everyone that the new Constitution could not succeed if the national courts could not strike down state laws that conflicted with it, but congressional enactments were different. Some argued that it was undemocratic to allow judges to supersede the collective wisdom of an elected legislature. Others replied that the judges could act as a restraint on a runaway legislature, to prevent the excitable masses from enacting unwise measures into law. In the end the drafters of the Constitution failed to mention it in the final document.

Against this unresolved dispute Chief Justice John Marshall threw his weight in the famous 1803 case of *Marbury* v. *Madison.* William Marbury, among others, had been commissioned to be a judge by President John Adams during the waning hours of the Adams administration in 1801. Adams had signed and sealed the commission and had sent it to the office of his secretary of state to be delivered to Marbury. But the secretary's office was vacant because he had just been appointed chief justice. When the new President, Thomas Jefferson, was inaugurated, his newly appointed secretary of state, James Madison, came upon the commission lying on his desk during his first days in office. Madison refused to deliver it, thereby preventing Marbury from assuming his position.

Marbury sued in the Supreme Court, asking for a *writ of mandamus* ordering Madison to deliver the commission. He was bringing the suit according to the Judiciary Act of 1789, which authorized an individual to go to trial directly in the Supreme Court when a federal government official declined to perform his job properly and thus caused injury.

Before Marshall could decide the case, Congress (controlled by the Jeffersonian Republicans) kept juggling the term of the Supreme Court, with the result that the Court did not sit for about a year and a half. But Marbury hung on with his lawsuit. When the Court finally met in February 1803, Marshall faced a tough problem.

He and Marbury were Federalists. Their party had been thoroughly repudiated in the election of 1800. He knew that an order to their vigorous rival Jefferson (through his appointee, Madison) would probably be ignored. The effect of that would be to point out to everyone the powerlessness of the Supreme Court, the only stronghold of the Federalists. Marshall was virtually impotent to compel Jefferson or Madison to comply. Yet to do nothing at all, in the face of Marbury's complaint, would be equally to confess weakness. There just seemed to be no way out of the dilemma.

But the resourceful Marshall produced a feat of remarkable statesmanship. He began a lengthy opinion with a stern lecture, in effect to Jefferson, on the duties that a responsible public official owes to the citizens of the country. And he castigated Jefferson (although not by name) for failing to meet those responsibilities in this case.

Marshall declared that Marbury was legally entitled to the commission; that Madison was lawfully obligated, indeed required by the function of his job as defined by law, to deliver the commission; and that the writ of mandamus was the proper judicial remedy to seek against an official who had failed to do his job. But, when it came to issuing that writ, Marshall ruled that he was *unable* to do so.

Marshall noted that this provision of the 1789 Judiciary Act had added to the original jurisdiction of the Supreme Court. But the Constitution had specified the only instances of the Court's original jurisdiction, and this was not one of them. Congress could not change that by statute, and the Court could not give effect to any act that was not made in pursuance of the Constitution. Such a law would be unconstitutional and void. Marbury had a just cause and an appropriate remedy, but he was in the wrong courtroom.

The significance of the decision was that Marshall established a tool of power for the Court—judicial review of congressional acts— without compelling Jefferson to do or to refrain from doing anything.

In fact, the outcome of the case—dismissal—was just what Jefferson had wanted initially. Jefferson, however, was furious, for he fully recognized what Marshall had succeeded in accomplishing. He had always opposed that principle, but here there was nothing he could do about it, except rant and rave about Marshall's usurpation of power.

Thus, the reason the Supreme Court can overrule Congress's acts is simply that it developed that way. To be sure, the Court used the power very sparingly in the next sixty years, at least until the country became accustomed to the "rightness" of it. Even today, the Supreme Court is reluctant to use this power for fear of losing the confidence of the people and diminishing the authority of its decisions. After all, it is only by suffrance that the Court still wields that power and that officials act in response to its commands.

Judicial review also extends to most of the activities of the executive branch when those actions are alleged to deprive individuals of certain of their constitutional rights. The techniques of statutory construction are used by the Supreme Court to review whether the acts of administrative officials are in accord with law. But many actions of the executive branch, most notably in foreign affairs, have not become subject to a similar judicial review. On questions such as whether the President can direct American troops in a foreign undeclared war or whether he can refuse to defend the constitutional rights of an American citizen in a foreign country, the Court can and does decline to answer, except perhaps to say it has no power to intervene.

Futhermore, when the highest court in a state renders a decision interpreting its own constitution, the Supreme Court will not intervene to review that decision, unless it tends to deprive a citizen of his or her federal rights. Even where the words of the state constitution are precisely the same as those of the federal Constitution, the Court frequently will not intervene.

The Structure of Court Opinions

The Opinion of the Court is most often the official reasoning of the majority in reaching its decision. On occasion, the majority members cannot all agree on one line of reasoning. In that case the Opinion of the Court is the argument adopted by more of these members than any other view. Only three or four justices might adhere to this view, whereas others file concurring opinions giving their reasons (as previously explained). On rare occasions, where the majority is split among several different lines of reasoning, the Opinion of the Court may become the minimum statement on which most can agree, in effect the least common denominator.

The Opinion of the Court has several parts: there is normally an argument, or line of reasoning; there are citations to constitutional provisions or to statutes; there is a series of cases supporting the Court's view (and/or reasons why those cases do not apply or are overruled); there are, perhaps, some observations about the facts in the case or some other legal principles; and there is a holding.

The *holding* is the most significant part of the opinion. It is what the Court actually decides in the case before it: usually an interpretation of a point of law. The other parts of the opinion have real significance only insofar as they support and are necessary to the holding. The holding determines what the Court's judgment will be.

If the Court makes an observation on fact situations or points of law other than what is necessary to the holding, that is known as *obiter dictum*. Such statements could conceivably have been left out of the opinion, but they generally tend to show the thinking of the Court that led it to the decision and are important in that respect. It is possible that such a dictum would support a somewhat different holding in a slightly different case, and dicta, therefore, are not authoritative in themselves. Oftentimes dicta in an opinion may give rise to concurring opinions, as one or more justices agree with the holding but not with the opinion's entire line of reasoning.

One of the major functions of an opinion is to make clear what kind of case is involved, so that, in the future, similar cases can be decided by lower courts in accordance with the Court's holding. The lower courts must be informed about what kinds of cases are covered by the Court's opinion. American courts place great weight on such earlier, or precedent, cases in interpreting the law. This is the principle of *stare decisis,* literally meaning "to stand as decided." It means that the matter in question, the legal point, has already been decided. The principle depends for its effectiveness on clear opinions describing as precisely as possible what kind of case is to be covered by the rule of law announced.

Precedent cases are the foundation of the common law and statutory construction. Although relying on precedent may lock courts into outmoded legal doctrines, it nevertheless adds to uniformity and predictability in the law. For these latter reasons courts are reluctant to overrule or ignore precedents and will only do so when it is shown that reliance on them leads to injustice in the present case. That is why it is important for lawyers to be able to distinguish unfavorable precedents—that is, to show that the present case arises from a distinctly different fact pattern than did the one that led to the apparently applicable precedent. It becomes even plainer, then, why the Supreme Court often writes a long opinion to make clear the kinds of similar cases to which its holding applies.

Judicial Administration

The Supervisory Task

The Supreme Court exercises a supervisory function over other courts in the federal judicial system. It oversees the work of the lower federal courts in order to assure that proper justice is done. This is a job that goes beyond reviewing cases to make sure that the lower courts are deciding them in accordance with the Court's holdings.

Because all new legal problems concerning constitutional or statutory interpretations arise first in the lower trial courts, the Court must see that serious new questions are decided consistently with the Court's views in related matters. Otherwise, the Supreme Court itself must change the doctrines to accommodate new problems. The lower courts cannot do this entirely alone.

Moreover, there are many "housekeeping" tasks involved in supervision. These range from taking steps to ease backlogs in case loads, to changing the hours and days at which the lower courts meet, to assuring that the funds appropriated by Congress are properly spent. The Court tries to keep the federal judicial system running as smoothly as possible.

The Supreme Court's supervision of state courts is limited mostly to decisions and practices that have constitutional implications. The Court does not attempt to assure that state court systems are run well, except insofar as faulty practices of a state's judiciary may result in depriving individuals of their constitutional rights.

The Federal Court System

The federal court system is best pictured as operating on three levels. At the top, by itself, is the Supreme Court. It is the court of last resort, where all appeals have their last stop.

On the level beneath that are the United States courts of appeals. The United States is divided into twelve circuits, each headed by a court of appeals. One circuit is comprised solely of the District of Columbia, because of the number of federal cases that arise there and the importance attached to those (most of them) that involve the federal government. Other circuits contain as few as three states (the second: New York, Vermont, and Connecticut; the third: Pennsylvania, New Jersey, and Delaware; and the seventh: Wisconsin, Illinois and Indiana) or up to as many as nine (the ninth: Arizona, California, Nevada, Oregon, Washington, Idaho, Montana, Alaska, and Hawaii).

These courts have **appellate jurisdiction** for almost all federal cases arising in the assigned states within the circuit. The courts of appeal serve to review lower court decisions as well as to screen out those cases that would take too much of the Supreme Court's time to review. This appellate level was created by Congress in the latter part of the nineteenth century primarily to save the Supreme Court's time and energy for the most important cases.

Litigants have an appeal by statutory right to a court of appeals from almost all lower federal courts. In no case can a court of appeals' decision be appealed *by right* to the Supreme Court. All such appeals are in the Supreme Court's discretion, primarily through the certiorari process.

The Supreme Court places a great deal of reliance on the decisions of the courts of appeals. The efforts of these reputable judges are not to be regarded lightly. Indeed, at certain times, the prestige of the court of appeals of one circuit or another has exceeded that of the Supreme Court. During the 1940s and 1950s, for example, the Second Circuit Court of Appeals, including at the time such legal luminaries as Learned Hand, Jerome Frank, and Charles Clark, was thought by many to be the finest bench in the country.

Also at the intermediate appellate level is the Court of Customs and Patent Appeals. This is one court for the entire country, as opposed to division into circuits. Its jurisdiction is confined by Congress to appeals from the United States Cutoms Court, the Patent Office, and the Tariff Commission (the latter two being administrative bodies, not judicial ones). It is generally comprised, therefore, of individuals who have made these fields of law their specialty.

Ranking beneath these appeals courts are the courts of first instance, which, as the label implies, are the places where the litigants go first to press a legal claim. The Customs Court is one of these. Its jurisdiction consists by law of reviewing the decisions of customs officials in the port cities of the nation. These officials may impound goods, lay and collect taxes and duties, and enforce other export-import regulations. Because of the specialized nature of this work, Congress thought it wise to provide for a system of judicial supervision apart from the regular federal courts.

The Court of Claims is another court of first instance. Its jurisdiction is also specialized, comprising primarily disputes between private parties and the national government. If, for instance, a federal contractor is dissatisfied with the government's payments to him for work done under contract, the contractor's resort is the Court of Claims.

But the most significant and numerous of the inferior federal courts are the United States district courts. These are courts of general jurisdiction—that is, they have **original jurisdiction** over all those cases that are not by law assigned elsewhere and that otherwise require federal resolution. They are also the trial courts for all federal criminal cases.

There is at least one federal district court in each state, each district having several judges. Some states, such as Maine, have only one district, whereas New York is divided into four districts (eastern, southern, northern, and western). Altogether there are about four hundred positions for United States district judges, although because of deaths, retirements, and subsequent appointments not all of these slots are always filled. Four territories that are not states (Puerto Rico, the U.S. Virgin Islands, the Canal Zone, and Guam) also comprise separate districts.

The district court judges preside over trials in the federal courts. For most cases federal court juries can be empaneled to decide the questions of fact that arise, although the parties may waive their rights to a jury and allow the judge to be the trier of fact. When a judge does so, he must submit written findings of fact and conclusions of law so that his decision can be properly reviewed on appeal. In some cases where only equitable remedies such as an injunction are sought, neither party is entitled to a jury trial and the judge is automatically the trier of fact.

The district courts may employ special agents to help resolve disputes without trial. Bankruptcy referees are provided for by statute for that type of case. The court may appoint a magistrate or other official who can help to arrange a settlement between parties and can, at a minimum, resolve numerous pretrial procedural problems without taking the time of the court. Such officials operate under the guidance and review of the court.

Federal judges at all levels are nominated and appointed by the President, subject to the Senate's confirmation. The procedure is the same as for a Supreme Court justice, although any hearings held are usually very brief. Yet the President has far less independence in his selection of lower court judges because of the practice of senatorial courtesy.

For the most part, senators allow each other a virtual veto over judicial appointments within their home states, although such power exercised by a senator not of the same party as the President is considerably less effective. If a Democratic President were to nominate a judge, the Senate would likely not confirm the choice unless the Democratic senator(s) from that state approved. This represents a source of judicial patronage for the Senate. It also means that the President is compelled to consult the senator(s) before nomination.

The considerations of the senator(s) vary in approving appointments. Some appointments are old cronies, some faithful party servants, and some are made to appease or to discipline factions of the state party organization. Some consideration is also given to the need for quality, with the result that there are some outstanding legal minds on the federal bench along with the others.

The senator(s) must juggle all these factors, although a few senators consistently regard the competence of the nominee as the significant criterion and take pride in the quality of the federal courts in their state. But disputes often arise when both senators from a state belong to the same party. For instance, in the early 1970s, four seats in the Southern District of New York lay vacant for nearly two years before Senators Jacob Javits (Republican) and James Buckley (Republican, Conservative), agreed on how to divide the positions between themselves. Republican President Nixon made no nominations until, in early 1973, Senators Javits and Buckley agreed to choose two judges each, the names of whom were then sent to the President. Needless to say, the nominations then breezed through the Senate without debate.

Court Rules and Reports

The Supreme Court has been authorized by Congress to establish procedural rules for the conduct of both civil and criminal actions.

These rules, together with periodic amendments, are subject to congressional approval.

Normally the Court appoints an advisory committee to study the existing rules (or a portion of them) and the way they work and to recommend changes if deemed desirable. The Court then takes the proposals, if any, under consideration. If approved, the Court publishes the rules with the proviso that they are to become effective on a certain date several months later. The rules will take effect on that date unless Congress disapproves, in which case the disapproved rule change is void.

The rules may not deprive litigants of any of their substantive rights. But disputes often arise in cases that reach federal courts because of diversity of citizenship, because here the court must apply state law. In such cases, however, the Supreme Court has ruled that the federal procedure must apply, even though the case is to be tried under state substantive law and even where the state procedure conflicts with the federal rules.

One significant purpose of these rules is to assure uniformity of practice in federal courts across the country, insofar as the conduct of the case is concerned. The Supreme Court leaves to local districts and circuits such matters as the calendar system of the court, the assignment of judges, the number of court officers, and other purely administrative tasks.

The chief justice may issue occasional reports on the state of the federal judiciary. The reports may deal with how well the court system is performing its task, where improvements could be made, and the like. It may include recommendations for legislative action, for example, to increase the number of judges or to alter the jurisdiction of the federal courts.

The Supreme Court does not like to be seen as engaging in lobbying or other pressure-group activities. The Court feels that this involves too much intrusion into the political arena. It prefers to think of itself (and to maintain a reputation) as a nonpolitical organ of government in order not to impair its function as an impartial arbiter of disputes.

But Congress may ask the Court (primarily the chief justice) to testify before it and advise it on proposed changes. Perhaps the most memorable occasion for this occurred at the time of President Roosevelt's "Court-packing" plan in 1937. Chief Justice Charles Evans Hughes overcame his reluctance to involve himself so directly in the legislative process and appeared on request before the Judiciary Committee of the Senate. He testified that there was no need for such a measure and that the court's work load was not too burdensome for the aged justices. Congress refused to approve Roosevelt's proposal.

Two Possible Changes

A Supreme Court-appointed committee, headed by Harvard Law Professor Paul Freund, proposed in the mid-1970s that a new layer in the federal appellate process be created. The work load of the Supreme Court has grown enormously in the last decade and shows few signs of letting up. The Court now receives more than 4,000 petitions yearly for certiorari or appeal, even though the number accepted for complete review and argument has held steady.

The proposal is to establish another court, called perhaps the National Court of Appeals, whose function would be to screen all appeals and petitions to the Supreme Court, to forward 700 to 800 of the most significant or the most wrongly decided in the lower courts, and to turn back all others, acting in the role of court of last resort for those cases. From those forwarded, the Supreme Court would then select for review about half: the same number as today. This procedure, the committee has urged, would significantly decrease the Supreme Court's work load, enabling it to give better attention to the truly serious judicial questions that are presented in the cases accepted for review.

The proposed National Court of Appeals would be manned not by permanent judges but rather through a system of rotation. Senior judges from the circuit courts of appeals would be chosen, on an annual or biannual basis, to sit as a five-, seven-, or nine-man body. After their term of service these judges would return to their circuits. Thus, the screening body would not be a rigid one and, at different times, different types of cases might be thought suitable for review by the Supreme Court.

But the proposal has met weighty opposition. Litigants would no longer feel assured that, given sufficient time and money, their case would at least be seen and thought about by the Supreme Court. Moreover, the Supreme Court would be prevented from reaching down, at its discretion, to take a case (properly decided below) in which it feels it is time for the law to change. Former Justices William O. Douglas and Arthur Goldberg declared that the Court was not overworked, that its present task was not unbearable, and that there was no need to abolish the Court's historic role as court of last resort simply in order to ease the justices' working day.

Congress, which must write a statute in order to bring the proposed National Court of Appeals into existence, has not seemed enthusiastic so far, although the chief justice has supported the idea. The Judiciary Committees of the House and Senate have not yet studied the problem in depth, but they apparently do not think that the situation is urgent.

Chief Justice Burger has suggested that one of the causes of clogged and overworked federal courts has been recent legislation by Congress that has enormously expanded the causes of action on which citizens may sue. As new rights are created, people tend to sue to enforce them. Burger has recommended that Congress consider the impact on federal courts whenever it writes a new legislation. This might lead to the preparation of a "judicial impact statement" with each bill (similar to the "environmental impact statements" required of federal agencies under the National Environmental Protection Act of 1970).

But again Congress has not seemed warm to the idea in the formal sense, although it undoubtedly has bolstered the arguments of opponents of new rights legislation, who can add to their opposition the claim that the courts will be overwhelmed by litigation concerning the new rights.

The Supreme Court in the Political System

The Supreme Court, like other courts, prefers to think of itself (and to have others think of it) as an impartial, nonpolitical umpire whose function is simply to resolve disputes. This, nonetheless, is one of the primary functions of a poltiical system. A governmental institution that carries out such functions is by definition an actor in the political system. As such, the Court is inevitably in a competition for power with other institutions. As a "separated institution sharing power" in our federal system, it has certain resources and some restraints on it.

Checks and Balances

The Court's most notorious resource is the power of judicial review. This is a check, or rein, not only on Congress but on the states and on the executive branch, to the extent that it implements legislation and acts within appropriate discretionary limits. The Supreme Court has been widely accepted as the arbiter of and ultimate authority on the Constitution. It is no small power but has widespread effect on the kinds of laws and governmental actions that take place in our society.

Possibly more significant than its power of judicial review, which is not often exercised, is the Court's activity in statutory interpretation and its capacity to define, alter, and remake the common law. The Supreme Court is the governmental organ that ultimately decides what the law says and determines what are permissible aims for the law to accomplish. The process of statutory interpretation may on occasion lead to results in practice that are unlike or in conflict with the original purposes of the statute. Quite often, administrative practices that depart from the statutory mandate have been brought into line through Court action.

Common law is little more than the collective decisions of courts. Consequently, because courts are less reluctant to change their own decisions than to overrule the decisions of lawmakers or administrators, judges feel freer to "make law" in this area than in others. Moreoever, it is their own province, for they have made it in the first place. Court-made law can be remade with less difficulty or hesitation, when shown to be unjust, than other law. The main inhibition for judges is their desire that the law be consistent and predictable. Judges do not like the idea of upsetting long-standing practices and rules that have stood the test of time. Because many common law rules have been in force for centuries, there exists constant tension between the need for stability and predictability in the law and the need for updating it to keep it responsive to present conditions. Only the awareness of judges of the reasons for a common law precept and their judgments about whether these justifications still hold can ease this tension.

The Supreme Court, thus, has powerful tools and resources with which it can order the lives of Americans. When properly presented to it, it can declare what law must be obeyed, which laws need not be obeyed, and when the law is to change to meet modern conditions. To a large extent the court decrees within what limits public officials (including policemen) may carry out their jobs and it can summon citizens before the bar of justice.

But the power of the Supreme Court is by no means unbridled. There are numerous restraints on the Court. Its members are selected by the other branches of government and they can be removed by impeachment and conviction. Congress can increase or decrease their number, their jurisdiction, the judicial bureaucracy, and the term during which they sit: in other words, the Court's capacity to assert its power.

Moreover, the Court's decisions can be overturned by other political institutions. The Sixteenth Amendment (income tax) was only one example. Statutes that the Court interprets in a manner Congress does not like can be rewritten. And statutory law can displace any of the Court's notions about the common law that seem outdated, harsh, or unjust.

Courts in general cannot intervene at will in the political arena, as can other institutions. Courts must be presented with a case or controversy to decide. Any political problem that is not translated into a legal dispute is beyond the ability of courts to decide. This is one of the most effective restrictions on the power of the Court.

The Supreme Court has found that it cannot exceed the limits of what the rest of society will tolerate, at least not consistently. Although it is not clear that the Court follows public opinion, there seems to be little question that, especially in critical times, the Supreme Court often defers to intense feelings in society. Freedom of speech, for example, often suffers in wartime as courts in general (and the Supreme Court in particular) refuse to protect speech that other institutions deem unfavorable to the war effort. At the height of the Depression-era Court-packing controversy, a Supreme Court that had been striking down President Roosevelt's New Deal laws suddenly found them tolerable and ceased its obstruction of government regulation of the economy.

The Court's central deficiency in power terms is its lack of enforcement capability. The Supreme Court must depend on other institutions, primarily the executive branch, to enforce its decrees. President Andrew Jackson, in a conflict with the Supreme Court, is reputed to have said, "John Marshall has made his decision. Now let him enforce it." Jackson knew the Court's weak spot.

The Court can persuade others to abide by its decisions only through its moral authority and reputation. Others must yield to it if the Court is to make its weight felt, to have the right to make those decisions and to determine what is right. The Court must maintain the confidence of society that it is properly doing its job, or else it will lose its powers when society no longer regards the Supreme Court as deserving to have the final word in social controversies.

It is an oft-repeated charge that the Supreme Court operates secretly and that this mysteriousness undermines its effectiveness. Justice Lewis F. Powell has recently pointed out that the extent of the Court's secrecy is more apparent than real. The courtroom doors are open; trials and arguments are public. Even votes on decisions are matters of record. The only element of the Court's activities that is not open to public view is the actual discussion among the justices, although the result of the discussion is printed and widely disseminated. Nevertheless, public misunderstanding is a constant threat to the Court's power.

Only rarely in other societies do courts have such independent power as in the United States. In most countries it is either the executive (in dictatorships, for example), the legislature (England), or a political party (the Soviet Union) that is supreme and to which courts defer. In order to preserve its ultimate right of decision of so many significant controversies, the Supreme Court must husband its power, and not waste it on minor matters but expend it where society expects (even demands) that the Court resolve the issue.

The Court's Constituency

As with other political figures or institutions, the Supreme Court has a number of close followers—those who are more deeply attentive to the Court's work than is the ordinary citizen. Such people, along with the nongovernmental institutions they have formed, watch, evaluate, criticize, and comment on the behavior of the Court. The Court, in turn, is responsive to this group, for the group helps the Court to evaluate its own role and performance in the political system and helps to make acceptable and to implement the Court's decisions. This is the Supreme Court's *constituency*.

The primary element in the Court's constituency is, of course, lawyers. They are the group who are most often and directly affected by the Court's work. All the justices have come from their ranks and it is attorneys who appear before the Court and directly address it. Lawyers are professionally as well as politically or personally interested in what the Court does.

Professional organizations of lawyers, known as bar organizations, speak with the collective voice of the legal profession, seeking to further the interests of the profession and its members. Courts have given to the various state bar associations some of the power to regulate the practice of law and the behavior of lawyers.

The legal literature is an important element reflecting the Court's constituency. This includes law reviews and journals written under the auspices of the nation's law schools, as well as treatises, textbooks, and articles published by private publishing houses or organizations. Such organizations range from bar associations that publish periodical journals, to organizations that are concerned with a particular field of law, such as environmental or insurance law.

Teachers of law, judicial scholars, and to some extent political scientists comprise another element of this constituency. Their writings and teachings can have an influence on those who seek to understand the legal process and the role of the Supreme Court in that process. They are close students of the Court's behavior, discerning trends and patterns in the Court's actions and evaluating those characteristics. They are also largely responsible for socializing new members of the constituency by passing on the collected wisdom of its older members and initiating them into the accepted modes of activity.

Finally, there are those persons in other fields who follow closely the work of the Court. This interested public or "attentive elite" may include those in the news media, policemen and others on whom the Court's work has some occupational effect, and private citizens. It is from these individuals that the Court can learn the public's impression of its behavior. Through them, the public at large receives many of its cues and information about the Court.

Because, given its constituency, the Supreme Court does not operate in a vacuum but must relate to others, there are opportunities for this constituency to influence the Court's behavior and work product. This may be called lobbying the Court, although such lobbies do not behave in the same mannner as the lobbyists who haunt the halls of Congress or the White House.

For example, direct approaches to justices are frowned on by the ethics of the profession. Wining and dining justices may be illegal. Justices cannot be threatened (or rewarded) by influencing the electoral behavior of their constituents or by campaign contributions.

But well-written pieces in the legal literature may persuade justices who read them to alter their views. Legal and sociological research, when published, may be effective. Bar associations can, through resolutions, conferences, and public statements, try to influence the Court. Other professional organizations and those interested in advancing legal rights in particular areas can do the same. The continuing press of litigation in certain fields may gradually erode judicial opposition to changes. When the Court feels that the public as well as the profession is ready for a change, it can take steps and render decisions that it would otherwise have been reluctant to undertake. Constituency pressure then can affect institutional behavior in the judiciary to much the same extent as in the other "political" branches.

"The Least Dangerous Branch"

Through the years, the Supreme Court has alternately risen and fallen in public esteem. The peaks and valleys roughly coincide with the degree to which the Court has made decisions in accordance with or opposed to the desires and beliefs of the nation's citizens. A Court that consistently opposes the wishes of the people risks losing its authoritative role as arbiter of the Constitution.

Because the Supreme Court depends to such a great degree on public acceptance of its right to make those great decisions, because it has no enforcement mechanism of its own, and because it must await a "case or controversy" and cannot strike out on its own, it has been called the least dangerous branch of government in the country. The concept of "judicial tyranny" seems farfetched, if only because the Supreme Court can do little on its own.

In a tyranny of some other institution (legislative, executive, bureaucratic, or party), the Court might well play a significant role, in alliance with or in deference to it, by placing a magisterial stamp of approval on illegal or unconstitutional acts. But that would be simply a ratification of accomplishments brought about by other means. The Court by itself has not the means to institute a tyrannical regime.

Although the Supreme Court's role as a protector of our freedoms may be controversial, we have little to fear from it alone. Although the Court could be corrupted or bulldozed by another institution, or may destroy itself, it represents little threat to dominate the American political system.

GLOSSARY

Appellate jurisdiction The power of a court to hear appeals.

Common law The collected decisions of courts over the centuries, interpreting and stating what the law is and sometimes making new law.

Concurring opinion Written by a justice who agrees with the judgment of the Court in a particular case but for reasons different from or in addition to those stated by the other members of the majority in the Opinion of the Court.

Dissenting opinion An opinion written by a justice who disagrees with the judgment of the Court in a particular case, citing his reasons for disagreement.

Judicial review The act of a court in ruling on the validity of a statute or of an administrative action.

Jurisdiction The power of a court over specific subject matter or parties to a dispute.

Opinion of the Court A statement, written by a member of the majority of the justices in ruling on a particular case, stating the reasons for the decision in the case, as agreed on by more members of the majority.

Original jurisdiction The power of a court to hear a case from its inception.

Political question A matter that parties have asked the court to resolve but that the court feels is more properly committed to the political branches of the government (legislature and executive) to resolve, refusing therefore to decide the matter.

Statute A variety of law that is an official enactment of a legislature, supreme over the common law and administrative decisions within the same jurisdiction, but subordinate to the Constitution.

Strict constructionist A judge who, it is thought, adheres very closely to the written word when interpreting a statute or the Constitution, refusing to adopt, as its meanings, the spirit or general purpose of the statute or constitutional provision. It is sometimes thought that a strict constructionist is politically "conservative," but the terms are not synonymous.

Term of the Court The period of the year, established by the Congress, during which the Court hears and decides cases.

Writ of certiorari An order granting review of a case, in a petition for which a party suffering an adverse decision at a lower level seeks to convince the Court to hear an appeal from that decision.

SUGGESTED READINGS

Abraham, Henry J. *The Judicial Process,* 3rd ed. New York: Oxford University Press, 1975

Bickel, Alexander. *The Least Dangerous Branch.* Indianapolis: The Bobbs-Merrill Company, Inc., 1962.

Corwin, Edward S. *The Constitution and What It Means Today,* 14th ed. Rev. by Harold W. Chase and Craig R. Ducat. Princeton, N.J.: Princeton University Press, 1978.

Danielski, Daniel J. *A Supreme Court Justice Is Appointed.* New York: Random House, Inc., 1964.

Harris, Richard, *Decision.* New York: E. P. Dutton & Co. Inc., 1971.

Horowitz, Donald L. *The Courts and Social Policy.* Washington, D.C.: Brookings Institution, 1977.

Lewis, Anthony. *Gideon's Trumpet.* New York: Random House, 1964.

McCloskey, Robert G. *The American Supreme Court.* Chicago: University of Chicago Press, 1960.

Murphy, Walter F. *Elements of Judicial Strategy.* Chicago: University of Chicago Press, 1964.

Richardson, Richard J., and Kenneth N. Vines. *The Politics of Federal Courts.* Boston: Little, Brown and Company, 1970.

5 Bureaucracy: The Permanent Government

Introduction

In this chapter we discuss the largest and, for most people, the most obscure part of the national government. The institutions of the federal bureaucracy are so numerous, so diverse, and, in some cases, so sprawling that it is difficult to find a focus. We begin by defining the word in its general sense. A *bureaucracy* is a way of organizing people; it is a plan for dividing authority and work among a group of people. Because nearly all the agencies in the executive branch are set up according to this plan, they are called "the bureaucracy." This is the word's second meaning.

We devote most of this chapter to describing the different agencies within the bureaucracy. How were they created? What are they supposed to do? What legal authority do they possess? What are the different kinds of bureaucracy? Why has this part of government grown so large?

Finally, we analyze the relations between the bureaucracy and the three traditional branches and the relations among the bureaucratic agencies themselves. We hope that by describing the bureaucracy's most important features we will be providing the basis for understanding the enormous power of the "permanent government."

Two Definitions

The word **bureaucracy** can mean either a kind of organization or a part of the federal government. Max Weber, the great German sociologist, provided the classic definition of bureaucracy as an organization. According to Weber's "ideal type," a bureaucracy consists of a hierarchy of specialized offices (or bureaus) that operate according to a set of rules and rely on written records called "files." Nearly all large companies—General Motors, Westinghouse, AT&T —are bureaucracies. So are the major churches and hospitals, the army, and the Mafia (sometimes files are secret). Not all modern organizations are bureaucracies. Within the federal government neither house of Congress nor the Supreme Court is a bureaucracy. Congress does have specialized units in its committee structure, and it keeps records of its activities. However, all congresspersons are formally equal and independent and all committees are formally equal and independent; there is no hierarchy of power. Supreme Court justices are also equal in formal stature and no record is kept of the Court's private deliberations.

Another way of saying that offices are specialized within the bureaucratic organization is to say that work is broken down into small tasks, each of which is performed by a particular person or group of people (the office). Functional specialization means that each office can become expert in handling its particular area. However, according to the theory of bureaucracy, the good bureaucrat, no matter how expert, is only supposed to act in accordance with the rules of the organization. These define his power and the procedures he is to follow.

In addition to the rules themselves, each official is subject to his superiors, whose authority is established by the same rules. This pyramid arrangement, illustrated in Figure 5.2, is another of the main characteristics of bureaucracy. All new rules, directives, and so on are supposed to come from the highest officials and are sent in written form (as memoranda—"memos" for short) to the ones below. In a familiar military example, the general tells the colonel, the colonel tells the major, the major tells the captain, the captain tells the lieutenant, the lieutenant tells the sergeant, the sergeant tells the private, and the private goes out for the general's coffee. In a government bureaucracy, such as a department, the chain of command would go from the secretary, to the undersecretary, to the assistant secretary, to the deputy assistant secretary, to the bureau director, to the section chief, to the worker.

The virtues of the bureaucratic form are its ability to provide direction and coordination to large enterprises, especially those doing complex jobs. Imagine the result if the general himself had to tell each soldier what to do during a battle, or if the president of General Motors had to instruct each assembly-line worker or to order each part for a new car. By dividing the work and the workers, and by providing a structure and rules to coordinate and direct their efforts, bureaucracy is supposed to provide the most efficient way of carrying out large, complicated tasks. Weber argued that bureaucracies were essential to the development of a modern society because they alone could provide the speed, precision, uniformity, and reliability essential to coordination in a large, complex society. We all know that bureaucracies don't always live up to Weber's ideal type.

Bureaucracy As a Part of Government

In reference to the national government, the term *bureaucracy* is used loosely to designate a group of organizations, most of which are

also bureaucracies in form. Many and various organizations are
included under this heading. The eleven **departments** are collectively, . . . the largest part. Also included are the **independent regulatory commissions,** the **government corporations,** the **unaffiliated
agencies,** and a potpourri of commissions and boards. In fact the
bureaucracy is overwhelmingly the largest part of the federal government employing more than 2.8 million civilians, and another 2
million military personnel, as of September 30, 1979. This alone is
a good reason for the conclusion of many analysts that the bureaucracy now constitutes the "fourth branch of government," and that
it has grown to be the most powerful part of the federal government—more powerful than the Congress and more powerful than
the Supreme Court, or the President.[1]

Because the bureaucracy is the least familiar of all the institutions
of our government, and because it encompasses such a large and
diverse group of organizations, we begin here with some very general
descriptive statements.

Origins: Where Do Bureaucracies Come From?

All the parts of the federal government, except those established
by the Constitution, were created by legislation or by executive
order. According to the regular procedures (see Chapter 3), a law
was passed that said, in effect, "There shall be established an agency
(or a department or a commission or a board) whose name shall
be . . . and whose functions shall be . . . and whose powers shall
be. . . ." Each year Congress passes laws that give the organization
the money to pay salaries, rent offices, and buy paper clips (see the
sections on authorizations and appropriations, p. 98). Congress has
by law given the President the authority to reorganize many agencies, subject to Congress's approval. For instance, President Nixon
used this power to expand the jurisdiction of the old Bureau of the
Budget, creating in its place the powerful Office of Management and
Budget. His more ambitious plans to reorganize many of the major
departments were blocked decisively in Congress.

Functions: What Do Bureaucracies Do?

In the simplest sense, bureaucracy is the action arm of the government. Nearly everything government does is done by people

---

[1] Francis E. Rourke, *Bureaucracy, Politics, and Public Policy* (Boston: Little,
Brown, and Company, 1969), p. vii.

Table 5.1
Full-Time Permanent Civilian Employment in the Executive Branch

Agency	As of September 30, 1979
Agriculture	83,899
Commerce	29,127
Defense—military functions	885,990
Defense—civil functions	28,592
Education	. . . .
Energy	19,005
Health, Education, and Welfare	141,945
Health and Human Services	. . . .
Housing and Urban Development	16,101
Interior	54,343
Justice	52,743
Labor	22,148
State	22,130
Transportation	70,166
Treasury	109,382
Environmental Protection Agency	10,153
National Aeronautics and Space Administration	22,633
Veterans Administration	193,641
Other:	
Agency for International Development	5,753
General Services Administration	32,787
International Communication Agency	8,020
International Development Cooperation Agency	. . . .
Nuclear Regulatory Commission	2,839
Office of Personnel Management	6,276
Panama Canal Commission	11,666
Small Business Administration	4,372
Tennessee Valley Authority	17,065
Miscellaneous	42,615
Subtotal	1,893,391
Postal Service:	
Full-time permanent	532,627
Total	2,426,018

Table 5.2
Total Federal Government Employment, Executive Branch

Description	As of September 30, 1979
Civilian employment in the executive branch:	
(Includes part time and temporary employees)	2,822,652
Military personnel on active duty:	
Department of Defense	2,024,444
Department of Transportation (Coast Guard)	38,565
Subtotal, military personnel	2,063,009
Total, executive branch employment	4,885,661

organized as bureaucracies. Judges do not carry out the sentences they pronounce. Congress does not enforce or implement the laws it passes. To make of these decisions and laws something more than mere words on paper, they must be carried out, put into practice, or "executed." (It is in this sense that the President is called the chief executive.)

To enforce a law prohibiting racial discrimination in housing requires investigators to check stories, lawyers to try cases, secretaries and clerks to type letters and keep records, and directors and coordinators to make sure that everyone else is working together properly. In short, it requires an organization—a bureaucracy. The same is true for a law such as the Social Security Act, or the various bills giving aid to schools or those providing money to build power dams. Someone must process the applications, draw up the plans, apply the standards that Congress sets forth, and supply the missing details. Someone must enforce rules of eligibility and write and distribute the checks. In the American federal government these jobs are nearly always done by bureaucracies.

In theory then bureaucracies do whatever the other branches tell them to do. (We shortly explain the ways in which bureaucracies gain independent power.) Sometimes duties are fairly straightforward. If a court says to incarcerate a prisoner, the federal marshals assigned to the case will take the person to the designated prison. However, if Congress passes a law establishing a federal institute to do research on disease, it may be necessary to go out and hire a leading scientist or physician. If a law is passed to conserve wildlife or to protect forests, the bureaucrats who carry out the law will be biologists, agronomists, and other experts. If the law provides money for building hospitals, the bureaucrats who administer the program will include construction engineers and architects.

It is important to understand that only a small fraction of the people who work in the federal bureaucracies are people who sit behind desks in Washington shuffling papers all day. Most of the people who work for the government do not work in Washington, and they carry on nearly as wide a range of activities as there are in the society itself. They are lawyers, doctors, statisticians, welders, truck drivers, doctors, and so on. The one clear difference is that fewer government workers than private workers are engaged in the manufacture of goods, although there are some special cases where the government has a monopoly, such as in the manufacture of postage stamps and the printing of money.

Most of the work done by federal bureaucrats is done "in the field" at local offices in cities and towns all over the country. The most familiar of these are the local post offices, but the pattern is a common one for government bureaucracies. These local offices are called the **field service.** Other common examples are the local offices of the Social Security Administration or the Federal Bureau of Investigation (FBI).

Bases of Organization

As the chapter on Congress indicated, passing a law is a political process requiring the support of groups and individuals in and out of government. The laws establishing bureaucracies are no exception. Over the years groups have made demands for different sorts of regulations and assistance, and Congress had responded in different ways to meet these demands. In the late 1890s farmers demanded protection against the unfair prices set by the railroads. (For a fuller treatment of this subject, see p. 179). Congress created an independent regulatory commission to oversee interstate commerce. On the other hand, when farmers sought help for themselves directly in matters such as aid for agricultural education and research, Congress created an agency that became the Department of Agriculture. Later, Congress added bureaus to meet other demands. For instance, bureaus were added to deal with the administration of farm price supports. Similar demands and pressures from other groups led to the establishment of the Departments of Commerce and Labor and to the creation of the Veterans Administration (VA). Such organizations, having a clearly defined constituency that maintains a close relationship to the agency, are classified as **clientele agencies.**

Agencies may also be organized according to one or more of the following principles: **process,** whereby an organization devotes itself to an area such as cancer research; **purpose,** in which the agency's function is defined by a goal—to protect savings bank deposits (Federal Deposit Insurance Corporation); or **geographic territory,** where an agency's power applies only in a particular area. The Tennessee Valley Authority (TVA) is one obvious example. These organizing principles are most often mixed together. Thus, the Bureau of Reclamation has a purpose: to provide irrigation and power dams; and an area: the far West; and, therefore, a clientele.

Lines of Authority

To whom Are Bureaucracies Responsible?

As Figure 5.1 indicates, only some of the agencies included under the heading "bureaucracy" are directly responsible to the President in his constitutional capacity as chief executive. This group of organizations includes two types: the departments and the unaffiliated or independent agencies. In both cases the institutions are headed by officials who are appointed by the President with the approval of the Senate and removable by the President.

Six bureaucracies report directly to Congress: the Architect of the Capitol; the United States Botanic Garden; the Government Printing Office; the Library of Congress; the Office of Technology Assessment; and the General Accounting Office. The last named is supposed to function as Congress's investigator, expecially in fiscal matters, and to keep tabs on the rest of the government.

Two other forms—government corporations and independent regulatory commissions—represent attempts to establish organizations that would have a degree of independence both from Congress and from the President. In the case of the government corporations, the original idea was that, once chartered by the government, they would be free to pursue their assigned goals without much control from the rest of the government. The TVA is an example of this type. More recently, in 1971, the Post Office Department was reorganized and became a government corporation called the **United States Postal Service.**

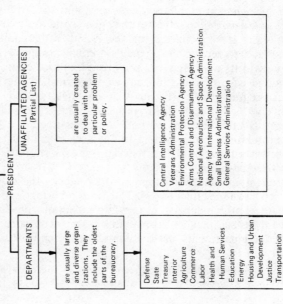

ORGANIZATIONS DIRECTLY RESPONSIBLE TO THE PRESIDENT

Both "Departments" and "Unaffiliated Agencies" are headed by
individuals who report to the President. The heads of departments
are called "Secretaries", and together they make up the President's
"Cabinet". The heads of the unaffiliated agencies have a variety of
titles. The most common is "Administrator".

PRESIDENT

DEPARTMENTS

are usually large
and diverse organ-
izations. They
include the oldest
parts of the
bureaucracy.

Defense
State
Treasury
Interior
Agriculture
Commerce
Labor
Health and
Human Services
Education
Energy
Housing and Urban
Development
Justice
Transportation

UNAFFILIATED AGENCIES
(Partial List)

are usually created
to deal with one
particular problem
or policy.

Central Intelligence Agency
Veterans Administration
Environmental Protection Agency
Arms Control and Disarmament Agency
National Aeronautics and Space Administration
Agency for International Development
Small Business Administration
General Services Administration

ORGANIZATIONS *NOT* DIRECTLY RESPONSIBLE TO THE PRESIDENT

**INDEPENDENT
REGULATORY
COMMISSIONS**
(Partial List)

Created To Act As
"Mini Governments"
To Regulate Particular
Parts of the Economy

Usually Headed By
A Board of Three or
More Commissioners

Interstate Commerce Commission
Federal Communications Commission
Federal Reserve System
Federal Trade Commission
National Labor Relations Board
Civil Aeronautics Board
Federal Reserve System

**GOVERNMENT
CORPORATIONS**
(Partial List)

Modeled after the
private corporation.
Designed to bring
greater efficiency
and flexibility

United States Postal Service
Tennessee Valley Authority
Federal Deposit Insurance Corporation
Overseas Investment Corporation
Export-Import Bank
National Railroad Passenger Company
(AMTRAK)

Figure 5.1. How the federal bureaucracy is organized.

171

Although the original purpose of creating government corporations was to make them independent and free of the red tape that hampers the efficiency of other government bureaucracies, Congress has moved recently to make them more subject to standard budgetary controls. Thus, government corporations have become more like the unaffiliated agencies, while retaining their distinctive form.

In the case of independent regulatory commissions (discussed on p. 179), Congress has made a clear attempt to establish organizations that would be divorced from the pressures of partisan politics emanating either from the President or the Congress. Thus, the regulatory commissions report neither to the President nor to the Congress. Their top officials—the commissioners—are appointed for lengthy terms, and the terms are staggered. Once in office, the commissioners may not be removed except for cause. Critics say that this system has worked all *too* well and that in cutting the commissions off from the President and Congress this scheme has also deprived them of needed support, leaving them the captives of the industries they are supposed to regulate.[2]

Legal Mandates: Where Do Bureaucracies Get Power?

An agency's duties, powers, authority, and structure are set forth in the same law that establishes the agency and are frequently modified by later laws. Congress and the President may amend the law, for instance, to reduce the agency's original powers, or, if they are pleased with its performance, to expand its jurisdiction and authority. In the case of the 1964 act that established the Community Action Program (CAP) of the War on Poverty, Congress reacted negatively to the early CAP programs and amended the act to reduce CAP's authority. In the 1966 amendments, CAP agencies were prohibited from engaging in any sort of political activity and money was channeled, or earmarked, into programs such as Head Start. (See page 101).

Frequently, Congress delegates to an agency the power to make rules that have the effect of law. The most important and well-known examples are the independent regulatory commissions (described on p. 179). Less conspicuous—but equally important—are the agencies *within* the departments and the unaffiliated agencies that have been

[2] See, for instance, Marver H. Bernstein, *The Job of the Federal Executive* (Washington, D.C.: The Brookings Institution, 1958).

given rulemaking authority. Such examples as the VA, the Department of Agriculture, and the IRS indicate the variety and breadth of the powers involved. The decisions as to how much compensation will be awarded a disabled veteran and the standards for the purity of drugs are made by bureaucrats. As decisions have become more complex and technical, Congress has delegated more and more authority to those bureaucrats who have the time and the expertise that Congress lacks.

Recruitment: Where Do Bureaucrats Come From?

A new President appoints about two thousand people to the top layers of jobs in the bureaucracy. This is about one job out of every thousand, a fact that indicates the limits on presidential power. From 1824 to the 1880s a new President could make appointments to most of the jobs in the federal bureaucracy. This system was called the **spoils system,** from the expression, "To the victor belong the spoils." Jobs were awarded to the members of the winning party toward whom the President felt especially beholden. The old officeholders were simply turned out. In the 1870s reform groups began to campaign against the spoils system, arguing that the increased technicality and complexity of goverment work required proven competence and experience. One dramatic episode greatly strenghtened their cause. In 1881 a crazed, unsuccessful office seeker shot and killed President James A. Garfield. In 1883 Congress passed the Pendelton Act, establishing the Civil Service Commission now called the Office of **Personnel Management,** and a **merit system** of hiring and promotion.

At first, only 10 per cent of the federal employees were selected by competitive examination. Over the years Congress—and the President, acting under authority given him by Congress—has increased the numbers greatly. Today about 75 per cent of all federal jobs are under the central merit system run by the Office of Personnel Management. Another 10 to 15 per cent are covered by the separate merit systems of individual agencies such as the FBI.

The Office of Personnel Management acts as a central employment agency for the government. It advertises jobs, encourages applications, and, most important, establishes, administers, and evaluates a system of competitive examinations: the merit system. The results of these examinations become the basis for hiring. When the administrator of a particular agency wants to hire someone, he or she notifies the Office of Personnel Management. They supply the names of the three top achievers on the appropriate exam. The administrator must choose one of the three.

After a six-month probationary period, a worker can be fired only "for such cause as will promote the efficiency of the service." Written charges must be presented to the employee, who has time to compose a reply and the right to several appeals. This cumbersome process makes firings difficult and infrequent. More important, it protects civil service workers from partisan assaults by the President or by Congress.

The top 1,100 jobs not covered by civil service go mainly to people within the President's party (a "minispoils system"). Many of the appointees will be the President's closest friends and political allies. Others will be representative of powerful groups whose support the President needs. Still others may be recommended by groups the President respects. At the level of the bureau chief, it is likely that a new President will retain many of the career employees whether or not they are party loyalists. Such people are often conspicuously well qualified for their jobs. Moreover, they have often been able to gain the support of powerful interest groups and congress persons. Some Presidents, such as John F. Kennedy in 1961, make an effort at bipartisanship by appointing members of the opposition to cabinet posts and other jobs.

Size and Shape

As previously mentioned, the bureaucracy includes many different organizations and a variety of forms. The largest and oldest are the departments, seen in the left-hand column below the presidency in Figure 5.1. The huge Department of Defense, known as the **Pentagon** because of the shape of its headquarters building, is the largest, employing nearly half of the government's *civilian* workers— about 9 million out of 2.4 million in 1979—and all of the military employees—another 2 million, for a total of 3 million people. By contrast, the Department of Housing and Urban Development, which is the smallest, employed only 16,101 people, less than 1 per cent of the Pentagon's total. In total the eleven departments employed 1.5 million of the 2.4 million civilian employees in 1979.

Departments, are headed by officials called **secretaries,** appointed by the President and approved by the Senate, who serve at the pleasure of the President. Together, the thirteen secretaries and certain other officials, such as the head of the CIA and the ambassador to the United Nations, make up the President's **cabinet.**

Most departments have one or more **undersecretaries,** who may function either as personal assistants to the secretary or as the heads of large parts of the department. For example, the Department of Housing and Urban Development has one undersecretary, who works directly for the secretary, and a deputy undersecretary who is responsible for field coordination (see Figure 5.2). At the next level are assistant secretaries, each of whom is responsible for a major function within the department. Within Housing and Urban Development (HUD), there are eight assistant secretaries with varying responsibilities. The assistant secretary for Housing oversees programs that include the production and financing of new housing and the preservation and management of existing federal housing. The assistant secretary for Community Planning and Development supervises programs under which money in the form of "block grants" is given to states, cities, counties, other units of government, and sometimes to community groups, who are supposed to use the money for projects that help low-land middle-income families by preventing or eliminating slums or by stimulating community development.

Within each division there may be several offices or bureaus. The division headed by the assistant secretary for Community Planning and Development contains thirty-six offices including an office that deals with small cities, four that handle environmental issues, and one that evaluates existing programs. Each office, or bureau, is headed by a director or an administrator. It is at this level that the President's appointment power ends. Secretaries, deputy secretaries, and assistant secretaries are all appointed by the President. Depending on the department and the law that created it and the bureaus within it, **bureau chiefs** may or may not be appointed by the President. About two thirds are appointed by the President. The one third that are not are protected from presidential removal by civil service regulations. Nearly all officials below the level of bureau chief are civil service employees.

A second major category within the bureaucracy we call here unaffiliated agencies.[3] The word *unaffiliated* is meant to indicate that these organizations are not part of any department, but stand on

---

[3] These are sometimes called independent agencies.

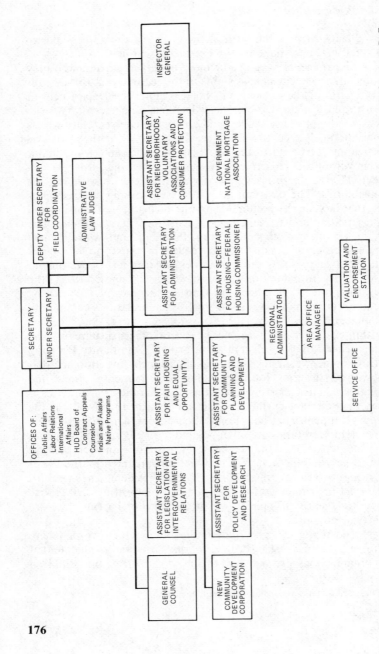

Figure 5.2. Department of Housing and Urban Development (*United States Government Manual, Washington, D.C.:*
U.S. Government Printing Office, 1979)

176

their own and are directly responsible to the President. The term is also meant to distinguish between these organizations and independent regulatory commissions, which are discussed later.

The top officials of unaffiliated agencies are called by various titles—administrator is the most common—and are appointed by the President with the consent of the Senate and may be removed by the President. Some of these agencies are very large, complex, and important. The Veterans Administration (VA,) which operates a national system of hospitals and administers other veterans' programs, employed more than 190,000 people in 1979. It is larger than any of the departments except Defense. Like the departments, the VA has an elaborate internal structure with many divisions and bureaus. Other important unaffiliated agencies are the National Aeronautics and Space Administration (NASA), which directed the effort to put a man on the moon, and the Environmental Protection Agency (EPA), created in 1970.

As these examples suggest, Congress uses the form of the unaffiliated agency to deal with special problems that do not fit well into the jurisdiction of existing agencies or departments. Congress may also feel that the problem needs the special attention and fresh approach that a new organization can provide. If a program is made part of an existing structure, it is more likely to be forced into conformity with that agency's practices and priorities. It may also be more difficult for the program to attract attention and support from the general public if it is one among many within a department. An unaffiliated agency gives its administrator the advantage of direct access to the President. The chief of a bureau within a department may achieve this access by reason of political power—J. Edgar Hoover did as director of the FBI—but the administrator has it by law.

Congress has also used the **government corporation** for certain special projects. This setup differs from a department or agency in that it is not subject to the same civil service regulations or budgetary procedures. These specially chartered corporations are created by the government to do a particular job. One familiar example is the **Federal Deposit Insurance Corporation (FDIC)** mentioned in all state bank advertising. After the bank failures of the Great Depression, Congress and the President created the corporation to protect people who put their money in banks. The FDIC insures the money deposited by individuals for up to $20,000, so that in case of the bank's failure, the money is not lost. The FDIC's budget does not come from congressional appropriations. Instead, the corporation is authorized by law to make assessments on member banks and to invest the assessments as a source of income. Thus, the corporation does *not* go to Congress each year to get new appropriations and to account for the spending of the previous budget.

The corporation's independence is protected by the appointment procedures for its top officials. Of the three directors, two are appointed for six-year terms and are subject to the approval of the Senate. The third is automatically the controller of the currency. The corporation's functions are fairly well specified in the legislation founding it and modifying its functions, which further limits the possibility of outside interference.

Perhaps the most famous government corporation is the TVA, created in 1933 to promote conservation and economic development in that region. TVA has established a large system of flood control and power dams that supplies electricity for "160 local municipal and cooperative electric systems, serving about two million customers in parts of seven states."[4] During World War II, power from these dams played an important part in the development of the atomic bomb. TVA also carries on research programs in agricultural fertilizer and in forestry, fish and game, and health services. Structurally, TVA is a corporation created and wholly owned by the United States Government. By law the TVA's power programs must be self-supporting, but it relies on regular appropriations for most of its other programs.

In 1970 the President and Congress created a government corporation, the United States Postal Service, which took the place of the old Post Office Department. Like the TVA, the Postal Service is a corporation wholly owned by the United States Government and directed by a board appointed by the President with the advice and consent of the Senate. It is the second largest government bureaucracy, employing more than 500,000 people.

The original reason for establishing government corporations was to promote efficiency by cutting red tape. Allowed to operate outside the usual regulations governing hiring and budget making, these organizations would resemble private businesses and would, therefore, be able to get the job done faster and better. Recently, Congress has felt somewhat disillusioned with this concept and has moved to

[4] *United States Government Manual 1973–74* (Washington, D.C.: U.S. Gov't. Printing Office, 1973), pp. 554–556.

reassert its budgetary control, making the corporations more like the unaffiliated agencies.

Another example of a special form created to deal with a special situation is the **independent regulatory commission.** These are often called institutional hybrids because they combine in one organization the power to legislate, to enforce, and to try cases. As we explain later, other parts of the bureaucracy also make rules that have the force of law. However, in the commissions this power is supplemented by executive and judicial power.

Independent regulatory commissions are headed by boards appointed by the President and approved by the Senate. The President is *not* entitled to remove commissioners, nor must they consult with him before taking action. The terms of commissioners are long—as many as sixteen years—and staggered—one commissioner is appointed, say, every six years—to minimize Presidential control. However, Presidents have often been able to use informal pressure to oust chairpersons and other members of commissions. As noted, the commissioners themselves have the legal authority to issue regulations that have the effect of law. Should these regulations be broken, the commission, through its staff, acts as a small executive branch and enforces the law. The staff apprehends the offender (usually this is a formality because the alleged transgressor is a large corporation) and presents the charges. Most often, the case is settled by negotiations between the companies and a staff person.

However, if this proves impossible, the accused party defends itself at a hearing before an administrative judge appointed by the commissioners. His decision may be appealed to the board of commissioners itself. Their decision may be appealed to the federal courts. Thus, to do its day-to-day business, the commission does not have to appeal to any other branch of government. The courts may review its decisions, and Congress has control of its budget and of its legal mandate, but unless and until these controls are brought into play the commission has the first and the last word.

The reason for this unusual concentration of power, which runs directly contrary to the idea of checks and balances, may be understood by examining the history of the first commission. Farmers in the Midwest and the Great Plain states, during the post-Civil War period, saw themselves as the victims of the railroads. In the farmers' view, the railroads charged exorbitant rates, thus taking advantage of their transportation monopoly. After the harvest, farmers had the choice of paying the railroads' prices or seeing their crops rot. Regulation by states proved ineffective, in part because the railroads "owned" many state legislators, and in part because of the inevitable conflicts and variations among the states.

The farmers turned to the federal government. In 1887, Congress created by law the Interstate Commerce Commission (ICC), modeled after the states' commissions. As with many major issues, the decision to establish a commission was by no means clear-cut. Many compromises occurred, key changes took place in the final congressional conference, and the will of the majority never was clearly defined. Nonetheless, some of the reasons for adopting a commission form were presented in the debates.

A commission provided the kind of day-to-day, expert attention Congress felt was required. Regulating railroad freight rates was a complicated, time-consuming business. Many congresspersons felt that Congress was not equipped to handle the details by legislation, especially in a situation where conditions changed rapidly and frequently. Perhaps most important, Congress saw a need to delegate authority to a body that was independent of Congress and the President. Thus separated from the evils of partisan politics, expert, rational, impartial judgment would prevail. As a bonus Congress would be off the hook. Relieved of the responsiblity to make decisions, Congress would antagonize neither the railroads nor the farmers.

In spite of the force of these arguments, it took some years before the ICC became a full-fledged, independent regulatory commission. Originally, its main function was to advise Congress and the courts as to what the rates and rules should be. Any orders issued by the commission itself could be reviewed in court, *before* they became effective. In practice this meant that the railroads could nullify any orders by taking them to the probusiness courts. In 1906, Congress changed the law to give the commission's orders the effect of law as soon as they were issued. The railroads could still appeal to the courts, but while the case was being tried, the regulations were operating. This shifted the burden of proof to the railroads and greatly strengthened the ICC. Further legislative amendments gave the ICC judicial power as well, so that by 1920 "it had begun to assume comprehensive regulatory authority."[5]

---

[5] Peter Woll, *American Bureaucracy* (New York: W. W. Norton & Co., 1963), p. 40. The description of the ICC's development is based on Woll's account.

Congress took the ICC as a model in creating other commissions. **The Federal Reserve Board,** which sets interest rates and runs a system of reserve banks ("banks for banks"), was set up in 1913. The **Federal Trade Commission (FTC),** charged with preventing monopolistic and fraudulent practices in commerce, followed a year later. The **Federal Power Commission,** chartered in 1920, was made independent in 1930. In 1977 its functions were transferred to the new Energy Regulatory Commission (ERC) in the Department of Energy. Among other functions, the ERC regulates the price of electricity and natural gas in interstate commerce. The **Federal Communications Commission** (FCC), which licenses and regulates radio and TV stations, began operation in 1934. In the same year Congress established the **Securities Exchange Commission** (SEC) to regulate stock market transactions and, a year later, created the **National Labor Relations Board** (NLRB) to carry out laws relating to labor management relations, especially the right of employees to organize unions.

In the field of air travel, Congress, in 1938, gave the **Civil Aeronautics Board (CAB)** the power to regulate fares and mergers and to decide which airlines could fly on which routes. A second agency, the **Federal Aviation Agency (FAA),** was created in 1958 and given authority to make safety regulations and to operate airport traffic control towers and other safety programs and installations. In 1967, the FAA became part of the Department of Transportation, where it is known as the Federal Aviation Administartion. The CAB remains independent.

The FAA illustrates a problem of definition and classification. By some standards it is an independent regulatory agency because it makes and enforces regulations that have the effect of law. On the other hand, it is not independent in the sense of standing alone as an organization and in the sense of being insulated from the President and Congress by special procedures of appointment. Some people would, therefore, argue that the FAA is better classified as an ordinary bureau, within the Department of Transporation, to which Congress has given certain regulatory authority.

Another ambiguous example was the old Atomic Energy Commission (AEC), which used to be one of the larger agencies outside the departments. The AEC was created in 1946 to control and promote the development of atomic energy both for peaceful and military purposes. It had the power to issue regulations and licenses for nuclear reactors, and it had the form of a commission, with one important exception: the chairman of the commission reported to the President. For many analysts this was sufficient to make the AEC simply an unaffiliated agency. In January 1975, the AEC was terminated and its functions were divided among two new unaffiliated agencies: the Nuclear Regulatory Commission and the Energy Research and Development Administration. In 1977 the latter became part of the new Department of Energy.

Reasons for Growth

In 1933, 600,000 people worked for the federal government; nearly half of them delivered the mail. By 1975 the number had quadrupled: five million people were working for the federal government.

Two factors account for the increase: First, the United States has established a "standing army," and the *civilian arm* of it is very large. Until the 1940s, America relied for its military defense on its two oceans and its potential strength. When war threatened, the ocean barriers to invasion gave us time to build our forces almost from scratch. At war's end, the forces disbanded, leaving only a skeleton.

The pattern changed following World War II. There was a substantial demobilization of troops, but considerably larger forces were kept in being than had existed in the 1930s. With the onset of the Korean War in 1950, the appropriations returned to wartime levels. In the cold war with the Soviet Union, military expenditures have averaged about 10 per cent of the Gross National Product (GNP), and sometimes have been as much as one half the federal budget. A good deal of this money has gone, not for weapons or for the armies themselves, but for *civilian employees*. It will be remembered that the Department of Defense is by far the largest employer of *civilians* in the federal government, hiring nearly a million of the 2.8 million in 1975. Some of these people are researchers; others are in logistics; still others are planners and designers. Were it not for the involvement of the United States in world politics, this enormous establishment would probably never have come into being.

Second, a major cause of bureaucratic growth has been the increased government involvement in the economy. In response to the Great Depression that began in 1929, Franklin Roosevelt's New Deal began programs of economic regulation, economic development, and economic relief and protection for individuals, groups, and the economy generally. The SEC (p. 178), the TVA (p. 180), and the Social Security Administration are prominent examples. Since that time, the federal government has extended its activities to education (the Elementary and Secondary Education Act of 1965 is one example) and to health (the Medicaid and Medicare programs). Most of these new programs have been administered by agencies within the Department of Health, Education, and Welfare.

One general stimulus to the growth of the "fourth branch," has been the increasing size and complexity of the society itself. The more people we have, the bigger the economy, the more TV stations, airlines, and so on, the more work for the bureaucrats who regulate them, and, hence, the need for more staff and bigger budgets. It should be noted that the federal bureaucracy has grown very little in recent years. In fact, total employment by the federal bureaucracy declined slightly between 1975 and 1979.

The Dynamics of Bureaucracy

Relations With Congress

The most fundamental legal part of this relation has been stated: Congress creates the bureaucracy; defines its power; and, in most cases, provides its budget.

One of the powers given by Congress both to independent regulatory commissions and to many other parts of the bureaucracy is the power to make regulations that have the effect of law. In this way the bureaucracy shares the lawmaking, or legislative, power granted to Congress and the President by the Constitution. In terms of their volume there is no question that the bureaucracy makes many more laws than Congress. It might also be argued that these laws, because they affect more people and more subjects, are more important than the laws made by Congress. Thus, even though the Constitution gave Congress sole possession of the legislative power, Congress has, ironically, created institutions that exercise a good deal of that power. Critics say that Congress abdicates its responsiblity by passing laws that are so vague that the bureaucrats have to make most of the decisions.

The bureaucracy also suggests many of the laws that Congress makes. Formally, of course, only a representative or senator may introduce a bill. In practice many congresspersons submit bills written by bureaucrats. We previously noted (p. 175) that in HUD, one assistant secretary heads a division of Legislation and Intergovernmental Relations. Nearly every bureaucracy has such an office whose job is to prepare bills, pass them on to friendly congresspersons, and then promote their passage. Agencies lobby for their bills, and against rival bills, in the same way that private interest groups do, and often with similar weapons. The Pentagon keeps three hundred lobbyists on full-time duty in Washington.

One powerful weapon in the hands of the bureaucrats is the control of expertise and information. Agencies often have a near monopoly of the information about a subject Congress is considering. This is especially true in military matters when the information is made less accessible by official secrecy. Control of information and expertise is also important in more mundane areas, such as in farm policy and aid to education. Few congresspersons have the time or the inclination to specialize sufficiently to acquire detailed knowledge of any one field. In a bureaucracy this is precisely what the official is supposed to do. The result is that congresspersons are at a considerable disadvantage. They often do not have sufficient information to evaluate a legistlative proposal coming from the bureaucracy.

When a bureau proposes a new law, or a change in an old one, Congress is faced with a barrage of experts, charts, statistics, and diagrams in support of the agency's position. Often, these resources carry the day because there is no equivalent competition. No one else can muster the same information or draw on the same experience as the organization that has been administering the existing law, perhaps for decades.

Administrative Oversight.   Similar considerations apply to the situation of congressional committees trying to make sure that the bureaucracy is following the intent of Congress as expressed in legislation. (Congress also attempts to make sure that the agencies are operating efficiently.) This function, known as administrative oversight, is carried out by committees and subcommittees (see Chapter 3). At best, administrative oversight is limited by the size and complexity of the bureaucracy. Neither the Armed Forces Committees nor the Appropriations Subcommittees assigned to the military budget can possibly know what the three and a half million people in the

Department of Defense are doing. Congressmen can follow up on rumors, or try to mitigate the most glaring inefficiencies, but it is impossible for them to exercise control and difficult enough to exert influence. This is not to say that the bureaucracies are entirely free of restraints, or that they make their own budgets. The assertion is that they have the resources to dominate the process.

Very often the congressional committee assigned to review a particular agency is itself the main ally and supporter of the agency. This is no accident. A congressperson from a rural area knows that he can best serve the interests of his farm constituents—and improve his own chances for reelection—by becoming a member of the Agriculture Committee. There he is in a position to know and influence the details of legislation and of bureaucratic practice. He is also in a position to make alliances with bureaucrats, to do favors for them, and, in return, to obtain favors for his district. Similarly, a congressperson from an urban area will press for a seat on a housing subcommittee; one from a mountain state will look for a seat on a committee dealing with electric power or forests. The result, more often than not, is a uniting of interests and ideologies. The committee and the agency share a view of what is good for the country and a view of what is good for the agency and its clientele groups.

Relations With the Courts

Decisions made by the bureaucracy could be appealed to the courts. There are two grounds for such appeals, both of which are subject to congressional limitations.

First, appeals may be made on constitutional grounds. A person (or group) may argue that a bureaucratic decision or regulation violates his or her constitutional rights. However, Article III of the Constitution gives Congress the power to determine what subjects may be appealed to the Supreme Court. Congress has never used that power, but the potential is nearly unlimited. Should Congress decide to do so, it could eliminate all bureaucratic decisions from the Supreme Court's jurisdiction and, by extension, from the jurisdiction of all the federal courts. In practice, appeals on constitutional grounds are infrequent and rarely successful.

The second basis for judicial review is established by Congress when it writes the law establishing the agency. There are three options: Congress may say that review by the courts is prohibited completely, giving the bureaucracy the final say. Congress may say specifically which of the agency's decisions may be appealed to the courts. Finally, Congress may say nothing, creating a vacuum that the courts may or may not enter, depending in part on their own interpretation.

The VA provides a good example of an absolute prohibition against review by courts. The VA's administrator—and, by extension, the agency staff—is given the last word on decisions with regard to such matters as disability payments and definitions.[6] Courts may review these cases *only* if there is a constitutional question involved; there seldom is. Thus, the agency becomes the final authority on the subject.

Relations With the President

The President is the chief executive. This title is derived from the clause in Article II of the Constitution that gives executive power to the President. The President is also made commander in chief and is given the authority and duty to "make sure that the laws are faithfully executed." The President may require in writing the opinions of the officers of the executive branch, and, as noted, he appoints them, with the advice and consent of the Senate, and may remove them.

In spite of these formal authorities and titles, and in spite of the charts (ours included) which put the President on the top of the bureaucracy, bureaucrats manage not to be ruled by presidents.

Sometimes Congress limits the President's power by specifying exactly what a bureau should do and how it should do it. More often, the power of the bureau is informal and is based on experience, expertise, information, and group support.

Most bureaucrats are careerists; they work in the same agency for twenty or thirty years. During that time they learn a great deal about their particular subject and about how to protect themselves politically. They build up contacts with congresspersons, with interest groups, with newspaper reporters, and with other bureaucrats. They see Presidents come and go.

By the time a person gets to be a bureau chief, he has learned how to get what he wants and how to avoid or neutralize the power of the President. Thus, when a President tries to change the bureau's policy, or cut its budget, or recognize its structure, the chief and his

---

[6] Woll, op. cit., p. 108.

allies in Congress, in the press, in other agencies, in organized interest groups, and in the public at large will fight back.

Hearings will be held before congressional committess. At the hearings, the bureaucrats themselves, representatives of interest groups, friendly congresspersons and senators, and various experts will testify. They will extoll the virtues of the agency's program and its staff. They will tell in graphic detail of the benefits received by groups, individuals, regions, the country, and perhaps the entire free world or even all mankind.

Newspapers will report the hearings, and individual reporters may add their own testimony. Lobbyists, some from the agency, will circulate through the Capitol, rounding up votes for the agency and its budget. Even if the President wins the final vote, he will have made powerful enemies who will oppose him on other issues.

Presidents know this and try to avoid disputes with powerful bureaucrats. One conspicuous example occurred at the beginning of the Kennedy administration. It was no secret that Kennedy wanted to replace J. Edgar Hoover, the bureau chief of the FBI. Nor was it a secret that after considering the strength of Hoover's support—in Congress, the press, and the general public—Kennedy decided to live with Hoover, rather than to pay the cost of ousting him.

Most bureaus have similar alliances—not as powerful as Hoover's, perhaps—strong enough to keep the bureau, its staff, and program intact through many administrations.

Another part of the limit on Presidential power is the sheer size of the bureaucracy. More than five million people worked for the federal government in 1975 (counting uniformed military personnel). Simply finding out what they are doing is a monumental job. Think how hard it is to keep track of your little brother or sister, or how well you have learned to conceal your own activities from your parents. Then consider the President's job. It is true that he has two thousand or so people to help him, and that he can appoint another two thousand or so of the top people in the bureaucracy. But these people are vastly outnumbered by the millions outside the President's control.

The story is told that Franklin Roosevelt, one of the most powerful of modern Presidents, woke one morning and, after looking at the newspaper, called in an aide, and said:

> When I woke up this morning, the first thing I saw was a headline in the *New York Times* to the effect that our navy was going to spend

two billion dollars on a shipbuilding program. Here I am, the commander in chief of the navy having to read about that for the first
time in the press. Do you know what I said to that?

. . .

I said: "Jesus Chr-rist!"[7]

Bureaucratic control of information and expertise limits the President's influence still further. It is only natural that the people who
run a program and have run it for years know more about it than
anyone else. Their natural advantage is strengthened by extensive
files and large computers. To get information about a program, the
President has no choice but to ask the bureaucrats in charge, and
they may answer when and how they please. They may answer fully
or partially, emphasizing as they see fit. They may even delay an
answer in the hope that the President and his staff will forget the
matter. Or, in an extreme case, they may suppress the information,
claiming that it is unavailable. If the President and his assistants are
not themselves experts in the subject, they may not be able to tell
when they are getting a straight answer.

In summary, although the President is supposed to be the chief
executive and to "make sure that the laws are faithfully executed,"
his ability to supervise and control the bureaucracy is very limited.
The officials at the bureau level and below, many of whose jobs are
protected by civil service, control resources that make them, to a considerable extent, independent of the President. They have legal mandates, expertise, information, and—most important—alliances with
congresspersons, other bureaucrats, and interest groups. In some
cases, such as the FBI, the agency also has a considerable public
reputation.

This is not to say that the President is powerless, but rather that
his power is limited. If a president is willing to concentrate on one
issue, he can probably defeat an agency and its allies. The victory
will, however, have its costs; the President will lose the resources to
fight other battles.

Should a bureau find itself engaged in battle with another bureau,
or under fire from Congress, the President's potential power will
increase dramatically. Because the bureau will then need the President, he can demand concessions from it. Instead of fighting to get

---

[7] Marriner S. Eccles, *Beckoning Frontiers,* ed. by Sidney Hyman, p. 336.

the bureau to change, he can simply require that they do so in exchange for his support. In any power relationship there is variation over time in who controls whom and at what price.

If the President is elected by a large majority, his "mandate" may give him power to defeat the bureaucracy, at least temporarily. (See Chapter 2.)

Bureaucratic Conflict

We have emphasized throughout this chapter the political nature of government bureaucracies; their origin in group demands; their alliances with groups and Congress; and their commitment to certain values and programs. It follows that agencies with different origins, alliances, and goals will come into conflict. In fact, conflict among bureaus is constant and sometimes heated. It is as much a part of politics in Washington as is conflict in Congress or between Congress and the President. In this section we attempt, by analyzing some examples, to indicate some of the main features of bureaucratic competition.

At the most general level all agencies compete for their share of the national budget. The battle of the budget proceeds within certain limits. It is unusual for an agency's budget to be cut more than a few per cent from the previous year, or for the budget to be increased more than a few per cent. For the most part the agency can count on getting about what it got the year before. Within such limits, however, the battle can be fierce.

Will the Defense Department get an extra $2 billion or will the money go to domestic programs in HEW? If the $2 billion goes to the Defense Department, will the air force, the navy, or the army get most of it? If the navy gets the lion's share, will it be spent on aircraft carriers or submarines? Agencies will battle on all of these questions along with representatives and senators, corporations, interest groups, and the President.

The resources we have discussed—information, access to the media, public reputation, and expertise—will be thrown into the battle. If the issue is regarded as especially important, top secret information may be leaked to the press. Frequently, when overall budget priorities are being set, information regarding the latest Russian missile developments is leaked to the press from the Pentagon. The purpose is to alert the public and Congress to the need for a big military budget. This is not to suggest that the men who leak the information do so casually or cynically, but rather that it is a standard bureaucratic technique.

Agencies also compete over legal authority and operational responsibility. This simply means who will do what job; which agency will have the responsiblity—and, therefore, the prestige—the budget, and the power that goes along with performing a particular function. In military politics a clear example is the struggle that occurred in the 1950s over which service would develop the nation's nuclear missile force. The primary contestants were the army and the air force, with the navy a surprise entry later on. To the victor would go a large appropriation, the prestige of protecting the country from the Russians, the glamour of working with the most advanced technology, and probably an expansion of personnel. As a result, the winner would gain power. Eventually, the air force's Minuteman missile carried the day.

In domestic politics a classic case is the conflict among four agencies—**The Army Corps of Engineers, the Bureau of Reclamation,** the Department of Agriculture, and the Tennessee Valley Authority—over the control of water resources policy. More specifically, the conflict is over who will build what kind of dam at which place on which river for which purpose.

The Army Corps of Engineers, an agency with both a civil and a military function, is the oldest of the competitors. The corps' philosophy emphasizes large-scale flood control projects built in the lower, or downstream, end of rivers.

The corps' political strength is legendary.[8] Although, technically a bureau within the Department of the Army subject to the directives of the secretary of the Army, the secretary of Defense and the President, the corps, in fact, is virtually autonomous.

The corps carries out projects dear to the hearts of congresspersons. A new dam or a dredged harbor lets constituents know, in a tangible and sometimes spectacular, way, that the congressperson is on the job. As a national agency, the corps is able to provide this proof for all of the 435 congresspersons and 100 senators. Congress reciprocates by protecting the corps from the wrath of presidents and budget cuts, consistently giving the corps what money it requests and ignoring presidential demands that projects be eliminated.

[8] The following description is based on Arthur B. Maass, "Congress and Water Resources," *The American Political Science Review,* **44**: 576–593 (Sept. 1950), and on Louis C. Gawthrop, *Bureaucratic Behavior in the Executive Branch* (New York: The Free Press, 1969), pp. 201–203.

The corps also benefits from its careful cultivation of powerful local groups and individuals. Planning for projects goes through twenty separate stages, including at least three public hearings and two consultations with local groups. By the time the corps decides whether to go ahead on a project, it has made many powerful friends. The corps is also the most prestigous of the agencies, partly because it is the oldest and has the longest relationship with Congress.

Established in 1902, the Bureau of Reclamation is a part of the Department of the Interior. Lacking the corp's strong ties to Congress, the bureau depends more on the support of the President and the secretary of the Interior and is, therefore, more subject to their influence. The bureau is oriented toward large irrigation and power dams, also constructed at downstream sites. Because it is limited by law to the seventeen western states and Hawaii, the bureau's appeal in Congress is more limited than that of the corps. In this semiarid and sparsely populated area, the bureau has concentrated on projects that involve more than one state.

Because both the bureau and the corps favor large dams built downstream, they come into frequent conflict. For the reasons cited, the corps usually wins.

Since 1936 the Department of Agriculture, through its Soil Conservation Service and Farmers Home Administration, has had legal authority to engage in projects related to the conservation of water. The program focuses on small projects built upstream to conserve watersheds. This emphasis brings the department into sharp conflict with the corps and the bureau, which favor large downstream projects.

The final combatant is the TVA, which, in its seven-state river basin, has built and operates thirty-one dams and many other facilities. The TVA's prime threat to the other three is as an example. Should other areas of the country set up similar authorities, the power of the corps, the bureau, and the department would dwindle.

As might be expected, the results of this sort of conflict are often a lack of coordination and the lack of a unified national or regional plan. To take one further example, there have been times when agencies in the Department of Agriculture were paying southern and midwestern farmers *not* to grow crops at the same time that the Bureau of Reclamation was building dams in the West to provide water to irrigate more fields so that *more* crops could be grown. Defenders of the system would argue that this sort of contradiction is inevitable in a democracy and is a small price to pay for the representation of different interests. They would also argue that competition and conflict are necessary in order to provide the experimentation and testing that offer the best basis for correct policy choices.

Summary and Conclusions

This brief survey of the national bureaucracy can only sketch its dimensions and variety. As suggested at the beginning of this chapter, the variety of activities of the federal bureaucracy nearly equals that of the society itself. In describing the different structures and programs and in analyzing the politics of the bureaucracy, we hope to have dispelled two stereotypes.

The first stereotype says that bureaucrats are **time servers;** that they are only interested in drawing their pay and doing as little work as possible. Surely there are some people working for the federal government (and private companies) who are like that; we have all met at least one. But in the important positions it is rare to find such a person. Instead, one finds deeply committed people who believe in their agencies and the agencies' programs. One also finds people who will fight long and hard for a program, which brings us to the second stereotype, the **mechanical man.**

By now it should be clear that bureaucrats are not simply robots who do whatever the President or Congress says. In very important ways, bureaucrats can be independent of the President and Congress. Bureaucrats control information and expertise and are frequently allied with powerful groups and corporations. Often, it is the bureaucrats and their allies who dominate the policymaking process.

Thus, this chapter is subtitled, "The Permanent Government," to call attention to these conditions. It is in this sense that President Kennedy referred to the bureaucracy when, in response to a policy suggestion, he said, "It sounds good, now let's see what the government has to say."

GLOSSARY

The Army Corps of Engineers   A bureau within the Department of the Army that has both civil and military functions. Its duties in regard to harbors and rivers have given it considerable political influence in Congress. It is one of the four agencies that competes for control of water resources policy.

Assistant secretaries Officials found at the third level of authority in the departments. Often, they are responsible for a major function within the department, such as research or legislation.

Bureau chiefs Officials of the federal government who head specific offices or bureaus. Some are appointed by the President and others are appointed according to civil service procedures. Often, bureau chiefs are able to accumulate great power that persists for many years. The most famous example was J. Edgar Hoover, who for many years headed the FBI.

The Bureau of Reclamation A bureau within the Department of the Interior, mandated since 1902 to build dams for power and irrigation in the seventeen western states and Hawaii. It is a competitor in the field of water resources policy.

Bureaucracy (1) A kind of organization that has a hierarchy of specialized offices (or bureaus); is governed by a set of rules; and bases its operations on written records called files. (2) A group of organizations within the federal government, including the departments, the independent regulatory commissions, the government corporations, the unaffiliated or independent agencies, and various commissions and boards.

The bureaucrat as mechanical man One of the stereotypes of the Washington bureaucrat that says that bureaucrats will do whatever the President or Congress tells them to do, in the manner of robots.

The bureaucrat as time server One of the stereotypes of the Washington bureaucrat that says that bureaucrats are only interested in drawing pay and doing as little work as possible.

Cabinet See the definition for departments.

Civil Aeronautics Board (CAB) An independent regulatory commission empowered by Congress in 1938 to regulate airlines' fares, mergers, and routes.

Civil Service Commission See "Office of Personnel Management."

Clientele Agency A federal agency having a clearly defined constituency that maintains a close relationship with the agency.

Departments A group of federal agencies that includes the oldest and largest of the federal bureaucracies. They are headed by officials called secretaries who are appointed by the President and approved by the Senate. The President may remove any secretary at any time for any reason. Together the secretaries constitute the President's cabinet.

Federal Aviation Agency (FAA) Established in 1958 to make safety regulations in the field of air travel and to operate airport traffic control towers and other safety programs, it was incorporated into the Department of Transportation in 1967.

Federal Communications Commission (FCC) Since 1934 this independent regulatory commission has licensed and regulated radio and television stations, among other functions.

Federal Deposit Insurance Corporation (FDIC) This government corporation was created following the bank failures of the Great Depression. Its function is to insure the bank deposits of individuals so that in case of the bank's failure the individual does not lose his savings. The corporation is headed by three directors, one of whom is automatically the controller of the currency. The other two are appointed by the President, subject to the approval of the Senate, for six-year terms.

Federal Power Commission Created in 1920, this commission was made fully independent in 1930 and became part of the Department of Energy in 1977. It is charged with regulating the price of electricity and natural gas in interstate commerce.

Federal Reserve Board This independent regulatory commission (see the definition of Independent Regulatory Commissions) sets interest rates and runs a system of reserve banks (banks for banks). It was created in 1913.

Federal Trade Commission (FTC) An independent regulatory commission that is supposed to prevent monopolistic and fraudulent business practices. It was created in 1914.

Field service The local offices of a government agency.

General Accounting Office One of the five agencies of the federal government that reports directly to Congress. Its job is to act as Congress's watchdog and to investigate other agencies.

Geographic territory The principle of organization that limits an agency to a particular area.

Government corporations Agencies of the federal government set up to resemble private corporations so that they can operate more efficiently. Examples are the Postal Service and the TVA.

Independent Regulatory Commissions Agencies of the federal government that combine the power to legislate, to enforce the rules they make, and to try cases arising under those rules. They are limited by law to certain areas or jurisdictions. For instance, the FCC concentrates on radio and television. They are usually headed by boards of commissioners (the number of commissioners varies from one agency to another) who are appointed by the President and approved by the Senate. The terms of appointment are long and staggered.

Mechanical man   The sterotype of the bureaucrat as mindless robot.

Merit system   The situation in which jobs in the federal bureaucracy are filled by competitive examination.

National Labor Relations Board (NLRB)   Created by Congress in 1935 to carry out the laws relating to labor-management relations, especially those giving workers the right to organize unions, the NLRB is considered by some to be an independent regulatory commission and by others to be an unaffiliated agency.

Office of Personnel Management   Known originally as the "Civil Service Commission" this agency acts as a central employment agency for the rest of the federal government. It advertises jobs; encourages applications; and, most important, establishes, administers, and evaluates a system of competitive examinations, the results of which govern hiring.

The Pentagon   The headquarters building of the Department of Defense, which includes the departments of the army, navy, and air force. The name comes from the shape of the five-sided building. This is the largest of the federal agencies, employing nearly one million civilians out of the total in the federal government of slightly more than two million.

Process   A principle of organization according to which an agency devotes itself to a particular area, such as cancer research.

Purpose   A principle of organization according to which an agency's function is to achieve a certain specified goal, such as defending the country from foreign attack.

Secretaries   See the definition for departments.

Securities and Exchange Commission (SEC)   Established in 1934 to regulate stock market transactions, this independent regulatory commission was initially headed by former Supreme Court Justice William O. Douglas.

Spoils system   The situation in which a victorious President could appoint his supporters to most of the jobs in the federal bureaucracy.

Tennessee Valley Authority (TVA)   A government corporation created in 1933 to promote conservation and economic development in the Tennessee River Valley. Its major activity is the production of electricity from power dams. It is one of the agencies involved in the competition for control of water resources.

Time server   The stereotype of the bureaucrat as lazy and uninterested in work.

Unaffiliated agencies (also known as independent agencies)   These organizations are part of the federal bureaucracy, but stand by themselves, without being part of a larger department. They report directly to the President, and their head officers, usually called administrators, are presidential appointees. Often, Congress uses this form to deal with a special problem that does not fit well into the jurisdiction of existing agencies. The largest unaffiliated agency is the VA. Other examples are NASA and the EPA.

Undersecretaries   These officials are the second highest in the departments, serving directly under the secretary. They may function either as his personal assistants or they may administer a large part or parts of the department.

The United States Postal Service   A government corporation created in 1971 to take over the functions of the old Post Office Department. Like the TVA, it is directed by a board appointed by the president with the advice and consent of the Senate. It is the second largest government bureaucracy, employing more than 700,000 people.

SUGGESTED READINGS

Bernstein, Marver H. *Regulating Business by Independent Commissions.* Princeton, N.J.: Princeton University Press, 1955.

Dox, Edward F., et al. *Nader's Raiders Report on the Federal Trade Commission.* New York, Grove Press, 1970.

Freeman, J. Leiper. *The Political Process.* New York: Random House, Inc., 1965.

Gawthrop, Louis C. *Bureaucratic Behavior in the Executive Branch.* New York: The Free Press, 1969.

Heclo, Hugh. *A Government of Strangers.* Washington, D.C.: The Brookings Institution, 1977.

Halperin, Morton. *Bureaucratic Politics and Foreign Policy.* Washington, D.C.; The Brookings Institution, 1974.

Rourke, Francis E. *Bureaucracy, Politics and Public Policy.* 2nd ed. Boston: Little, Brown and Company, 1976.

Seidman, Harold. *Politics, Position and Power.* New York: Oxford University Press, 1970.

Weber, Max. "Bureaucracy," in *From Max Weber.* Hans Gerth and C. Wright Mills, eds. New York: Oxford University Press, 1946.

———. *Theory of Social and Economic Organizations.* Trans., by A. M. Henderson and T. Parsons. New York: Oxford University Press, 1947.

White, Leonard D. *The Federalists.* New York: Macmillan Publishing Co., Inc., 1948.

———. *The Jeffersonians.* New York: Macmillan Publishing Co., Inc., 1951.

White, Leonard D. *The Jacksonians.* New York: Macmillan Publishing Co., Inc., 1955.

———. *The Republican Era, 1869–1901.* New York: Macmillan Publishing Co., Inc., 1958.

Wildavsky, Aaron, *The Politics of the Budgetary Process.* Boston: Little, Brown and Company, 1964.

Wilson, James Q. *The Investigators.* New York: Basic Books, 1978.

———. *The Politics of Regulation.* New York: Basic Books, 1980.

Woll, Peter. *American Bureaucracy.* New York: W. W. Norton & Company, Inc., 1963.

6 Interests and Pressure Groups

The Structure of Group Activity

Interests

Large societies are inevitably characterized by a rough division of labor in which not all the members of the society are engaged in the same occupation or contribute in the same manner to the welfare of the society. This is unlike a small social entity, in which each of the members (save for the distinction in gender roles) performs nearly the same tasks as any other. They may at times be warriors or farmers or fishermen, but all partake equally of the tasks.

As societies grow, the members differentiate themselves, becoming primarily farmers, soldiers, traders, craftsmen, and so on. Specialization thus takes place, depending on skills, expertise, intelligence, preferences, and a host of nonoccupational characteristics such as class, wealth, and others. The larger and more complex the society, the greater is the number of these specializations. With industrialization, the number grows astronomically.

All those engaged in any one specialization, when considered together, are obviously different to some extent from the collection of individuals engaged in another specialization. Each of those collections of people can be said to represent an **interest**—that is, in political terms they seek to further the interest involved in their own specialized activity or to make their activities more rewarding, whether in a material sense or intangibly.

An interest, then, is a collection of individuals who have significant characteristics in common. An interest may be occupationally defined: all ironworkers, for example, have a common interest in their occupation. So do farmers. But interests can be defined by other criteria. The nation's poor comprise an interest, as do members of the middle class. An interest may be represented by a religious group or sect; or by those whose primary concern is the preservation of civil liberties or the right to own guns: or by businessmen who employ workers: or by those whose concern is the improvement of the status of particular racial or ethnic groups.

Individuals who are represented by or are members of an interest have in common that they share certain values and characteristics of their activity or status. These are, in fact, the bases of their common bond. There may be individual variations, especially in personal values, but the values peculiar to their commonness are generally quite widely shared with others.

Moreover, those who comprise the interest generally have common goals and objectives that are the product of their specialized activity or status. They may have a common desire to achieve certain results or to rearrange the political and social order for their benefit. They may want to see others behave the way they do, without personal or material gain being involved, or they may want simply to be let alone in their uniqueness. Or they may want to have their status improved, whether or not they have a clear idea of how to accomplish it and whether or not their interest is in opposition to someone else's.

A complex society is composed of many interests. To this extent, the concept is one of a **pluralist** society. People are rich, poor, workers, unemployed, employers, professionals, laborers, members of various ethnic or religious groups, and so on. There may be an "establishment" or "elite" group that dominates the society and manipulates the perceptions and desires of everyone else for its own benefit. Individuals may belong to or consider themselves part of several different interests. But all this does not contradict the basic description of separable interests in society.

A public official generally has one or more of such interests as part of his **constituency.** If he is an appointed official, he will usually be in a position in which he works closely with not more than one interest or mediates between that interest and all others. An elected official, on the other hand, ordinarily has a more complex constituency with which to contend. Within the district from which he or she was elected, especially if it is the size of a congressional district (about 450,000 people) or greater, several interests will usually be represented. The voters—his or her constituents—thus are not homogeneous, but belong to different interests. Although one may predominate, others are nonetheless present.

Organized Interests

Not all interests have or seek to have influence in the political process. For some, their influence is felt even without exerting a positive effort to affect the process. Other interests, no matter how large they may be, have little or no effect. But most of them attempt, in one fashion or another, to persuade public officials to act in their favor.

An organized interest—that is, an interest that organizes itself in order more adequately to reflect and further the views of its members—is called an **interest group.** The organizing normally takes the shape of a more or less permanent structure or organization. It may be an elective body, such as in a union, or a voluntary association. The members of the interest support the organization through membership, dues paying, volunteer work, or other contributions. These interest groups (often called *pressure groups*) try to affect the political process in such a way that the outcome of the process is beneficial to the group's members.

Such interest groups may be separate and unassociated, seeking influence only for the benefit of their own narrow following. Or they may see themselves as part of a broad coalition of groups like themselves. Farmers, for example, ordinarily are concerned only with agricultural policy and the effects of government action on farming, whereas organized plumbers regard themselves as part of a broad-scale labor movement. Although it is conceivable that some governmental activity will affect only plumbers and not, say, ironworkers, most of the time the values and policies that affect plumbers are shared with other labor unions. The interests of plumbers and ironworkers rarely, if ever, conflict, so that they and all similar interests can be unified in a single, overall framework. This is, broadly speaking, the labor movement.

The purpose of interest groups is to secure the common objectives of their members. For a number of reasons (to be discussed later), group activity is more potent than the actions of individuals in determining the direction of the public policy of the United States. An organization that exists to perpetuate the aims and goals of the individuals who compose it can direct its activity knowledgeably and pointedly at the spot in the governmental process where it is most likely to succeed.

The legislative arena is the place that most easily comes to mind when thinking of the location of interest-group activity. It is there that the statutes are made, and statutes incorporate the public policy of the state. The legislators are chosen by the people in order to make these laws. Interest groups seek to have public policy reflect their own policy preferences, their own values and objectives. And, to the extent that legislation embodies public policy, it is crucial for an interest group, therefore, to be able to affect and influence the composition of those laws.

The relationship of interest-group activity and legislation is a many-sided one. The most straightforward example occurs where a group tries to get a law passed whose purpose is to benefit the group. Farmers, for example, might want the government to buy all the excess crops produced and would try to get the legislature to pass such a bill. Labor unions might want a law requiring all government-funded construction activity to be performed only by union labor. Or religious groups might want the government to pay for building their schools. In all these instances the interest group is the direct and intended beneficiary of the proposed law.

But this does not indicate the complexity of the relationship between interest groups and legislation. Groups seek not only favorable laws but protection from onerous ones. The American Medical Association (AMA), composed of doctors, was vigorously opposed to Medicare legislation because of its anticipated adverse effects on the medical profession. The National Rifle Association (NRA) has continually fought legislation regulating the sale, use, or ownership of guns, deeming such laws inimical to its members interests.

An interest group that has been favored by past legislation will strive to maintain its protected position against any change in current laws. A group may seek to be exempted from the operation of laws aimed at controlling an industry, several industries, or the entire economy. If an ongoing program requires new funds each year or a new determination about the level or percentage of funding, then in each year there must be another effort by the relevant interest groups to influence the appropriation of funds.

Legislation is not the only object of interest-group activity, although it is perhaps the most visible. Officeholders in the executive branch constantly have to make policy choices that affect groups in society. Many such choices must be made during the interelection period—that is, when voters are not exercising their direct control over policy. These executive policy choices are subject to influence by interest groups in much the same manner as legislation.

The goal of influencing executive policy choices is perhaps even more vital to the group than is influencing legislators because, at virtually all levels of government, the chief executive is the most significant force in procuring laws or defeating proposals he does not favor. The executive is an important ally for an interest group because of all the resources and influence he commands. He and the appointed officials who work for him, are consequently a focus of interest-group activity.

If an election is approaching, interest-group activity shifts to the selection by voters of candidates favorable to a group's values and preferences. Groups can direct their efforts at the candidates themselves, trying to get an expression or implication of agreement with the group's position. They can also attempt to influence the political party organization, in an attempt to influence the party leaders' selection of the candidate or to affect the writing of the party platform.

Whether in a general or a primary election, an interest group can direct its activity toward influencing voters to choose the candidate who is most favorably inclined to its position. The group's ideal, naturally, would be an election in which both candidates are equally (and strongly) committed in its favor. Any general election in Iowa, for example, is likely to find both the Republican and Democratic candidate strongly in favor of high agricultural subsidies. An election in New York, however, may find one candidate in favor of, and one opposed to, aid to parochial schools. The concerned interest groups may have a significant role to play in influencing voters to choose between the two candidates.

A vital, but often hidden, locus of interest-group activity is at the level of administrative and regulatory decision. Executive agencies, empowered to carry out the public policy as pronounced by legislation, must necessarily have some discretion in operation. And the "appropriate" exercise of that discretion is the object of the interest group's actions.

The administrators may be civil bureaucrats, quasi-independent functionaries under the direction of the chief executive, or independent commissioners or agents. These less often regulate some of the larger, more important industries in the country. Although the techniques used to influence each of these types of administrator may vary, the objective is the same: favorable rulings and decisions.

A commission authorized by law to regulate an industry or a public service can make the difference between profit and loss for the concerned companies, or, perhaps more realistically, between large and only moderate profits. A commission-regulated rate structure is only the most obvious mode of control. Discretion exercised by the commission may also determine such factors as quality of service, employment requirements, safety hazards and practices, level of competition, and volume of business. Each of those decisions is the object of attempts to influence them by the concerned interest groups.

Agency bureaucrats perform similar tasks for virtually all the operations of government as regulatory commissions do for regulated industries. Such wide limits of discretion are frequently necessary, if only because legislation cannot be so detailed as to deal with every task that must be performed in implementing a law or other piece of public policy. Moreover, legislators themselves are not always totally familiar with the entire range of problems, with the "nitty-gritty" involved in the area governed by the legislation. They can provide only guidelines and overall boundaries in many cases. The administrators must implement the program—and not always under the watchful eye of the legislature. There is, thus, ample opportunity for the influence of interest groups to be felt at the ground level, whether to sharpen or to dull the cutting edge of the legislated public policy.

Judicial decisions can be and often are the object of interest-group activity. This is more likely where judges are elected (or chosen by political parties) for fairly short periods of time than when they are appointed for lengthy or lifetime terms. In the former case, the judges are subject to the same influences as legislators are, with a few modifications, although they operate within quite a different context.

But even lifetime judges can be influenced less directly. Many court decisions, especially at the highest levels, reflect policy choices. Constitutions continually have to be updated by reinterpretation in the light of contemporary affairs and concerns. Even a settled body of common law may have to be revised or abandoned when its original rationale is undercut by social or economic changes. Strong representations by interest groups *in litigation* can hasten the judicial recognition of changed circumstances and the need for a new path in the judicial construction of the law, even without the same kind of lobbying activity that affects legislators and bureaucrats.

In each of the operational branches of government, therefore, the influence of interest groups can be felt. This influence can be directed at any one of them or at any combination when necessary. Quite often, the interest-group activity or **lobbying** is directed and performed by paid professional persuaders called lobbyists.

The term *lobbyist* developed from the practice of speaking to legislators about pending matters in the lobby just outside the legislative chamber. A regular occupant of the lobby, whose function was to try to influence the legislators, came to be called a lobbyist.

An interest group whose organization can raise sufficient funds may hire a person to be its permanent representative, with instructions to act so as to further the interests of the group. Hiring a lobbyist (sometimes called a public relations specialist or a legislative consultant) helps to ensure that the group's interests are continually made known to the decision makers in government, that effective arguments on the group's behalf are presented in the proper places, and—through a kind of watchdog function—that pending official action anywhere in government that might affect the group is brought to the group's attention.

If the group is large enough, its lobbyist may, in fact, be a small army. Numerous organizations maintain offices in Washington and many of them employ upward of a dozen or more persons to act on behalf of the group. The lobbying staff may include, in addition to a director and his immediate assistants, liaison officials for the component organizations, researchers, copywriters, an editorial crew, specialists with contacts in different branches of government, and an appropriately sized clerical staff. The larger the interest represented, the more sophisticated its lobbying operation can be.

Although it may once have been the case, lobbying nowadays is no longer concerned solely with leglislative activity. The myriad of government functions and offices means that any interest group may be affected by the actions of large numbers of public officials. Consequently, lobbyists must direct their activity not simply at the legislature, but at various regulatory and administrative agencies, cabinet departments, and high policy levels within the executive branch.

Types of Pressure Groups

Three types of interest groups try to influence governmental decisions. The first and most common is the permanently organized interest. This variety of pressure group consists of those interests that themselves are more or less permenent components of society and, conscious of their distinctiveness, are continuous competitors in the political process. Their status and objectives require repeated efforts to further and protect them. Each group in this category has to pay constant attention to its political fortunes. Gains won during one political season can be lost in the next unless the group's representatives remain alert.

Groups of this type are most often occupationally or ethnically defined. A given ethnic group or employment type is not likely to disappear after a short spell in the social system. It remains as a constituent element in the political structure, constantly seeking at least to maintain, and more often to improve, its position. To the extent that the resources that society has to allocate are scarce—that is, there is not enough to make everyone happy—and that intergroup values are not harmonious, the group's interests are continually endangered or hindered in progressing.

Moreover, because such a group is more or less permanent, its specific aims will vary as time passes. At one time it may want favorable tax treatment from the government. Having achieved that, its next specific objective may be to secure government regulation of a competitor. After that issue is finally decided, the group may then seek certain export privileges to foreign or Communist countries. This changing universe of objectives requires continual pressure-group activity directed at various institutions of government, to protect prior gains while securing newer ones.

Permanently established interest groups are the most likely groups to hire and maintain lobbyists. This professional interest representation may range from a one-man part-time operation in a hole-in-the-wall office to a staff of hundreds in an entire office building just off Pennsylvania Avenue, depending on how much the group has to protect and how much it is willing to spend to protect and further its interests.

The Petroleum Institute of America, the Committee on Political Education (COPE) of the AFL-CIO, the NRA, and the National Association for the Advancement of Colored People (NAACP) are examples of large, influential, and permanent pressure groups. Each seeks to further its own interests on a continuing basis, and each maintains an elaborate lobbying organization centered in the nation's capital for that purpose.

The oil lobby has had a broad range of specific interests on the contemporary scene. These extend from protecting the oil depletion allowance, to fighting the windfall profits tax, to securing drilling rights off the Atlantic coast, and to the strict regulation of nuclear energy power plants. It has sought to further and protect those interests by directing its lobbying and pressure group activity at the Congress, the presidency, administrative agencies, and the courts of the nation.

COPE's interests have been equally varied in recent years. Labor has sought and continues to seek the elimination of wage controls and guidelines (while retaining price controls), the repeal of right-to-work laws, the extension of minimum-wage coverage to all workers, and the exemption of personal services from accounting under campaign finance laws. These reflect the continual existence of organized labor as a pressure group, representing the interests of an occupationally defined group of people.

The NRA, the chief organization in what has been referred to as the gun lobby, keeps watch on government activity that threatens to affect public access to guns. Comprised mostly of sportsmen, both hunters and target shooters, its interests are narrower than those of, for example, COPE, centering on such topics as gun registration and sales, shooting contests, and hunting seasons. The NRA is not an occupationally defined pressure group, but more a recreational one. Although it rests its legal arguments on the Second Amendment's "right of the people to keep and bear arms," it has no particular political or philosophical ax to grind and it consequently supports (or opposes) politicians of varying political affiliations.

The NAACP is an ethnically based pressure group whose primary interest is the "advancement" of the interests of blacks. Its objectives, however, have moved at times beyond simply the removal of legal obstacles to racial equality. It has supported (or opposed) policies and programs not specifically aimed at colored people but whose impact on blacks and other racial minorities would be beneficial (or detrimental). It has, for example, supported minimum-wage legislation and Medicaid, and opposed such measures as wiretapping laws and immigration regulations that favor Europeans over Africans or Asians. Because racial minorities are permanent elements of our population, the NAACP and groups like it can be expected to play continuing roles in American politics.

A second type of interest group is the issue-oriented, *ad hoc* organization. In contrast to the permanent pressure group, which has continuing and often widespread interests to further and protect, this type is transient and centered on one public policy issue or on a very narrow range of issues. It tends to come into existence to struggle over that issue and to disappear when the issue is no longer a subject of controversy. It normally does not represent a class or subclass of people who can be defined by any of the ordinary socioeconomic criteria. It can consist of people with a broad spectrum of political values and beliefs, so long as there is agreement on the fundamental issue providing impetus for the group's activity.

Although such a group can focus attention on a public issue that otherwise might not command such concern, it operates at a considerable disadvantage compared to more permanent ones, especially when it collides head on with a permanent pressure group. The *ad hoc* pressure group's members are often inexperienced politically; they may not know the most effective ways to direct their pressure-group activity because they have never had reason to learn them. They often lack the resources to conduct appropriate and effective activities even if they know how. They cannot hire the professionals: the lobbyists. If they are in conflict with a permanent group, their influence may be less heavily felt because public officials will not easily be inclined to alienate a permanent contestant in the political arena for the sake of gaining the favor of a group that will soon disappear.

But some of the factors leading to the weakness of issue-oriented, *ad hoc* groups can become sources of strength. First of all, without such a group an issue might never receive any attention at all in higher circles, or there might never be any opposition to conventional policies. The group can mobilize previously unmobilized and unheard voices. It can bring together all who favor a certain position on a matter of public policy without having to make a broad philosophical appeal to a class of citizens. It can, at least temporarily, unite diverse elements of society. The group's public appeal may be strengthened by its lack of sophistication and newness to the political scene, especially where politics and special interests are dirty words. Finally, the concentration on one issue may mean that there are no entrenched groups in opposition. Consequently, there may be little significant pressure against which to compete.

Issue-oriented, *ad hoc* interest groups are most often characterized by their opposition to a particular government policy or to a threatened action by the government. They are predominantly "anti" groups, although quite often what they are opposed to is a lack of government action or the absence of a policy. And as soon as the policy is changed or the desired action is taken, the group's *raison d'être* no longer exists and it disappears from the political scene.

Many of these groups can be observed in local or neighborhood politics. Groups may organize themselves to fight off the installation of parking meters, to oppose the presence of a drug-rehabilitation center, or to save a park from destruction to make room for a highway. Or they may organize to bring pressure for a better traffic control system on a major street or for a new school in the area.

Local conflicts are sometimes reflections of larger national issues, and a small group, formed to fight a local proglem, may subsequently join a larger, although still issue-oriented and *ad hoc,* pressure group. A small organization designed to oppose obscene or pornographic movies at the town's only theater may soon join a larger state- or nationwide group whose purpose is to ban pornography in all theaters. Or the national group may inspire the formation of smaller affiliated groups on a local level.

Some examples of issue-oriented, *ad hoc* pressure groups on a national scale are the loosely knit collection of individuals and organizations called the China lobby, the antiwar movement of the 1960s, and the antiabortion forces. The China lobby (discussed further in Chapter 9) is a large, informal pressure group comprised of several smaller and offshoot organizations plus influential persons from various parts of the United States. It was formed during the Chinese civil war in the late 1940s, which ended in the removal of the Nationalist government to Taiwan. Its purpose was to maintain American involvement on behalf of Chiang Kai-shek and in opposition to the Communists, who had won control of the mainland. Among its constituent elements were organizations such as the "Commitee of One Million," which consisted of individuals opposed to the admission of the Chinese Peoples Republic to the United Nations.

The China lobby was supported by widely diverse elements of American society, ranging from business and industry, church groups, a number of influential labor unions and organizations, professional anti-Communist groups, and politicians of all stripes. In its heyday in the early and mid-1950s, it wielded a good deal of influence in the formulation of American foreign policy. But changes in the climate of opinion here and in the international situation as a whole have diminished its influence. President Nixon's trip to China in 1972, the subsequent admission of Red China to the U.N. and the displacing of the Nationalists, recognition of the communist regime on the mainland, and the diplomatic advantage of a counterforce to oppose the U.S.S.R. have undermined the group's efficacy. The issue is, in effect, disappearing as a public policy matter of major importance. The questions no longer deal with whether, but rather how, we should conduct relations with mainland China. Should Taiwan be reabsorbed within China, the China lobby will no longer have any purpose, as there would be no Nationalist government left to support. The issue will not exist and the *ad hoc* groups involved will pass out of existence.

This process happened in the antiwar movement that sprang up to oppose the Vietnam War. Although it included some permanent organizations such as the Quakers, the antiwar movement was primarily a loose coalition of organizations such as the Fifth Avenue Peace Parade Committee and others. The movement made attempts to encompass a number of other issues, but it was opposition to the Vietnam War around which the groups coalesced and from which they drew strength. The movement forced the public and the government to debate whether we should be fighting the war, and later how best to end it, rather than have widespread acceptance of the proposition that there was no other proper policy than to fight it. This pressure group is widely credited with providing the impetus for a change in American policy on the war and with forcing President Lyndon Johnson in 1968 to decline to run for reelection, although it failed to determine the timing and the structure of the peace that followed.

But when the Vietnam War ended, the issue also ceased to exist. Because the movement was not founded on a broad political philosophy or on a continuous competitor in the political system, it failed to survive the issue that gave it life. Although vesitgal remains are left to deal with some issues like amnesty and veterans' rights, the movement itself is no longer a significant force.

An *ad hoc,* issue-oriented interest group is the antiabortion movement. Subsequent to the revision of abortion laws in several states and especially to the Supreme Court's 1973 ruling that most state restrictions on abortion were unconstitutional, groups such as the Right to Life Committee began to organize themselves to repeal the revised legislation, to seek a constitutional amendment to outlaw abortion, and to oppose proabortion politicians. Abortion is a currently controversial issue around which *ad hoc* groups can organize in order to influence government decisions in the matter. Groups that favor abortion have also formed, although many of them are in effect revivals of the earlier groups that opposed abortion laws. These organizations on both sides will persist until the issue is finally decided one way or the other and removed from public controversy.

The third type of pressure group is the citizen lobby or public interest group. These groups normally distinguish themselves by claiming that they speak for and support the common, or public, interest, as opposed to special interest that seek unwarranted favors from government. (A "special interest" in political discourse is a pejorative term for an interest group, lobby, or representative that you oppose. The "good guys," the ones you favor, are usually referred to in terms something like an "interested organization.") Public interest groups resemble the *ad hoc* ones in that they are comprised of diverse elements that cut across ordinary political and group ties, representing no definable class or sublcass of people. But they are similar to permanent interest groups in that they are interested in a range of issues and they intend to become continuous competitors on the political scene.

Pressure groups on behalf of the public interest are not an especially new phenomenon, but in recent times they are becoming more numerous and better publicized. Ralph Nader's various organizations and a group called Common Cause are examples of this kind of interest group. Nader's forces have been concentrated in the area of consumer protection, beginning with his book about the automotive industry, *Unsafe at Any Speed,* but have branched out into all kinds of products and processes that may prove harmful or dangerous. Common Cause has interests in virtually every area of public policy that can be said to affect the country's population. Its interests are narrowed only to the extent that it lacks the resources and funds to tackle everything it wishes it could.

Some groups, such as environmental protection organizations, are more like *ad hoc,* issue-oriented groups because they are interested in a narrow (although significant and active) field; yet, the nature of the issue is such that the groups are probably here to stay. Environmental issues are not likely ever to be fully resolved and noncontroversial. The groups are, thus, compelled to become permanent political contestants representing, they claim, the public interest, not a private one.

Public interest pressure groups direct their activity at all the major institutions: executive, legislative, bureaucratic, and judicial. One of their major tools is the lawsuit on behalf of an otherwise unrepresented class; but they are capable of developing skilful lobbying activities and many permanent lobbyists have been retained to pursue their objectives.

The Behavior and Activity of Groups

The Means of Influence: Pressure and Policy

Interest groups by definition seek to further the interests of the members of the group. They seek governmental decisions in their favor. They do not merely *hope* for favorable decisions from the various branches of government; they actively persuade decision makers by applying one or more of several persuasive tactics or pressures. Some are designed to affect the decision-maker's judgment on the merits of the issue. Others are aimed at influencing more personal or political factors in the decision-maker's judgement. Some require use of specialists; others can be used by virtually anyone.

Whatever the common image of a lobbyist, it remains the fact that one of the lobbyist's most significant activities is simply to disseminate information. A legislative committee will often take up an issue or consider a bill without its members initially knowing very much about the issue. When it does so, the committee normally wants to inform itself about what is involved in the question so that it can make a reasoned judgment as to the specifics of the new legislation. In order to obtain this information, it invites all interested parties to submit statements or any other matter that might be helpful to the committee. Some groups are called to testify before the committee; others may request to do so. Lobbyists must remain alert to provide this information whenever it is requested.

Moreover, the interest group involved often possesses the only real information concerning an issue. No other group or agencies may be able to provide what the legislators need. The group's personnel are the experts in the field, and their advice must be considered seriously if only because no other individual or group knows as much about the subject as they do. This command of sources of information and expertise creates a powerful tool with which to influence policy.

The committee will want to know not only what the facts are, but also what are the views of groups and organizations that are concerned with the issue—groups who will be directly affected by the legislation and will have to live with it. The legislator wants to know who cares about the issue, as well as where powerful groups line up on it. In all these respects the lobbyists, or any other representative of an interest group, can be of significant assistance to the legislative process and in a perfectly legal, aboveboard manner. They can exert influence on the outcome of the process even without resorting to some of the cruder forms of persuasion that are commonly called pressure.

This same means of influencing policy can be brought to bear on the executive or administrative branch of government. A legislative policy must be implemented by rules and regulations adopted to deal with the specific problem of administration. Bureaucrats ordinarily have some discretion in formulating, administering, and enforcing the rules. Interest-group representatives can make known to the bureaucrats what the views and preferences of the interested parties are, so that the laws can be executed in the light of what the parties directly affected by them desire. The interested groups may all agree on what is preferable, or they may be in conflict, in which case the administrators must choose among different bureaucratic schemes or levels of enforcement. But, in either case, the views of the interest groups, when made known to the administrators, can have an effect on policy at this juncture that may very nearly amount to determining what the law is.

To inform a policymaker, whether he or she is a legislator or an elected official in the executive branch (or an appointive official working for an elected one), of the views of an interest group is, of course, not simply to contribute to the policy maker's overall knowledge. It is to imply, at least, certain other measures or persuasive tactics that more nearly fit the common notion of the activities of pressure groups. Public officials need to get elected and reelected, and pressures to influence policy are very often designed to operate at that level.

One of the most common of these pressure tactics has been the campaign finance contribution. Organizations (especially larger groups) generally have access to financial resources. They prefer to see candidates who are in favor of their interests elected over hostile candidates. Consequently, because campaigns cost money, these groups may make contributions to candidates' or officials' campaigns. The amounts they contribute may vary from purely nominal sums of $100 or so up to the rumored several million dollars promised by an organization of milk producers to former President Nixon's 1972 reelection campaign. Often, as in the case of some legislators, the amount contributed is a regular sum given each election year. The explosive growth of political action committees (PAC's) in recent years enables interest groups legally to target vast sums of money to or against certain candidates, and especially working to the advantage of the interest groups in closely fought elections.

Campaign contributions permit the hiring of campaign aides; the printing and distribution of literature; the purchase of television and radio time; the use of cars, buses, and even planes in order to get around; as well as some living in style, such as expensive hotels and dinners, new clothes for the candidate and even for his wife, and perhaps a vacation trip. The promise of continued giving, and the threat—if they are dissatisfied—to discontinue such gifts are among the powerful tools of pressure groups.

Contributions to campaign finances can be made in ways other than money being handed over or passed through a bank account. Interest groups can contribute services, such as free printing of literature or copywriting of advertisements. An employer may assign an assistant of his to work temporarily on the staff of the candidate. Or, interest-group members may volunteer their time and effort to the campaign, with or without the express direction of the organization leaders, on or before election day. These hidden contributions are perhaps even more valuable than the overt kind.

Another means by which interest groups exert pressure is the exercise of vote-pulling power and the mobilization of support. The interest group's leadership can encourage its membership to vote for or against a particular candidate. And the members will often proselytize among family and associates for similar votes. If the group can act monolithically, or nearly so, the promise to offer group endorsement to the official or candidate (or the threat to withhold it) carries weight. The larger the group and the more monolithically it acts, the greater the weight it can throw around in this manner. It is naturally more effective at the margin—that is, in closely contested districts or elections. But where the group is the largest component of an official's prior support at the polls, it can wield influence even where an election is not expected to be close, by threatening to withdraw and create an uncertain situation or a possible loss.

If interest groups can affect the results on election day, they may, in some cases, be even more influential in the nominating process. If there is a direct primary for the party's nomination, then the groups can exercise influence by much the same means as in a general election: through finances and votes. But, if the nomination is granted by a party leadership structure, or if the party leadership's choice is normally the heavy favorite in the primary, then the groups to whom the party leaders listen can, in effect, control the nomination. The party leadership tends to select candidates because of their appeal to key interest groups, either groups who regularly support the party or those who the party is trying to win over in the upcoming election. In this way an interest group controlling the nomination can (provided the candidate wins) be assured that an official is elected who is sympathetic to the group's interests and whose decisions in office will presumably reflect that feeling.

Between elections, or when an appointed or nonelected official wants to have a particular policy implemented or bill passed by the legislative, the support of an interest group can be vital to the success of the policy or bill. The threat to remove that support, or actively to oppose a policy or legislative proposal, constitutes another instrument of pressure. The group's ability to mobilize support or opposition is a measure of the influence it can wield even in a nonelection framework.

These means of influence and pressure work on public officials more or less indirectly, either through information control or by means of the selection process, both past and future. That is, the policymaker is affected by his chances of being "allowed" to stay in office. But there are other means of influence that work more directly. Outright bribes are, of course, the prototypes (along with possible blackmail threats) and sometimes the line is very thin between bribery and what are called **conflict of interest** situations. Many jurisdictions have statutes prohibiting certain defined forms of conflict of interest, but these are not agreed on uniformly.

Conflicts of interest come in a variety of forms—in the most obvious one a legislator votes for (or an executive administers) a measure that directly benefits him. But other conflicts are more subtle and may involve "the acquisition of unwarranted influence" (in President Eisenhower's words) by pressure groups. For example, many regulatory commissions are so specialized and require such intimate knowledge of the regulated area that the only persons who are thought qualified to do the regulating are persons whose careers have been in the regulated industry. Often these individuals have worked for companies being regulated and, because a commission appointment is not normally a preretirement position, they will return to one of the regulated companies when they leave office. Can such an individual regulate in the public interest when he knows that soon he will be employed by the private interest he is supposed to regulate? Or will the private interest exercise a good deal of influence over the official's decisions, even without an outright bribe or job offer?

The Federal Power Commission offers an example here. The commission chairman may be an eminent lawyer, knowledgeable and competent in the field of public utilities and production of power. But he may have made his career as counsel to a power company and, because he is likely not to be near retirement age, he will likely return to the industry, if not to the same company. Will he put the industry's needs before the public's needs, or will the public come first? Or, most likely, will he tend to equate the good of the industry with the good of the public, so that a ruling favorable to the industry becomes, in his mind, one that benefits the public first?

Similarly, the Department of Energy has recruited many persons who came directly from oil companies and will return to those companies when their governmental "tour of duty" is over. These persons are necessary to the department because few other people have equivalent expertise or access to information to allow them to function properly in the job. An official cannot make effective energy policy unless he or she has knowledge of all of the factors affecting the energy industry to which the policy relates. Yet the official's career is not likely to be permanently in government. A "healthy" oil industry is critical to his or her future and friendly contacts made while he or she is in government service increase one's chances of gaining a good job afterwards.

The federal government's Bureau of Mines is another example. This agency is responsible for, among other things, enforcing mine safety regulations. Most of its leadership personnel, no matter which party is in power, comes either from the high ranks of mining companies or from university departments of mining (between which two positions individuals often move easily and rapidly). Few other people know enough about mining to be able to administer such an agency; yet, the presence of a conflict in loyalty, if not provable interest, is apparent.

In most states a legislator's elective job is not a full-time one and the legislator must continue to work at his normal occupation, taking time out to journey to the capital during the legislative session. Many legislators are lawyers and continue to practice law, either individually or as a partner in a firm. (Former Senate Minority Leader Everett McKinley Dirksen from Illinois remained associated with his law firm throughout his many years in Washington.) Legislators who have clients with matters pending in bureaucratic agencies are in obvious conflict-of-interest situations, a good number of which are prohibited by law. But what if the legislator's law firm has the client? Or if the firm is counsel for a regulated industry or company or one that is subject to pending legislation? Even if the legislator is required to sever his or her connection with the firm, he or she may be influenced by his former activities or he or her may may intend to rejoin the firm when his or her term in office is over. Legal fees paid to a firm or to an individual legislator may be little more than indirect and concealed bribe.

Conflict-of-interest situations are normally thought of as instances in which money passes (either simultaneously or by deferred compensation—that is, a later job) in exchange for favorable action or inside information on matters properly within the discretion of the official. But the line is not a clear one. A farmer-legislator who votes for agricultural subsidies for which he or she is eligible and that he or she collects (such as Senator James Eastland of Mississippi) may be thought to have crossed the line. But what about a labor union member-legislator who votes on bills affecting union rights and finances? Or a priest-legislator who votes on aid to parochial schools? Or an army reservist-legislator who votes on military appropriations, including funds for reserve officers? Or, for that matter, lawyers who vote to regulate (or rather to refuse to regulate) the legal profession? In each of these cases the interest group concerned has "its" representative present to watch out for its interests and to influence policymaking. In fact, the legislator is himself a member of the interest.

A final means of influence, which has been gaining popularity, is the lawsuit. Interest groups unable to sway legislators or administrators in their favor, or who seek an alternative course of action, may go to court not simply to preserve their known rights but to secure unacknowledged ones. A large interest group that can afford batteries of lawyers and has unlimited time has an obvious advantage over a poorly endowed group. Research and mobilization of support within the legal profession can serve to influence (even to pressure) courts to rule in favor of one group over another. The lawsuit may shed public light on previously unknown, unadmitted, or hidden facts whose exposure alters the public sense of rightness. Continued litigation in the same general subject area may accomplish the same purpose.

On occasion the law protects groups with lesser means of influence, acting as a corrective to the pressure that large organized interests can exert. An example is that some of the recent environmental legislation, by which a small group with limited resources, but representing a wide public following, can challenge, on a relatively equal footing, powerful interest groups in court. Although the law most often reflects existing power relationships and older social values, sometimes even the threat of a lawsuit is enough to force a settlement of grievances.

The lawsuit as a means of influence or pressure affects public policy by generating (indeed, forcing) decisions of courts on these policy matters. The development of the class action suit and its increasingly widespread use by groups of environmentalists and consumers was one such technique, but the courts have been limiting that device as a means of exerting influence. A recent Supreme Court decision requires that notice of the lawsuit be given to all members of the class on whose behalf relief is sought. If one is trying to bring a legal action on behalf of a class of a million or so people, that is an impossible requirement to fulfill, effectively preventing the lawsuit.

The Style of Influence: Getting the Message Across

The means, or exact pressures, being used to exert influence sometimes dictates the style or mode of applying the pressure, but not always. Often there is a choice of ways, some more direct than others, in which to approach and influence officials. Arm twisting and the use of overt threats are not always necessary and can be counterproductive unless used sparingly and with discretion.

When an interest group deems it necessary to exert pressure on an official, it often seeks a face-to-face meeting between the official and the group's representatives. The group wants to explain its position. Its implied weapon—to award or withhold group support during the next election—is not always helpful, depending on how many other groups can effectively use the same tool. And the group's plea is most likely to be made not in raw terms of special group interest, but by equating the group's position with the public interest —with right as against wrong. Not all officials are "up for sale." They may have to be persuaded by reasonable argument in addition to "political realities."

If the face-to-face discussion can be judged the most productive (or, at least, satisfying) opportunity to sway a policymaker, then it can be seen that getting access to the appropriate officials is a key problem. An interest group wants to make sure that its voice is heard and its message is getting across. The best way to be sure of that is to speak to the official himself. One of the key functions of lobbyists and other professional representatives of interest groups is to open the right doors. (Similarly, one of the significant effects of a large campaign contribution is that it may open that same door.)

Having a "friend in court" is one way to be sure that the door is open. An industry with "its man" on the regulatory commission or in a key position in an agency almost automatically has access. It can be sure that, at least, its side of a controversy will be heard by the decision maker. Thus, even if there is no outright conflict-of-interest situation and even if the interest group cannot "control" the official, it has an important advantage over competing groups that have no comparable way of being heard directly.

But often the interest group has no direct connection. It must rely then on intermediaries to gain access for it. It can hire, as a lobbyist on a permenent basis or as a "public relations expert" on a more *ad hoc* basis, a former government employee who "knows his way around." He or she may be a retired bureaucrat or an appointee of previous administrations (or of the current one if he or she has since quit).

This is a technique used by numerous private interests as well as groups, and it has two advantages. First, the former official knows to what agency, channel, or department a question should be routed. His or her experience provides him or her with the knowledge of what part of government will be handling a particular problem and what bureaus are likely to be most sympathetic to the needs of the interest group's efforts. This familiarity with the terrain is important to a group that does not know exactly how decisions are made or implemented.

But the hired intermediary provides a second and possibly even more important advantage, for he or she may also be familiar with those who occupy positions. In addition to knowing by title which official to call about a particular problem, he or she may also know the official personally. He or she may have worked with, for, or above the official. Or, he or she may have reason to expect that the official knows of him or her even if they have never met. In any case, the lobbyist can provide access for the interest group to the official who will be making the relevant decisions or who can open still another door. A network of personal relationships is vital to a lobbyist's success at the highest levels.

It is quite common for defense industry companies to hire retired generals and admirals not because the general knows a lot about manufacturing bullets but because he knows who in the government is going to buy the bullets. Similarly, President Nixon's congressional liaison, Robert Timmons, was the chief lobbyist for Proctor & Gamble, a job he left to join the Nixon administration, and which he had received after working in the Eisenhower administration. Larry O'Brien, a former Kennedy and Johnson administration official, opened up a public relations office in Washington after he left the government. Many of his clients did government business or were affected by government decisions, and O'Brien was an effective door opener.

The institution of the "Washington law firm" performs the same service. A company, industry, or interest group that faces legal problems with the federal government can hire as its counsel a law firm whose leaders were formerly government officials. They, too, know who to call and where to apply the pressure. Moreover, they often know the ins and outs of the laws the client might be concerned with, having administered them at one time. The law firm of Arnold and Porter (formerly Arnold, Fortas and Porter) is the prototype in this respect—both Thurman Arnold and Paul Porter were Roosevelt administration officials. Such firms, or at least their leaders, do not have to try a case because they can often resolve a problem by arranging settlements. Yet, they can have an effect even in court, as was illustrated when former Secretary of Defense Clark Clifford, arguing a private case (unrelated to the defense industry) before the Supreme Court in 1969, was inadvertently addressed by one of the justices as "Mr. Secretary." (He won the case.)

Interest groups and their representatives can gain access to officials in other ways, too. All congressmen have legislative aides and staff personnel. They advise the congressman, who does not have time to keep up with everything, as well as prepare summaries of pending legislation, do research, and help draft the congressman's own proposals. Access by the group to the congressman's staff members or even to only one of his or her legislative aides may be enough because the aide then can pass on the information to the congressman. Enlisting the aides in the group's cause can create an influential force in the group's favor. Congressmen have, in the past, given speeches and proposed legislation written by an interest group that were given to the congressman through his or her aides.

Interest-group representatives who are on good terms personally with a public official can capitalize on that friendship. A lobbyist may call an administrator on behalf of an interest group using the telephone belonging to a congressman. He or she can then begin the conversation by saying, "I'm calling from Congressman Doe's office," thereby implying that Congressman Doe is personally interested in the matter and may even be right there listening. This tactic is even more effective if Doe happens to be on a committee that oversees the administrator's agency. Influence peddling of this sort may be illegal, but slight variations are commonplace.

Interest groups often make their facilities available to public officials in situations where no business is either mentioned or transacted. An official in a hurry may be flown across the country in a corporation's private jet, or be given a helicopter flight from the office to the airport, or be lent a car for a time. Taking an official to lunch in a posh restaurant is another frequent occurrence. An interest group may hold a convention or conference in a resort area and "invite" a public official to come down to the conference (with or without his wife) and present the government's views on problems being discussed, all expenses paid.

Lobbyists hold cocktail parties, cookouts, and the like, to which they invite agency officials and legislators, as well as the interest-group leaders. These social contacts can ripen into acquaintanceships that at the least open doors for the interest group to present its views and that may even help to create a sense of obligation on an official's part, especially if in addition he has received some minor favors from the group.

Pressure on behalf of an interest group, thus, can be applied in a style or fashion in which it may not even seem to be pressure. One might call it subliminal—that is, it does not pass the threshold of recognition as pressure. Although there is little doubt that threats and arm twisting do sometimes occur, the exertion of influence is most often a much more subtle and many-faceted process.

The Effects and Effectiveness of Group Activity

Interest groups try to affect all aspects of public policy, no matter by whom or in what manner made. Groups try to influence the legislative process by affecting how legislators vote on a particular bill, the content of the legislation, whether a certain bill is introduced and supported, the size of appropriations, and all other substantive results. They affect the executive branch by influencing policy choices, regulatory decisions, administrative practice and procedure, and proposals made to the legislature. They try to affect judicial decisions by bringing cases for courts to decide and influencing the outcome of those cases.

This represents a lot of bases to touch. An interest that is not organized is a loosely guarded one. Changes in public policy affecting it may be brought about in numerous ways; organization helps to keep track of all those ways, so that the group will be aware of any threats to its interests.

Maintaining an organization helps a group to plan strategies to protect its interests and to further them. It enables the group to define precisely what constitutes a threat to those interests and what steps, actions, and policies might further them. And, with organization, strategies can be implemented in more than a haphazard manner. It becomes possible to coordinate tactical steps in various forums in order to achieve the optimum effect. An ongoing organization helps to build a network of connections to persons who are in positions of authority who will be making the decisions that affect the group. Over time, the organization can develop an expertise in using its connections as well as in knowing when and where to apply the appropriate amounts and kinds of pressure. And an ongoing organization becomes a focus for raising funds—funds necessary to perpetuate the organization itself, as well as to be expended where they will do the most good.

But perhaps the greatest advantage of good organization is in its capacity to mobilize political support in favor of, or in opposition to, a policy or candidate. Concentrated power is almost always more effective than a diffusion of effort. The ability to say to a public official that the group leadership can direct the casting of a specific number of votes, or the expenditure of a certain amount of campaign resources, or the efforts of volunteers is an important weapon—probably the most powerful one in a group's arsenal.

An organized group that responds to its leadership has this tool. Most Americans belong to some kind of organization and many to more than one. The influential organizations are the ones that are not only large but have a membership that takes its voting cues from the leadership and that can sway those who are not formally associated with the group but who sympathize with it. When policy decisions are made that distribute society's scarce resources, it is such groups that get a healthy share.

Political scientist Theodore Lowi has called this concept "interest group liberalism." The country's resources and values are divided among competing interests scattered around the "bargaining table." Everybody there gets a piece of action; the stronger—that is, the better organized—a group is, the larger the slice of the pie it gets.

The chief advantage that organization confers on an interest is a place at the table. Generally speaking, only organized interests are represented there. An interest without organization, one that is not an interest group, may be represented by someone else (as, for example, Harry Truman considered the President to be the "people's lob-byist," protecting their interests against the encroachments of special interests), but more likely it will not be represented at all. Consequently, the unorganized interest gets little, if any, of society's resources allotted to it. Such a group's interests go unprotected.

An interest group can increase the size of its share through an alliance with one or more other groups. Some of these coalitions achieve a regularity that seems almost like permanence, depending on the absence of conflict between the groups over a period of time. The labor-civil rights coalition of the postwar era has been one such near-permanent alliance, benefiting both groups by increasing the power of each through the effective mobilization of political support by one on behalf of the other. The agreement was, in effect, "You scratch my back; I'll scratch yours." Yet, this coalition broke down at times when underlying conflicts came to the surface and prevented common action. The business-farming coalition has been one of long-standing regularity that is still a frequent phenomenon in American politics.

Our political parties have, for most of their history, represented loose coalitions of certain interests and interest groups. The groups and interests have shifted over the years from one party to the other and sometimes back again for various reasons, with the major shifts coming at critical, divisive times in our history. The parties have made generally uneasy accomodations with the groups. Since Franklin D. Roosevelt's time, for example, it has been common to think of labor, liberals, minorities, and intellectuals as being within the Democratic party; conservatives, businessmen, those from rural areas, and upper-income people have been Republicans. But minorities, especially Negroes after the Civil War, intellectuals, and even labor were at one time or another identified with the Republican party, and conservatives and people in rural areas were at one time thought to be within the Democratic party. Even now, there are Democratic businessmen and Republican trade-union members; no interest is monolithically within one party or the other.

Some Reflections

How effective are interest groups in serving as a mechanism for the distribution of scarce resources and values in society? This is a loaded question, in the sense that anyone's answer to it will be based on often-unexpressed values and assumptions about society. For instance, in order to answer this question one would have to decide whether it is appropriate and right for persons to be interested chiefly in the welfare of their own primary group or have their chief interest in the welfare of the society as a whole. In any case, the answer is beyond the scope of this chapter, which has been concerned with a description of the structure and behavior of interest groups.

There are other questions whose answers require extensive investigation and empirical research. To what extent do interest groups represent "real" interests or self-perpetuating cliques? To what extent do they actually represent, further, and protect the interests of the members? How much do they influence their membership? Do they serve a valid public purpose? And, whether they do or not, is there anything anyone can do about it, or will they always be with us in roughly the same form and style?

There can be little doubt, however, that interest groups are a primary extraconstitutional element of American politics. Understanding the role they play, what they look like, and how they act provides an essential foundation for understanding the nature and operation of the American political process.

GLOSSARY

Conflict of interest A situation in which a public official is required to deal with opposing personal loyalties, obligations, or interests in the performance of his duties.

Constituency The supporters, friends, voters, and/or members of the same interest or interest group of a public official, to whom he must, or desires to, listen for guidance in the performance of his or her duties.

Influence The power or persuasiveness that determines how a public official performs his or her duties.

Interest The desires, values, or objectives held in common by a number of individuals.

Interest group An organized interest, desiring to exercise influence in order to achieve its goals and to see its interests become public policy; also known as a pressure group.

Lobbying The activity carried on by an interest or interest group that is aimed at influencing public officials.

Pluralist A concept describing a society in which many interests or interest groups vie through the political process to achieve their objectives; as opposed to monolithic, in which one interest or group dominates the process to the exclusion of the interests of others.

SUGGESTED READINGS

Bauer, Raymond, et al. *American Business and Public Policy,* 2nd ed. Chicago: Aldine Publishing Co., 1972.

Cloward, Richard, and Frances Fox Piven. *Regulating the Poor.* New York: Vintage Books, 1971.

———— *Poor People's Movements.* New York: Vintage, 1979.

Dahl, Robert. *Who Governs?* New Haven, Conn.: Yale University Press, 1961.

Kariel, Henry. *The Decline of American Pluralism.* Palo Alto, Cal.: Standford Univ. Press, 1961.

Key, V. O. *Parties, Politics, and Pressure Groups.* 4th ed. New York: The Crowell Publishing Company, 1958.

Lowi, Theodore. *The End of Liberalism,* 2nd ed. W. W. Norton & Company, Inc., 1979.

McConnell, Grant. *Private Power and American Democracy.* New York: Alfred A. Knopf, Inc., 1967.

Mills, C. Wright. *The Power Elite.* New York: Oxford University Press, 1956.

Schattschneider, E. E. *The Semi-Sovereign People.* New York: Holt, Rinehart, and Winston, 1960.

Seidman, Harold. *Politics, Position, and Power.* New York: Oxford University Press, 1970.

Truman, David B. *The Governmental Process,* rev. ed. New York: Alfred A. Knopf, Inc., 1971.

Wilson, James Q. *Political Organizations.* New York: Basic Books, 1973.

7 Public Opinion, Political Participation, and Political Parties

Introduction

In this chapter we concentrate on the manner in which people in the United States think about politics, what some of their opinions are, and how they participate (or fail to participate) in the political system. In the last sections of the chapter we concentrate on one form of political activity—political parties.

Public Opinion

Political Socialization: Definition

The process by which people acquire their political ideas and opinions is called *political socialization.* In part, political socialization is simply a learning process. This book is an example of political learning. It is an attempt to convey information: the number and forms of Senate committees, the processes of bureaucratic politics, and so on. The other major part of political socialization is developing attitudes, or values, about politics: opinions about what is good and bad. This we try to minimize; we leave to the reader the decisions about what is good and bad.

It is very important to understand that political socialization in both these aspects does *not* necessarily stop at a certain age. The experiences we have as children influence us greatly in politics as in other matters; but they do not shape us irrevocably. We are not finished products at the age of twelve or eighteen or sixty-six. Anyone who has lived in the United States for the last fifteen years knows that the opinions of many people, old and young, have changed enormously in response to the events of Vietnam and Watergate, and, more recently, the holding of American hostages in Iran, and continuing economic distress at home.

The Process

People get most of their beliefs and opinions from other people, especially groups of people. The family is the first, and often the most important group. Later on in life, peer groups—other people of the same status—may become influential.

Thus, the earliest political learning occurs in the family. Children pick up knowledge and beliefs from their parents. Sometimes children also learn a lesson about politics from the structure of their families. For instance, children raised by a strict and harsh father may develop the attitude that authority always knows best and should be followed without question.

Because politics is not a matter of great concern for most Americans, there is very little formal indoctrination in family life. Parents do not sit down with their children and teach them what to believe and whom to follow in politics. Parents' conversation, their reaction to newspaper stories or television news, and their comments about people and life generally are the main influences on children.

As they grow older, children are exposed to influences outside the home and family. Frequently, the most powerful of these influences are found in schools. First teachers, then peer, groups may powerfully change or reinforce the attitudes children bring with them from their family. In the early grades it seems likely that teachers and the curriculum of the school are the most significant forces. Later on, when teenagers begin to form the separate culture that characterizes adolescence in the United States, peer groups become more powerful. Teenagers are at a level of intellectual and social development at which they discuss politics with each other.

A less tangible, but important source of influence is the general climate of opinion at a school, which creates assumptions and impressions that may differ widely from those of the students' homes. Thus, if an institution is predominantly liberal, conservative students will find themselves under social as well as intellectual pressure to conform to the prevailing ideology.

Adults are often influenced most strongly by the peer groups in their job situations, but other groups such as church groups, unions, social clubs, neighborhood organizations, and ethnic groups may also be important. Such groups may influence a person even when he or she is not active in the group or even in contact with group members. In such a case, we call a group a **reference group,** meaning that the individual refers to the group and is guided by its position without being in personal contact with the group. For example, a machinist from Boston who has retired to Santa Fe, New Mexico, may still accept the opinions in his union's newsletter. An upper-class woman raised by conservative parents may continue to use them as her reference group long after she has left their home; or, she may adopt the liberal beliefs of some of her college teachers.

For many Americans, political parties are important reference groups, as are ethnic, religious, and occupational organizations. Another way of expressing this point is to say that people's opinions are determined by their identifications, by the answer to the question: Who are you? "I am a Protestant, a union member, a Democrat, a liberal, a member of the middle class."

In situations where the individual sees and talks frequently with the influential group, the name given to it is **primary group.** By now it should be clear that many of the most influential groups are, at least temporarily, primary groups. The family, peer groups, and job groups all fit into this category. Research indicates that within such groups, the pressure to conform to the group's opinion is stronger the more often the group is together, the smaller the group is, the longer the group has been together, and the more related the group is to the issue in question. Thus, family influence is likely to be particularly strong on such issues as the integration of schools and housing, which affect the family itself.

The influence of primary or reference groups helps to explain why people sometimes have opinions on subjects about which they know very little. Often, these ideas have come from the groups. Having heard a friend say that the TVA is a good thing, the person may adopt that view without having much idea of what the TVA is.

One way of seeing the process by which public opinion takes shape is to consider the leaders within primary groups and reference groups generally as one category, and those people who follow the leaders and the reference groups as a second. The first group may be called **opinion leaders,** or the attentive elite. They are the ones who follow politics, form opinions, and try to communicate their ideas to others either informally in primary groups or through the written word and the other more formal mechanisms of reference groups. Thus, there is a flow of information and opinion from the leaders to the general public. There is, as well, a flow in the opposite direction as the public accepts or rejects what it receives. A group or a leader who can convince the attentive elite has gone a long way toward convincing the public generally.

The Media. The media gain influence in the process just described because the media inform the attentive elite. Thus, information and opinions pass from the media to the attentive elite, and from the attentive elite to the general public. The media have indirect influence—their contribution is filtered through the attentive elite.

A second theory is that the media influence the general public directly. According to this idea, individuals get their information for themselves from newspapers, television, and radio. They may accept the opinions in the media or form their own. If they accept what they read and hear, they are subject to manipulation by whoever controls the media.

In practice, both theories may apply to some extent. Some people may be influenced more by the media, others by the attentive elite. Media influence may increase in a time of crisis when there is little chance for discussion. The attentive elites may have more power on issues that develop more slowly or that touch organized interests such as unions, which act as reference groups. We discuss this issue more thoroughly in Chapter 8.

Results

Obviously, not all opinions and attitudes are equally important. Whether a person favors bigger defense budgets is not as important as whether he or she believes that all politicians are dishonest. Perhaps the most important attitudes that develop in the socialization process are those relating to the individual's own place in the political system and those relating to the system itself. Most Americans learn as children that the United States is a great and good country, that our economic and political systems are the best, and that everyone has a chance here. These ideas, first in the world acquired in the family, are powerfully reinforced at school. The notion of America the beautiful is stressed both in such rituals as the daily flag salute and Thanksgiving pageants and in academic work. Most textbooks and most teachers celebrate American virtues and overlook our faults. According to Herbert Gans' recent study, the media reinforce this view by presenting the idea that we have a good system that suffers from occasional corruption by bad leaders.

There is also some evidence to suggest that early schooling promotes a concept of citizenship based on obedience rather than independence and criticism. Several studies indicate that the message conveyed to middle- and lower-class students is to accept the policies of the government and not question the leaders.

College experience seems to encourage independence, at least from parents' opinions. College in particular, and school experience generally, provides the individual with other sources of information and opinion. Over all, the higher the individual's level of education, the greater is the deviation from the views of the parents. Shifts in status may also change people's views. Those who rise from blue-collar to white-collar jobs are likely to become more conservative and to switch from the Democratic to the Republican party.

Among the attitudes that define a person's relation to the political system, two are especially important. **Political efficacy** (or political self-confidence) is the term applied to the feeling of being powerful, of feeling able to influence the system. Political efficacy is thought to be an important cause of political involvement. If people are confident at their ability and of government's response, they are more likely to get involved. Closely related to political efficacy is **political trust**—the attitude toward the political system. Do people feel that the government is operating effectively and honestly? Do they have faith in the government to do the right thing most of the time?

Before 1970 the general pattern in the United States had been for children to develop considerable trust in government and a high sense of political efficacy. As they grew to adulthood, some of these rosy views changed, but for the most part they persist. Some groups may have felt less efficacious than others—women generally scored lower in this category than men—but most people accepted the system and felt confident about their own place in it.

For certain groups, however, the results were quite different. Poor, white children who lived in rural Appalachia were much more negative and cynical about the government than the average child. Instead of seeing the President as more honest than most men, these children, before Watergate, saw the President as less honest than most. Instead of seeing the President as more capable than others, they saw him as less capable. Instead of a basic trust in government, they exhibited strong feelings of skepticism and cynicism. They viewed the government as uncaring and unresponsive. It seems likely that the children's views, to a considerable extent, reflected the feelings of their parents. In turn, the poverty and isolation of the communities probably shaped the parents' views.

Black children also developed attitudes different from the majority's. As they got older, they lost their original liking for the national government and their confidence in its ability to act for the people. White children retained this confidence to a much greater degree and also retained a more favorable overall view of the government.

In recent years, however, there has been a widespread decline of faith in government and in political efficacy. Vietnam, with its credibility gaps, and then Watergate, with its revelations of political corruption, have reduced the people's confidence in government. Participation seems to have declined as a result. The turnout for the 1980 presidential elections was the lowest in thirty-two years. The relationship between attitudes and activity is the subject of our next section.

Attitudes, Social Characteristics, and Participation

Among adults, those who have higher incomes, more prestigious occupations, and more education tend to have higher levels of political efficacy. The young and middle-aged, males, and longtime residents of a community also tend to have a stronger political self-confidence than the elderly, females, and transients. Of all the factors associated with political efficacy, education is associated most strongly. In a group with the same jobs and income, those with more education show considerably higher levels of political efficacy.

This attitude, and the social characteristics that go along with it, are in turn linked to levels of participation. People with a high sense of political efficacy tend to participate more in politics. They vote more often, and write letters to their representatives more often.

Different explanations have been offered for this pattern. Some writers say that middle- and upper-class people are more active because they have a greater stake in the system. Another view is that being successful economically and socially gives one the confidence to be politically active. These views emphasize the importance of the individual's experience and character. A contrasting explanation says that the pattern is caused by a bias in the system. According to this view, the political system discriminates against the poor and minorities, especially when they are not well organized. Either they are kept out, as blacks were for years kept out of southern politics, or they see that they will not get a fair deal and don't even try to participate.

Forms of Political Participation: Voting

For most Americans, voting is the basic political act. Only a minority go beyond voting to contributing money or time to a candidate, to engaging in political discussion, or to joining an interest group. At most, 25 per cent of the people engage in such activities.

For about 60 per cent of people, voting is the only form of political participation.

In a presidential election, the turnout is likely to run about 60 per cent of the voting-age public. Turnout falls off sharply in congressional, state, and local elections, and in primaries.

Voting Choices. Having an allegiance to a party is the most important influence on how a person votes. This **party identification** does not mean that the individual is a dues-paying, active member of the party. It is enough if a person thinks of himself or herself as a Republican or a Democrat. Of course, there are variations. Some people are died-in-the-wool party stalwarts who would stick with their party even if it advocated a return to monarchy. Others are weak party identifiers who are more easily swayed to vote against their party.

Sources of Party Identification. Children tend to acquire their parents' party allegiance, especially if their mothers and fathers agree. Nearly 75 per cent once adopted the same party as their parents, but more recent studies indicate that only 60 per cent do. In addition, there has been a general weakening of party identification in the United States. More and more people have abandoned the political parties and are becoming independents. Therefore, fewer children are inheriting a party preference.

As with other values and opinions, party identification can be changed by later experiences. Friends, job situations, a college education, or an increase in social status may have this effect. In general, the higher an individual's education and income level, the more likely he or she is to be a Republican. This does not mean that there are no rich Democrats or poor Republicans. We are stating a generalization: More higher-income people are Republicans than are Democrats.

Party identification influences more than voting. For most people, party is a key reference group for the political thought as well as action. If a Republican President goes to China, Republican party identifiers are likely to see it as good diplomacy. If a Democratic President makes the same trip, Republicans are more likely to see it as a sellout or a blunder.

In regard to voting decisions, party identification is the most important of several factors. One analysis refers to the electorate's **standing decision.** By this is meant that many people will vote Republican or Democratic, according to their party identification, year in and year out, unless something unusual happens to break the pattern. In other words, party identifiers tend to stick by their party. Their decisions were made before the candidates were even nominated.

Because there are more Democrats than Republicans, this kind of party voting tends to favor the Democrats. Their candidates know this and stress party appeals. Republicans try to shape appeals that will win over some of the opposition.

Voters are also influenced by the candidates, by issues, and by groups. In the 1972 presidential election, the late George Meany, then president of the AFL-CIO, made it clear that he preferred the Republican candidate, Richard Nixon. As the leading spokesman for organized labor, Meany may have influenced those union members (and others) who look to the AFL-CIO as a reference group.

Meany seemed to be affected by the Democratic candidate George McGovern's personality and by certain issues: He disliked McGovern and disliked some of McGovern's views, especially his stands on welfare and foreign policy. In both of these ways, Meany typifies processes by which a voter chooses a candidate. He was evaluating McGovern as a person and in terms of his policies. For many Democrats, either McGovern was not the sort of person they wanted as President or his stands on the issues were unacceptable. People who had voted Democratic for years, and who voted for Democrats for Congress in 1972, did not vote for George McGovern.

In 1980 nearly half of all union members voted for the Republican Ronald Reagan, despite the fact that union members generally vote Democratic. Some disliked Reagan's opponent; others objected to what they saw as a decline in America's international prestige and power. Still others wanted a change in economic policy. The combination of personality and issue voting helped to overcome party loyalties and to produce the Reagan victory. Whether this is a permanent or a temporary shift remains to be seen.

Among independents (those people who do not have a party identification), the factors of personality, issues, and groups play a much greater role. Because more and more Americans have become independents, these factors are increasingly important in deciding elections.

Elections

The primary mode by which ordinary citizens actively participate in politics is voting in elections. The act of voting is an individual one, not concerted or organized in groups although individuals may choose to vote in response to organizational preferences. In the United States, voting is by secret ballot. Not even a court of law can compel someone to reveal the manner in which he or she cast his or her vote. In many areas of the country, especially when there is a heavy turnout, voting is done by machine; in other areas, paper ballots are used. Anyone unable to be present on Election Day can vote by absentee ballot.

Congress has established a day on which, throughout the country, all votes for federal positions are to be cast: the first Tuesday after the first Monday in November. Almost all statewide elections in the fifty states are held on that day, and many localties have followed suit for their elections. Although state and municipal elections are of vital importance to interests and parties everywhere, their patterns and peculiarities will not be described at length here because the emphasis is to be on elections on a nationwide scale.

As noted in prior chapters, presidential elections are held every four years; every two years elections are held for one third of the Senate seats (for a six-year term) and for every seat in the House of Representatives. Elections held in nonpresidential years are called midterm elections because they occur halfway between presidential elections. All congressmen may run for reelection indefinitely; a President may run for reelection only once, unless he has served for less than half of the term of his predecessor, in which case he can run twice.

Congressional Elections: House and Senate

Members of the House of Representatives are nearly all elected in **single-member districts.** This is a defined area that is entitled to send one, and only one, delegate to Congress. Each voter has one vote. The candidate who received the most votes wins the election. He or she is the district's sole representative,regardless of how many votes his or her opponent(s) received.

In a number of state or local jurisdictions, there exist **multimember districts.** This is an area that is entitled to send two (or more, whatever is specified) delegates to the legislative assembly. The voter may have more than one vote that he or she is able to cast. Under some procedures, if the voter has more than one vote he or she may cast them all for the same candidate (bullet-voting), but more often than not, the voter may cast only one vote for a candidate. If the voter wants to exercise both of his or her votes, he or she must vote for two people. The candidates with the most votes are awarded the legislative seats, whether they are of the same or different parties.

There have occasionally been multimember districts for election to the House but, most recently, these have only been in periods of instability during reapportionment in some states. Senate elections are technically all in multimember districts because each state (district) is entitled to two delegates. But they are, in effect, single-member districts because, on all but very rare occasions, only one senator's seat from a state expires in any election year. Since 1913, candidates for the Senate have been voted on directly by the voters, and it is a winner-take-all contest.

In every even-numbered year, the entire composition of the House may change, while two thirds of the Senate will remain. This adds a theoretical element of instability to the House that is not present in the Senate. But, in practical terms, the theoretical element is severely diminished by the high rate (more than 90 per cent) at which incumbents in the House are reelected. In the 1974 elections, for example, it appeared that a dramatic upheaval had taken place when more than ninety new members were elected to the House. Yet, this result came largely because about fifty House members chose not to run again, not because ninety members were defeated. Most who ran for reelection were sent back to Washington in the same capacity. Such figures also indicate there is little reason to suppose that, because of its frequency of election, the House is any more responsive to the "will of the people" than is the Senate.

Presidential Elections

Unlike members of congress, Presidents are not elected directly by the people. There is an intervening mechanism known as the **electoral college,** which was established by the Constitution expressly to prevent direct election of the president by country's ordinary citzens.

The college is a group of persons, selected by the voters of each of the states, that does the actual voting for President. These **electors** transmit their votes to the president of the Senate at the seat of government of the United States. Each state selects a number of electors that is equal to the total number of members of congress (senators plus representatives) to which it is entitled. (In addition, residents of the District of Columbia may select three electors, the same number as the least populous state.) Thus, a state like New Jersey is entitled to seventeen electoral votes (that is, votes for the President by electors): one for each of its fifteen representatives and one for each senator.

The electors are chosen on Election Day every four years. Voters actually vote for them, and not directly for a candidate. The voting machine or ballot generally lists only the candidate; but the vote is actually cast for a group of electors (New Jersey's seventeen, for example). Or, perhaps, even more accurately, the voter in New Jersey casts seventeen votes simultaneously, for seventeen persons each of whom has pledged to cast his electoral vote for the named candidate. Each candidate whose name appears on the ballot has (in New Jersey) seventeen persons pledged, if they are selected, to cast their electoral votes for that candidate. All of the states except Maine, where electors are selected indiscrete districts follow this procedure.

The Constitution does not specify that the states must hold elections to determine the electors. Indeed, in the early days, the state legislatures in most states selected the electors. This presented no problem, either practically or in terms of democratic theory, as long as everyone was going to vote for George Washington anyway. But with the passing away of unanimity, the mode of choosing electors became important. And, gradually, states began holding elections that grew to be more than merely advisory. Finally, the uniform practice came to be to choose—by popular vote—between opposing slates of possible electors, so that the people's choice could be reflected in electors who agreed with that choice.

Occasionally, an independent slate of electors may run without pledging in advance for whom they will cast their electoral votes. Such an "unpledged" group of electors was successful in Mississippi in 1964.

Although prospective electors generally pledge themselves to cast their electoral votes for a specific candidate, there have been instances of electors violating their pledges and voting for someone else. State laws vary in their requirements for pledging. It would probably be unconstitutional for a state to punish someone for failing to live up to the pledge, even if taken under oath. Yet, such failure by an elector certainly violates the promise made to the voters and, in effect, takes away the voter's choice in voting.

In order to be elected President, a candidate must secure a majority of the votes in the electoral college—at present 270 of 538. If no one achieves a majority, the election is decided immediately by the House of Representatives from among the top three vote getters.

Each state's House delegation casts one vote; a majority—at present twenty-six—is necessary to win. If no one has a majority and more than two have won votes, the person with the fewest votes is dropped and another vote is taken; they continue to vote until one of the two persons achieves a majority. If there is no decision by Inauguration Day, January 20, the Vice President acts as President until one is selected.

Votes are cast in the electoral college for Vice President in the same manner as for President and by the same electors. Again a majority is necessary, but if no one gets it, the Senate selects the Vice President from among the top two, with the senators voting individually; a majority of all the senators is necessary for election.

Several proposals have been made to modify this awkward procedure. The two most prominent are (1) direct election—simply counting all the votes and awarding the office to the victor, perhaps requiring him to receive at least 40 per cent to avoid a runoff, and (2) a modified electoral vote system where the electoral votes of a state are awarded not on a winner-take-all basis but rather in proportion to the votes cast for each candidate. Both proposals would try to avoid the anomaly that, as can happen now, the most popular vote getter nationwide may not win the most electoral votes and may, thus lose the election.

The last time this occurred was in 1888, when Benjamin Harrison, although receiving fewer popular votes than the incumbent President Grover Cleveland, won a majority of the electoral votes and was "elected" President.

Some Notable Elections

National elections have often signified basic attitudes or changes in the American body politic. Yet, on occasion, idiosyncratic factors have led to some unusual results.

The election of 1800 was decided in the House after two Republicans (Thomas Jefferson, the party's nominee for President, and Aaron Burr, the vice-presidential nominee) tied for the lead. Jefferson's bitter opponent, Alexander Hamilton, the defeated Federalist candidate finally threw the election to him because of his (Hamilton's) even more intense dislike for Burr, who was relegated to the vice presidency. Burr later killed Hamilton in a duel in Weehawken, New Jersey, and was subsequently tried for (and acquitted of) treason in a matter unrelated to the duel.

The election of 1824 was also decided by the House when Andrew

Jackson, the leading vote getter, failed to achieve an electoral vote majority. The House selected John Quincy Adams over Jackson. Jackson won on his own in 1828 and 1832, reforming the Democratic party in the process. In 1860 Abraham Lincoln won a majority of the electoral votes although he failed to achieve more than half of the popular votes. In 1876 Republican Rutherford B. Hayes became President after a congressional commission of eight Republicans and seven Democrats voted 8 to 7 to award the contested electoral votes of three southern states to him. Although Democrat Samuel Tilden won more popular votes, the commission's decision gave Hayes an electoral vote majority of one.

The year 1888, as was noted, was the last occasion in which the leader in popular votes (Cleveland) received fewer electoral votes than his opponent (Harrison). But then, in 1892, Cleveland became the only President to come back to win another term after having been defeated for reelection. The 1896 victory of William McKinley marked the beginning of a generation of Republican dominance in national politics.

In 1912 Woodrow Wilson became another "minority" President, receiving fewer than half of the popular votes but achieving 435 electoral votes. Former President Theodore Roosevelt, running as the candidate of the Bull Moose party, received more popular and electoral votes than the Republican candidate, incumbent President William Howard Taft, ironically Roosevelt's hand-picked successor, who received eight electoral votes for reelection. After three successive Republican victories, Franklin D. Roosevelt, in 1932, fashioned the first of his four overwhelming popular majorities, beginning a stretch of Democratic dominance in national elections—the exceptions having been Republican Congresses in 1946 and 1952 (and a Republican Senate in 1980) and the election of Republican Presidents Dwight D. Eisenhower in 1952 and 1956, Richard M. Nixon in 1968 and 1972, and Ronald Reagan in 1980. Presidents John F. Kennedy in 1960 and Nixon in 1968 were both minority presidents like Wilson in 1912, although Nixon was overwhelmingly reelected in 1972.

The facts that (1) the House has not had to decide an election since 1824, and (2) not since 1888 has a President been selected by the electoral college who received fewer popular votes than his opponent have dampened the movement for reform of the presidential election process. It seems safe to predict that, should either occur again, the pressure for modification might be irresistable.

Election Issues and Decisive Factors

Although we do not explore fully the complex determining factors in national elections, nonetheless a few comments can be offered.

First, incumbents, whether they be Presidents, members of congress, or others, have an enormous advantage. Statistically they only rarely get defeated at the national level, despite recent presidential history.

Second, the critical national issues in presidential elections have been domestic in nature and predominantly economic. Occasionally, a war hero gets elected (Eisenhower, Grant, Jackson), but it is most often the popular judgment of who is more competent to lead us to prosperity that determines the winner. Foreign policy only occasionally is a truly significant issue, such as in 1916, 1944, and perhaps 1964 or 1968.

Third, personalities (or that elusive term *charisma*) often are a decisive factor. The campaigning abilities of Truman over Dewey in 1948 and Nixon over McGovern in 1972, as well as the apparent abrasiveness (plus his Catholicism) of Al Smith in 1928, demonstrated that a choice based on issues is frequently not the primary one made in a presidential election.

Fourth, Presidents have coattails—that is, they attract voters to their party during an election. The consequence of this phenomenon is that the Congress elected during a presidential election year tends to be more heavily weighted toward the President's party than would be suggested by the numbers of adherents of each of the national parties. A further consequence is that, in the off-year congressional elections (when the President is not running), the natural balance reasserts itself and the President's party tends to lose seats in Congress (even more so when the President was overwhelmingly elected two years earlier).

Political Parties

Political parties are the most significant *organized* mode of citizen participation in politics and, except for the act of voting, are the most important of all acts of participation. Parties provide a means for citizens to classify the choices available in elections, and they enable citizens to interpret the results determined by the electoral process. In the remainder of this chapter we deal with parties essentially from a national perspective, but it is well to keep in mind that, for many purposes, American national parties can be most easily understood as temporary coalitions of the fifty state parties with the same name. Nonetheless, American parties are perceived by both officeholders and private citizens as national in scope and function.

The Party as Group Contestant

American society is comprised of many different and competing groups. One of these identifiable types of groups is the political party, of which there are presently two major ones: the Republican party and the Democratic party. The names have only historical, and not ideological, significance. Moreover, these have not always been the only parties in America, nor even the only *major* ones.

The definition of what a political party is has been the subject of controversy. William N. Chambers have given perhaps the most helpful definition. He calls a party a "relatively durable social formation" with three major characteristics: (1) it seeks power in the state, (2) it has a structure that helps to connect the people with their government, and (3) it generates symbols of loyalty to itself. Distilled to its essentials, leaving the remainder as implied, this definition approaches Allen Sindler's notion of a party as simply a stable organization seeking control of the government.

Two factors are noticeable and significant in these and most other definitions. First, a party, properly speaking, is conceived of as being organized and as lasting for a reasonable lengthy period of time. It is not a fleeting phenomenon but a recurring one, a permanent competitor in the political arena. The time necessary for an organization to qualify as a "party" is not clear, but it is certainly more than the duration of one election campaign and somewhere short of a generation.

Second, to be defined as a party, it is not necessary for the organization to reflect any particular social or economic interests. Although a party may encompass within it, or be comprised of, an interest group or class, it need not do so. Or, specific interest groups may shift their allegiances from one party to another over a period of time.

In this respect parties are unlike other group contestants in politics. Whether a party wins or loses in an election may, in effect, advance or retard one or a set of societal interests, but this need not be the result. Moreover, parties perform a wide range of functions or services for society that are not related to other group activities. These functions or services can be divided into three categories: those that are involved with *organizing the electoral process;* those in which the party helps to *organize the government;* and those where the party serves as an *agent of social control.*

The first set of services concerns the ballot box. Parties put forward candidates to run in elections and for specific offices. They help to define and make manageable the choices that the voters face, concerning both personnel and policies. They put together campaigns that help to pass on information to the voter about public issues. And they provide a means of identification of persons and policies, especially for those public offices about which voters know little and for which they often have no other way to distinguish among the candidates.

The second set concerns running the government. Parties provide a ready source of personnel to fill vacant jobs, especialy at the policy level. Recruits for these appointive jobs thus have at least a nominal loyalty to the chief executive and a minimum incentive to follow his directions. Parties help to mobilize support for the government's programs and provide a focus for approval or disapproval by the populace. The party serves what has been called a brokerage function: it can act as an agent of representation, a point of connection between the citizen and his government. On occasion the party may be a source of policy, either acting independently or by reflecting the position of a constituent group.

The third set of services, or functions, performed by political parties consists of what has variously been called integrative, socializing, or constituent functions. Parties serve society in several ways here. They provide a conduit through which established interests can make their weight felt in government. They incorporate both new interests and groups into the political process. They educate such interests into the acceptable pathways for securing their goals. They help to channel social conflict into a framework in which it can be resolved peacefully. They provide coalition structures for contestants in the political process, so that power can be achieved and shared by varying interests.

There is no inevitably about parties and their activities. Any or all of these services and functions might be (and some are) performed as well or better by other institutions. Parties might even perform predominantly different tasks (as they have at times in the past). These are, to a greater or lesser extent, simply what parties do for American politics today.

In addition to what political parties do for the system, there in a sense in which the party may be looked on as an interest group, as V. O. Key has written. Like other "permanently organized interests," a party is a continuous competitor in the political process. It has two objectives that it seeks to satisfy. First, it seeks policy preference. That is, it attempts to use control of the government to incorporate its preferred policies into the public policy of the country. Such policies are, in the American system, not often ideological. Nor are they the same policies year after year, except as, for example, the Democratic party generally prefers pro-labor policies and the Republican party has generally been pro-business. The policies sought to be furthered by each of the interest group-parties change over the years and even from election to election. When a party achieves power, it may then put its preferred policies of the moment into effect.

Second, and perhaps even more important, a party seeks jobs for its professional membership. At the federal level, thousands of positions are not civil service (as are many thousands more at the state and local levels). The occupants of these positions serve at the pleasure of higher appointive (or elective) officials. These jobs represent the party's stake in elections. Party organizations generally have a small payroll themselves. They depend on the public payroll as the source of employment for their most valued, hardest-working, and most necessary officials, in return for which the officials devote significant blocs of their time to party affairs. The jobs serve also as a reward for loyal party followers, as incentive for greater achievement by party regulars and for those being groomed for higher office, and as an attraction for recruits and new blood into the organization. Thus, as an interest group, a party competes with other interest groups for the resources of society.

Types of Parties

There are several different kinds of political parties in America. The most significant are the **"permanent" parties,** of which there are now two: the Republican and the Democratic. These parties regularly contest elections on a nationwide basis. They are represented in all fifty states (although in some states one or the other is quite weak—most notably the Republicans in some of the states of the Deep South), and in most of the political subdivisions of each of the states (although, again, in some localties one party or the other may be virtually nonexistent because of lack of support).

The Democratic party has had a traceable existence for almost all of the nation's constitutional history, although in its earliest stage it was named the Republican party. The present Republican party began in 1854 and has been a significant contestant in all nationwide elections since 1856. Prior to that, the Federalists (from about 1793–1816 or so) and the Whigs (roughly 1828–1852) exhibited characteristics of "permanent" parties.

With the possible exception of the first few decades of the Republic, none of this country's permanent parties has been the bearer of a consistent ideological viewpoint. To this extent the permanent parties in the United States differ markedly from the idealized version of parties on the European, or continental, model: organizations that offer distinct and coherent social, economic, and often class-based programs for the approval of the voters. America's permanent parties are coalitions, or conglomerations, of varying interests of which it can hardly be said there is anything approaching a coherent program to unify them. Moreover, because European parties quite often in fact do not offer distinct programs (for example, the 1974 British elections), and because it appears that political parties made their first appearance in modern guise in the United States, it might well be argued that the European model is the mutation, not the ideal.

Another variety of political party in America is the phenomenon known as the **third party.** As the label implies, it is generally a third force superimposed on an ordinary two-party contest. Third parties on the national level have not been permanent—in the sense that they never contested a series of elections over a period of time, at least not with any substantial effect. They have been limited to a surprising or influential showing in very few national elections, only once (in 1912) securing more electoral votes for President than a permanent or major party.

Third-party movements have most often arisen around a narrow social or economic policy preference or have centered on a particular candidate. Because the effort to secure majority status and acceptability for the views of a third party almost inevitably involves the party in a search for allies, it has been the recurrent fate of such movements, once having located allies, to be swallowed up by one or the other of the major parties with those adherents it has sought to ally. In this manner, third parties most affect the political scene by leaving it.

Third parties arising from popular interest in one prospective candidate do not often survive the political life of that candidate and have not been very common. Nevertheless, the third-party movement that was organized around Alabama Governor George C. Wallace was a substantial force in elections.

At the state, or local level, third parties have, on occasion, been more long-lasting. The liberal party in New York since 1944 and the Conservative party in the same state since 1962 are some recent examples.

Third parties, even though they may later merge with a major party, ought to be distinguished from an apparently similar phenomenon that is more properly characterized as an **insurgent movement.** Periodically, within a major party, factions may develop around particular policies or leaders that so deeply divide the membership that the minority, or losing element, within the party cannot reconcile itself to the current leadership. The challengers, or insurgents, may then conduct a campaign for control of the party, in the course of which they may refuse to lend or provide any support to the existing leadership or to the party itself.

It is this tactic that creates the similarity to the third-party phenomenon. The distinction lies in the insurgent movement's origin within the party and its struggle expressly for control of the party, not to displace the party or to add a third force of the electoral competition. Insurgents, like third parties, can be bought off by policy concessions or even through patronage, or they simply can be ineffectual and unsuccessful. Occasionally the insurgent movement wins and displaces the existing leadership, although this more often happens at lower levels than at national levels, especially in those situations in which one party is dominant and the insurgents provide a focus for all political opposition to the existing leadership.

Political Party Alignments

The most common and, in that sense, ordinary arrangement of political parties in America is in a **two-party system.** This is considered to be one in which both parties (and only those two) have at least a competitive or perceived chance to win the election. The parties need not alternate in control. Indeed, one party may go decades without achieving majority electoral support. But each must be *thought* to have a chance to win. The competition between the parties then finds its rewards in patronage, policy preference, interest-group success or failure, and increased chances of winning the next election.

We can discuss a two-party system because, in electoral contests for national power, either the Republican or the Democratic party has a chance to win. Although the Republicans have not won control of Congress for more than two decades, nevertheless they have always been a threat to win and they have, in fact, won the presidency in 1952, 1956, 1968, 1972, and 1980, and the Senate in 1980.

But a national two-party system does not mean a two-party system in every subdivision and locality. In some areas one of the two parties may not exist or, if it exists, it may have no perceived chance to win. This may be true where there are powerful historical reasons for a strong preference for one party over another, or where the interest groups allied with one party so predominate within a locality that the other party has no chance.

In such cases a one-party system emerges. An example of the former case is the South, or rather most of the former Confederate states. At the state level and most local levels there, the Republican party of Lincoln and the Union never took root after the Civil War. The latter type of one-party system arises, for example, in cities, where the Democratic party coalition embraces most of the residents (unions, liberals, ethnic groups, intellectuals, the pool , and so on). Northern New England, solidly Republican, is a mixture, with historical Unionist attachments as well as rural, conservative, and nativist predominance.

Another type of party system, rare in this country at any level, is the multiparty system, in which any of several parties has a chance to win or to become influential in the government. In many European countries such a party system exists, requiring parliamentary coalitions for purposes of governing to be formed after the election, rather than beforehand within the party structure.

Although it is not altogether clear why the two-party system is the dominant one in America, we can cite some significant reasons for it. The single-member district and the selection of executives independently of (that is, by vote separately from) the legislature are both winner-take-all governmental structures. This tends to force coalitions to be arranged *before* the election and probably accounts for the absence of multiparty systems. The existence of popular elections and the fact of a plethora of contending, opposing interests probably prevent a nationwide one-party system. "Congruent preferences"—that is, that people tend to vote for the same things or the same labels (a perceived equivalence) at all levels—tend to extend the national system down to political subdivisions and to structure contending forces within a preexisting, convenient two-party framework. Moreover, the probabilities are that a random distribution of party loyalties among all the political subdivisions of the country would yield some concentrated areas of support for one party or the other, even without historical of sociological factors present. Thus, we would expect to find some one-party states or localities in any national two-party system, but most of the subdivisions would have two contending parties.

American National Party Systems

There have been five fairly distinct periods in the history of political parties in America. Each one can be characterized as a separate party "system," although all have been two-party systems. The last three have had the same two parties, and one party has lasted through all five periods. The major distinctions among the systems have concerned the social or economic elements aligned within each of the parties during a period and the political background of the times. The years assigned to each system are mostly benchmarks rather than cut-and-dried chronological dividing lines.

The first party system arose in the last years of the eighteenth century, about ten years after the Constitution took effect, and lasted for about twenty years. The major parties were the Federalists, the party of Alexander Hamilton, John Adams, and, at least by association, George Washington; and the Republicans, a party so closely related in the beginning to the fortunes and politics of Thomas Jefferson that it is often referred to as the Jeffersonian party.

The tensions involved in the early struggles to make a new nation and the new Constitution work drew the leaders into recurring patterns of association and conflict, based on their mutual, or at least nonantagonistic, interests. The group that became the Federalist party basically respresented commercial, banking, and trade interests. They sought a strong national government capable of enforcing obligations, paying debts, and generally creating a favorable milieu for activities of commerce, especially in cities and in the populous

North. Jefferson and his allies represented rural, agricultural interests (stereotypically, the small independent farmer in the countryside) and vigorously opposed a strong nationally oriented central government that would take power away from state and local governing bodies.

The Republicans first took national power in the election of 1800 and thereafter never relinquished it to the Federalists. As the Jeffersonians (especially after Jefferson) became more accustomed to national power and as commerce prospered under Republican rule, the Federalist party disintegrated until, in the years around 1820, it disappeared altogether. The "Era of Good Feeling" during the administration of the fifth President, James Monroe, was essentially a one-party era.

The beginning of the second party system was marked by the election of President Andrew Jackson in 1828. Jackson refashioned the Republican party (which had become known as the Democratic-Republican party and was soon to be shortened to the Democratic party) as a vehicle for his election and reelection and to perpetuate its own organizational interests. The party system was an election-oriented system, without too much emphasis on policy preference. The Jacksonian era marked the integration of new interests from the West into the political process, as well as a significant expansion of the franchise.

The opposition of Jackson centered first, in the late 1820's, around Henry Clay of Kentucky, and was given a shot in the arm by adverse reaction, especially in the South, to Jackson's choice as successor, Martin Van Buren of New York. By the late 1830s these interests had coalesced into an organization known as the Whig party, which elected a President in 1840.

This second-party system existed without significant ideological or consistent policy competition, although it was national in scope, devoid sectionalism, and focused on organizational victory in elections. It eventually broke up over the issues of slavery and sectional rivalry—on the inability to come to grips with those terribly divisive problems. The Whigs disappeared after the 1852 elections, but the Democratic party survived (probably because it was better organized and more thoroughly rooted in people's minds and habits).

The third-party system is usually dated from 1865, the year the Civil War ended and politcs returned to "normal." But the new Republican party had been born in 1854 (absorbing may old Whigs), ran a candidate for President in 1856 (General John Frémont, who was soundly trounced in finishing second to James Buchanan), and elected its first President, Abraham Lincoln, in 1860 (although with only about 40 per cent of the popular vote in a four-man race, as the Democratic party split three ways). Moreover, as analyst Eric L. McKitrick has shown, the Republican party was a vehicle for political control in the Union during the Civil War. And Lincoln gave explicit recognition to the two-party nature of the system by dumping Republican Vice-President Hannibal Hamlin of Maine in 1864 and selecting Union-Democrat Andrew Johnson of Tennessee to be his running mate in a play for bipartisan support.

The Republican coalition, down to the 1890s, tended to comprise old Unionists, business interests (especially since they were mostly northern), blacks (for obvious reasons), Protestants, farmers, and "nativists." The Democrats (referred to in the 1880s by their opponents as the party of "Rum Romanism, and rebellion") brought within their wing southerners, Catholics, new Americans (predominantly immigrants from northern Europe), and some city dwellers. The Panic of 1893, and the Depression that followed, during Democratic President Grover Cleveland's administration, stigmitized the party for a generation as incompetent in economic affairs.

The year 1896, bringing with it William Jennings Bryan's "Cross of Gold" speech, marked the beginning of the fourth-party system. The Republicans maintained their influence with business interests, blacks, and Protestants, but gained the loyalties of immigrant families, many urban dwellers, and early organized labor (a seemingly unholy coalition) because of their apparent economic competence. Meanwhile, Bryan brought rural dwellers, farmers, populists, nativists, and anti-imperialists into a Democratic coalition in which southerners were still influential.

The only Democrat elected President during this party system was Woodrow Wilson, elected with around 40 per cent of the popular vote during the year (1912) of a split in the Republican ranks. Wilson was reelected in 1916 on an antiwar platform, a position he rejected one month after his second inauguration. Again it was an economic event that triggered the breakup of the fourth-party system and the formation of the fifth: the Stock Market Crash in 1929 and the ensuing Great Depression during the administration of Republican Herbert Hoover.

The benchmark of the fifth-party system is normally regarded as the election of Franklin D. Roosevelt in 1932, although a Democratic

Congress has been elected in 1930, the first since Wilson. The Roosevelt Democratic coalition (the essence of which still exists) continued its relationship with southerners, Catholics, and populists, but lost Bryan's rural area dwellers, nativists, farmers (to some extent), and the anti-imperialists and isolationists. In their place the Democrats picked up labor, blacks and other ethnic minorities, immigrants, the poor, the unemployed, and intellectuals, bringing about the virtually complete destruction of big-city Republican party machines. The Republicans held on to business interests (now opposed to organized labor, within a party structure, for the first time) and Protestants, picked up the remnants of the Byran coalition, and acquired an overall conservative tinge. Thus, this system began to present a vague, uncertain ideological character that had been absent from the party system since Jefferson's time.

The fifth-party system is extant, after five decades. This has been the longest stretch of any of the party systems and, for that reason alone, one probably ought to be looking for a new alignment of the horizon.

It is difficult to foresee whether the impetus for a realignment is present and whether some present departures from the existing coalitions are harbingers of the future or mere aberrations. For instance, some of organized labor (led by the Teamsters) has supported Republicans Nixon, Ford, and Reagan, and some influential black leaders, such as Rev. Ralph Abernathy, came out for Reagan in 1980. Does this portend a breakup of the Democratic party coalition? Prediction here seems especially difficult. Among the possibilities that have been offered as the fundamental split are liberal versus conservative; coastal versus rural interior areas; urban versus rural; rich and poor versus the middle class; business and big labor versus the unorganized; and so on. And the nature of the event that would be necessary to trigger a realignment demands equal speculation.

The Structure of Political Parties

The bulwark of the American political party system is the state party organization. Each major party is organized in each of the states under the laws of those states. Together these fifty "separate" parties make up the national party. They are the fundamental building blocks of the national party, as well as the vehicles through which elections are contested and other party functions discharged. When party workers and officials speak of "the party," they are most often speaking of the state party (or even, in some cases, the county organization), not the national party. Although state parties will not be described here at any length, their significance must be kept in mind.

National Party Structure. American national political parties are really coalitions of separate elements, with an overlay of structure that is national in scope but only skin deep. There are two senses in which the national party is describable as a "coalition."

First, each of the state parties is independent of any of the others. None has any control over, demonstrable effect on, or significant interaction with even a neighboring state's party organization, much less the party in another corner of the country. This independence, and the jealousy with which it is guarded, means that the national party is a conglomeration of those fifty elements, a cover organization constantly struggling for a separate identity. Its powers are limited to what the constituent parties are willing to grant it (or can be tricked into granting it). It is, thus, a coalition structure, unified only by (1) attachment to a common label; (2) perhaps some extremely general agreement on principles; and (3) a common interest in winning the national elections. Of these, the last is probably the most significant for the national party and accounts for most of the structure of the national organization.

In a second sense the national party is a coalition of interests and interest groups. This is the sense in which, historically, the different party systems have been distinguishable. Parties, in order to win votes, have had to incorporate appeals to various groups of voters who have certain policy preferences (usually in accord with their interests and values). And various interest groups have chosen to affiliate themselves informally with one or the other of the parties, either in order to maximize their chances of translating their preferred policies into law or because an opposing, directly antagonistic interest is affiliated with the other party.

The diverse elements of this coalition may have virtually nothing in common with one another, except for party label. Each party is an aggregate of interests rather than a unified interest. Thus, it is possible (indeed, built into the system) that the coalition may fragment over specific policy choices at any one time or, ultimately, when a catastrophic social or economic event forces the realization among some interests that they would fare better in a new coalition.

Achieving national power, then, is the driving force behind national party coalitions. Consequently, the national party acquires most of its significance at four-year intervals, when a Presidential election occurs. Congressional elections in the off-years do not acquire nearly the same significance because the national organization has virtually nothing to do with selection of the candidates or conduct of the election. The four-year cycle, together with an inability to direct state party operations, leaves the national party practically moribund (except for the party cohesiveness of legislators) most of the time.

Each major party has a national committee that maintains a continuous existence throughout the cycle. Reflecting the state party coalition nature of the national party, this national committee is composed of two members from each state party organization (usually a man and a woman). Its function is not at all clear in practice, but its purpose is to be the embodiment of the national party and to maintain organizational continuity during the dry spells between elections.

The national committee elects a chairman who, together with as much staff as the party can afford (which is rarely much), implements the decisions and policies of the committee and, within the limits of the committee's tolerance and his or her own aggressiveness, works to improve the party's chances at the next election. Neither the national committee nor the chairman can issue instructions to the state parties about how to run state parties. Their only authority extends to national organization and to the quadrennial national convention at which a Presidential nominee is selected.

The national committee can appoint what are, in effect, subcommittees or special committees during interim periods or to serve at the convention. Such committees make rules, determine procedures, check on the eligibility of delegates, and help to draft platform statements (the statement of the principles and objectives on which the party officially bases its appeal in the upcoming election). They are significant insofar as the balance of contending forces within the coalition is worked out by these special committees.

In 1974 Democratic party held the first-ever interim convention, or miniconvention. Its purpose was to draft rules and procedures for the 1976 convention and to promulgate a statement of policies for the party. Whether this midterm convention will continue as a permanent feature and will spur the Republicans to do the same remains to be seen and depends on political judgments of its utility to the party.

The quadrennial national convention is easily the crowning event of the national party organization. Ostensibly a meeting to determine the favorite candidate of the party membership for President, it has been characterized as a diplomatic conference among the representatives of independent fiefdoms, as a circus, and as a manipulated puppet show. In reality, it displays all those characteristics. As a coalition structure, the party meeting must of course bring together the chiefs of the constituent elements. The convention is a pageant designed in part to entertain and inspire the party faithful. And, quite often, the formality of choosing a candidate is merely a pretense, little more than the ratification of the prior choice of powerful elements in the party organization.

Aside from a ruralistic need for pageantry, the future of the convention is uncertain. It was the creation of the second-party system, intended to replace the congressional caucus of the first-party system as a more "democratic" mode of selecting the party's nominee. It has since been modified by such innovations as primaries and elected delegates. A nationwide presidential primary, as well as several other options, could destroy the essential purpose of a convention, despite the subsidiary functions of writing the **party platform** and socializing.

Leadership of the National Party.   The President of the United States is generally considered to be the leader of his party on the national level, especially if he is eligible to succeed himself. The party was geared to his election. His influence is strong enough to dominate the national committee and often to influence the selection of its membership. The chairman of the national committee is effectively the President's appointed choice. His patronage power is huge and involves appointment to powerful, visible, and well-paid positions. The party will rise or fall to a large extent with the fortunes of the President and therefore will reflect his leadership.

Although the leadership situation is ordinarily fairly clear for the President's party, the "out-party" faces a leadership gap. There is no structural position in national party organization that is capable of the kind of influence a President can exert on his party. The heads of state parties (governors or otherwise), who are jealous of their independence, are unwilling to concede leadership to one of their number or to authorize the national committee chairman to exercise independent leadership. An individual may have influence derived from his stature, but that is not an institutional position. The out-party's defeated candidate in the last election is widely known as the "titular head of the party" but, except for his personal influence and that derived from his status, the title is all that the position is worth.

It has been supposed that the out-party's congressmen, especially if the party has a majority in Congress, could exercise effective leadership. After all, they are in a position to make policy and are actually helping to run the government. But as the Democrats in the first half of the 1970s learned and are now relearning in the 1980s, leadership by the congressional faction is difficult to achieve. Rank-and-file party members in Congress are reluctant to give very much more power to the congressional leadership; and, despite their desire to head the party, congressional leaders are reluctant to have ties to the national committee for fear of coming under the dominance of a noncongressional force and, thereby, compromising their own independence in Congress.

The lack of a structure of party leadership in national party organization prevents the formation of what the British call a **shadow government**—that is, a government in waiting ready to take over depending on the results of the next election. The advantages of such an institution are in predictability (knowing who the next leaders will be and what positions they will occupy), leadership (giving direction to the opposition and offering alternatives), and expertise (training for the job before assuming it). Newly elected American Presidents must choose assistants whom the voters may not know and who may not be familiar with the tasks to be performed. They are all rookies, rather than having been executives in training. Moreover, the public may have made a different choice had they known who would be the top officials of the new administration.

Party Responsibility

A generation ago, the American Political Science Association sponsored a report by a special Committee on Political Parties. The report urged, in effect, that the current party structure, with its absence of clear committment to consistent, specified policy alternatives, be modified to produce a more **"responsible" party system** in which voters would know what each party stood for, could cast votes to register clear preferences, and could develop mechanisms to hold officials accountable for not pursuing the voters' desires. Under the then- (and still-) existing structure, the major parties do not offer clear alternative programs; voters cannot, therefore, register explicit policy preferences; and accountability, either within the party or in the general electorate, is difficult to bring about.

In the years since then, some of the report's authors have withdrawn their allegiance to it largely because the desirability of party responsibility seems not so clear on reflection. If parties are a coalition of interests, party policy may have to be a compromise of many interests, rather than a clear, consistent program. Nor is it so clearly demonstrable that the model system for party responsibility—the British system—actually performs in a "responsible" manner. And the idea of accountability, or adherence to party programs and policies, may run afoul of the system of primary elections.

In any case, it is difficult to conceive of the device with which to bring about the proposed system, even if it were shown to be desirable. And it may not represent much of an improvement on the present structure. Modern political parties, with the constraints imposed on them by American society and values, appear to be responding to some of the structural needs of American politics. Only that social and political fabric will determine the future of the American party system.

GLOSSARY

Congressional caucus   A meeting of a party's representatives in Congress that, in the early 1800s, selected the party's nominees for national office; it was replaced as a nominating mechanism by the convention system.

Electoral college   A group of persons, selected by the voters in each state, that officially elects the President and Vice President.

Electors   Persons chosen by the voters of each state and empowered to cast a vote directly for the President and Vice President; they equal in number the total of senators and representatives to which the state is entitled.

Insurgent movement   A faction within a permanent party that seeks to displace the existing leadership or to change its policies.

Multimember district   An area represented by two or more persons in a legislative assembly.

Opinion leaders (the attentive elite)   People who follow politics, form opinions, and try to communicate their ideas to others, either informally in primary groups or through the written word and other formal mechanisms.

Party identification The feeling of an individual that one party is *his* or *her* party and deserves his support because it represents his or her point of view.

Party platform A statement, produced at a convention, of the party's position on or beliefs about the issues of the day.

"Permanent" parties Political parties that regularly and for an extended period of time contest elections on a nationwide basis.

Political efficacy The feeling of being able to influence the political system, of being able to get the results one wants.

Political party A stable organization that seeks to control the government by competing in and winning elections.

Political socialization The process by which people acquire their political ideas and opinions.

Political trust The feeling that the political system is operating effectively and honestly, that people in the government can be counted on to do the right thing most of the time.

Primary group A group whose members have frequent, fact-to-fact contact.

Reference group A group to which an individual looks for guidance on issues, such as who should be President, or whether schools should be integrated.

"Responsible" parties Parties that offer voters clear alternative policies and possess mechanisms by which party officials who do not pursue those alternatives can be removed from their positions.

"Shadow" government A group of leaders of the party not in power (the out-party) in which members of the group are assigned leadership posts corresponding to positions in the government, thereby readying them to take up such positions should their party win the next election.

Single-member district An area represented by one (and only one) person in a legislative assembly.

Standing decision The pattern by which many Americans who are party identifiers vote for their party's nominee, year in and year out. Only an unusual factor, such as the personality of the candidate, can change this more or less permanent decision.

"Third" parties Political parties that, although stable for a brief period of time, either do not last for long or fail to displace a major party.

Two-party system A political system in which two and only two parties have a competitive or perceived chance to win an election.

SUGGESTED READINGS

Burnham, Walter Dean. *Critical Elections and the Mainsprings of American Politics.* New York: W. W. Norton, and Company, Inc., 1970.

Campbell, Angus, et. al., *The American Voter.* New York: John Wiley & Sons, Inc., 1960.

Chambers, William N., and Walter Dean Burnham. *The American Party Systems.* New York: Oxford University Press, 1967.

Dawson, Richard, and Kenneth Prewitt. *Political Socialization.* Boston: Little, Brown and Company, 1969.

Erikson, Robert S., and Norman G. Luttberg. *American Public Opinion.* 2nd ed, New York: John Wiley, 1979.

Gosnell, Harold G. *Machine Politics.* Chicago: University of Chicago Press, 1937.

Greeley, Andrew M. *Building Coalitions.* Franklin Watts, 1974.

Greenstein, Fred. *The American Party System and the American People.* Englewood Cliffs, N.J.: Prentice-Hall, Inc., 1970.

Jennings, M. Kent, and Richard G. Niemi. *The Political Character of Adolescence.* Princeton, N.J.: Princeton Univ. Press, 1979.

Key, V. O. *The Responsible Electorate.* Cambridge: Harvard University Press, 1966.

Ladd, Everett Carll, Jr. *Where Have All the Voters Gone?* New York: W. W. Norton, 1978.

Milbrath, Lester W., and M. L. Goel. *Political Participation.* 2nd ed. Chicago: Rand McNally 1977.

Nie, Norman H., Sidney Verba, and John R. Petrocik. *The Changing American Voter.* Cambridge, Mass.: Harvard University Press, 1976.

Orwell, George. *Animal Farm.* New York: Harcourt Brace Jovanovich, 1946.

Pomper, Gerald M. *The Election of 1976.* New York: Longman, 1977.

―――― *Party Renewal in America.* New York: Praeger, 1980.

―――― *The Election of 1980.* Chatham, N.J.: Chatham House, 1980.

Sorauf, Frank. *Party Politics in America.* 3rd ed. Boston: Little, Brown and Company, 1976.

Sundquist, James. *The Dynamics of the American Party.* Washington, D.C.: The Brookings Institution, 1973.

Verba, Sidney, and Norman Nie. *Participation in America,* New York: Harper & Row, Publishers, Inc., 1972.

8 The News Media

Introduction

As noted in the preface, we have devoted a chapter to the news media for two reasons. First, the media have power. Other people and institutions, including politicians, lobbyists, and bureaucrats, do things differently from the way they might because of the media. Furthermore, the media's power is increasing. This chapter describes the different ways in which that power is exercised and considers some of the reasons for its growth.

Second, the media provide most of us with most of our information about politics. In this chapter we describe how this is done. The process affects the results. Knowing how a story gets into the newspaper or onto the evening news enables us to evaluate that story. For instance, we can become aware of the possibilities for "slanting" a story. More important, we can know the limitations of that particular medium. How much information can a ninety-second television report deliver? What kinds of material does television emphasize and what kind does it omit? What are the problems that face a newspaper reporter who tries to give a complete account of events he or she witnesses? What are the sources for the hourly news broadcasts on local radio stations? What are the pressures faced by reporters in all media when they try to deal with controversial materials? The descriptions that follow provide the information for answering these questions.

The Press

Structure

The main component of the print media is the newspaper. This is a regularly issued unbound publication that purports to present the "news"—a description and summary of information and events of interest to its readers.

There are more than eleven thousand newspapers in the country and only a few people never see or do not have the opportunity to buy one. Yet, contrary to what might be supposed, far more than half of the papers issue only weekly editions and not daily ones. Although the total number of people living in rural (as opposed to urban and suburban) communities is low, the number of rural communities is high; they are served by weeklies largely because they cannot support the costs of a daily paper. A significant portion of these weekly papers, especially in suburban areas, is local advertising handouts with a sprinkling of news, and many are distributed without cost.

American newspapers predated the Revolution by nearly a hundred years. Regular publication began early in the 1700s, although the first true *daily* paper did not arrive until after our country's independence. Benjamin Franklin was printing his Philadelphia paper more than forty years before the birth of the nation.

Both before and after John Peter Zenger's libel trial in 1735 (the first great landmark in the struggle for a free press), American newspapers were characterized by their partisan political tone. Separating fact from polemic in the early papers was difficult for the reader to do. The goal of the "objective" reporting of events, with opinion confined to the editorial pages and specified articles or columns, did not become widespread until the latter half of the nineteenth century and is even today the subject of controversy. Yet, today's reader expects to find factual reporting of news about which he or she can form his or her own opinion.

Daily newspapers are mostly located in cities, whose sizes vary. There are fewer than 1,800 dailies and, although the trend became a downward one after World War I, it seems to have leveled off in recent years. New York City alone lost three of its dailies at one time in 1966 (following a newspaper strike) and another a year earlier, but nationally the number of newspapers has been stable in the last generation. Most dailies print on weekends as well, but some publish only a Saturday or Sunday edition. Their circulation extends beyond the borders of the city of publication but is largely confined to the suburbs of the city.

The circulation of daily papers has risen along with the national population. Yet, competition among newspapers has fallen dramatically as many papers have folded. In 1930 more than 20 per cent of all American cities had competing daily newspapers owned by different persons; now it is fewer than 3 per cent. Here is a paradox: Newspaper circulation has risen while city dailies are dying. One explanation cites the fairly constant population of larger, older cities and the growth of newer cities. In places where circulation cannot rise, the increased costs of competing cause papers to fold. Circulation rises in newer, growing areas that have only one daily. Costs prevent a competitor from trying to break into the market.

Although we tend to think of newspapers as dispensing "news," most papers, even big ones, consist of advertising by more than half. It is advertising that supports a paper; the purchase price is only a small part of the revenue a paper needs to keep going. And, although a paper is local in origin and circulation, the average proportion of space allotted to local news other than sports or family-oriented features is a good deal less than 10 per cent. The remaining space, about a third of the paper, is devoted to material originating elsewhere: national or international news picked up from sources other than the paper's own reporters, comics, sports, syndicated columns, and the like.

Advertisers hope, naturally, that readers will look at the ads, but the reader who skips them finds that less than a fourth of the news concerns local events. Newspapers tend to emphasize state and national events, even where they can only print secondhand material because their own reporters do not cover those events. This emphasis contributes to the wide distribution of information about national and governmental events, which may be a favorable effect from the perspective of inhibiting provincialism and encouraging national unity. However, such emphasis is costly in terms of keeping readers only barely informed about events of local significance.

Despite this overall pattern of newspaper coverage, the influence of local papers on local matters may still be fairly high. Especially in discrete instances, whether of a recurring nature (like local elections) or on a particular issue (a controversial zoning change, a school-busing decision, or the sighting of a shark in coastal resort waters), newspapers grasp public attention. On such occasions, coverage is broader and deeper than usual, information from other sources is scarce, and the purchasers of the paper read the news more thoroughly than otherwise. They may even read the editorials (the paper's express and personal opinions), which most readers ordinarily neglect. The paper may become a forum in which the issue is contested publicly, and the style and content of the coverage may help to determine the outcome.

A few daily papers have come to be loosely known as **national newspapers.** Some, such as the *New York Times* (which likes to consider itself the "paper of record" because of its lengthy coverage of major events) and the *Washington Post,* have a predominantly local circulation and do extensive local reporting, but they are read widely by important national figures, especially in government. Others, such as the *Wall Street Journal* and the *Christian Science Monitor,* are oriented toward a national audience and are sold (or mailed) to readers across the country. These papers do little state or local reporting and, although they may exhibit special concern for a particular group of readers (as evidenced in their origins and name), they primarily report news of national significance. But these American national dailies do not compare, in terms of the pattern and volume of circulation, to the national papers in other major capitals of the world.

Newsmagazines. Weekly **newsmagazines,** such as *Time, Newsweek,* and *U.S. News and World Report,* developed in the twentieth century. They are exclusively national in orientation and serve as a sort of news-of-the-week-in-review. Although they occasionally originate news stories, their basic purpose is to summarize and report the news of major national significance of the past week. Their circulations are far larger than daily papers and are patterned after the distribution of population nationwide. (*Time* sells or mails more than six million copies, whereas even the *New York Times* has a circulation of only about 800,000.)

Advertising takes up most of the space in the weekly newsmagazines, just as it does in newspapers. In the remaining space, the news is usually divided into topics. Only two departments (usually called national and international) cover essentially governmental or political events. The other departments deal with social and cultural issues. Increasing government involvement in all aspects of society causes these departments to report political matters as well.

The emphasis in newsmagazines has traditionally been on digesting the highlights of the week's events in the different topical areas. During the last decade or two, however, the newsmagazines have increasingly developed feature writing—that is, a deeper, more exhaustive treatment of particular issues or events that qualify as news, whether current or recurring. This development is partially in recognition of the fact that they cannot often "break" stories—that is, provide the reader's initial exposure to a news item (as daily newspapers do)—but they can afford to provide a much more thorough exploration of the context and significance of a news story or social event than a daily paper is able to do. It is a way of attracting and retaining readers who want more than a rehash of the week's news that they probably read elsewhere.

The newsweeklies perform a significant "nationalizing" function. A story that appears in one newsweekly is disseminated to all the corners of the country at once. For newspapers to perform that function, there would have to be a nearly simultaneous agreement of hundreds of separate, independent decisions. Although, in a "hot" story, such agreement might well be forthcoming, other important, but not so noticeable, events or issues can be overlooked by a fair proportion of the newspapers. Moreover, the coverage of big stories is uniform nationwide, rather than underplayed in parts of the country and sensationalized in others.

Journals of Opinion. Still another component of the print media that has some political significance is what might be called **journals of opinion.** These are periodical, nonacademic publications, that appear at regular intervals (weekly, monthly) and are aimed at a more specialized audience than the general public. The *New Republic,* the *Nation,* and *Human Events* are examples. As the general label indicates, most journals of opinion are published from a particular perspective on events and issues. They present lengthy treatments of the issues, although usually not exhaustive ones.

Most of these journals are characterized by a determinable editorial bias. Consequently, their appeal is limited to those who are somewhat sympathetic to that bias. Here, the tension between "objective" reporting and "point-of-view" journalism is particularly great. Further limiting the circulation of journals of opinion is the fact that they do not digest or review prior news, as the newsweeklies do in appealing to a mass audience. Rather, they concentrate on only certain stories that interest the writers or publishers. The extent to which the potential readership shares that opinion or interest and appreciates the writing determines the level of circulation.

Some of these journals intentionally maintain one or more writers who do not share the overall bias of the publication. For years, the late Alexander Bickel, a moderately conservative law professor, wrote regularly about the Supreme Court for the liberal *New Republic.* A journal might be trying to broaden its appeal by appearing to present a balanced approach to the range of issues it covers. The writer might be so accomplished and skillful that even an opposing view of the issues is tolerated for the sake of quality. Or, he or she might be a "straw man" or convenient target for the journal's other writers to demolish.

Occasionally, these journals do **investigative reporting.** Their reporters uncover what becomes (when the other media pick it up) a major news story, usually an exposé of the nefarious activities of political figures whose views are not shared by the journal. But the primary emphasis is on critical commentary on a regular basis of national political issues or events.

Wire Services. The **wire services** are a major element in the structure of the news media. The Associated Press (AP) and United Press International (UPI) are the two major independent wire services in this country. They provide news reporting to papers all over the country that subscribe to their service. A paper may subscribe to one or both wire services.

AP and UPI employ hundreds of reporters. Some are assigned regularly to cover certain "beats," such as the White House, the U.N., or an election campaign, or to be available on assignment to cover a breaking news event, and some are **stringers,** who are not regularly employed but who report events happening in their vicinity when a regular wire service reporter is not around, and who are paid on the basis of each story they file that the service puts on the wire.

A newspaper that subscribes to the service need not use all the stories that come to it over the wire. Normally, there are far too many stories for a paper to use, so it must make its own decisions based on its need and its readership. But the services assure that information about major events is distributed throughout the country. To that extent, they too perform an important nationalizing function. The contribution of the wire services is even greater than that of the newsmagazines because a wire service story that is printed widely by the papers can reach a far larger circulation.

The emphasis of the wire service is on breaking news stories. They do little analysis or commentary and even less feature-length treatment of issues. Because of the nationwide nature of their distribution and the different audiences to which their subscribers appeal, the services attempt strictly to adhere to "objective," "just-the-facts" reporting. Were they to do interpretative or opinion writing, they would risk losing subscribers who did not share their writers' views. But this neutral stance has led to some criticism. For instance, if a reporter hears a politician speaking what the reporter knows is an out-and-out lie, he or she cannot say so for fear of appearing to be biased. The reporter is compelled to report simply what happened— what the politician said. This in itself may be misleading, for readers of the report may have no context or prior information with which to evaluate the statement made and may, therefore, miss the full significance of the event. The criticism, thus, is that truth is sacrificed on the altar of objectivity, the original purpose of which was to preserve the truth.

Wire services exist because most newspapers cannot afford to have a reporter regularly assigned to cover all major events and places. Only major newspapers have even a Washington correspondent (although some of them have entire bureaus) and even those that do have "their" man in D.C. cannot cover the whole spectrum of events. The wire services can do this relatively easily and cheaply by spreading the cost among their subscribers.

For the same reasons, many papers also subscribe to overseas news services. Reuters and Agence France-Presse are two of the most prominent wire services that relay news of the international scene to American subscribers. And some of the largest American papers, such as the *New York Times* and the *Chicago Daily News,* operate news services of their own to which smaller papers may subscribe. Individual writers like Jack Anderson and William F. Buckley, Jr., write articles that are syndicated regularly to subscriber newspapers. These syndicated articles can be opinions and commentary or they may be the result of investigations. They may appear daily or less frequently and, like wire service reports, the subscribers do not necessarily print every one.

Ownership

The pattern of ownership of American newspapers is a mixed one. Early papers were owned and operated by individuals. But, as in most other aspects of American life, the trend toward concentration took hold. Publishers of successful papers bought other papers and used the profits from those to buy still more. First, these empire builders bought papers only in other cities, but then they bought out competing papers in the same city. Newspaper chains—groups of papers in different cities owned by the same person or company— began in the late nineteenth century. They reached their peak in the decade after World War I and gradually subsided to their present level. Today's pattern is three-part: large chains of five or more papers stretched across the country; two papers in the same city owned by the same person (usually one is a morning paper and the other an afternoon paper so as to avoid direct competition); and a flock of individual owners of one paper. Even in the class of small, one-paper cities, there is no standard formula; the paper may be individually owned by a local publisher or it may be part of a chain.

Concentration was in good part the product of increased costs, which compelled the reliance on advertising to produce the necessary revenue. Rates for advertisements were cheaper as the number of papers serving an area diminished and as massive circulation of only one paper became practical. As Ben Bagdikian has indicated, American papers became fewer but fatter. The costs of entering the competition were nearly prohibitive. Consequently, few new papers are started any more, even though existing ones may die off, and there is little likelihood that American newspaper ownership will become less concentrated in the future.

Internal Organization of a Newspaper

A newspaper is organized much like any other business that produces something. Under the head of the company and his executive assistant(s) come the heads of the major division or units: (1) the planning and design unit, which determines what the product will look like and does all the necessary work to prepare it for manufacture; (2) the production unit, which physically makes the company's product; and (3) the sales and marketing unit, which sees to it that the product is distributed and revenue obtained. Each of these units is further organized to properly allocate the specialized tasks of the particular business.

In a newspaper, as Figure 8.1 indicates, the major units, or departments, are generically labeled editorial, mechanical, and business. Any newspaper may vary the names of the positions as well as some of the command and control lines, but this structure is a functional prototype to which all newspapers adhere to a signifcant degree.

As can be judged from the chart, the reporter, who is commonly thought to be the key person on a paper, is merely one of numerous types of employees on a paper's staff, and is fairly low on the totem pole. He or she works for a department editor, who in turn works for the managing editor, who in turn is subordinate to the head of the editorial department (sometimes called an executive editor), who again in turn may be subordinate to an immediate deputy of the boss—the publisher. Each of these "chiefs" may supervise the reporter's work and, in addition, the reporter's product may be influenced by others in the process of "doing" a story, as seen in the next section. Moreover, if the reporter works for an out-of-the-office bureau (for example, the Washington bureau of a major newspaper), he or she will have another layer of officials above him or her because that bureau may be only a division of a major department (for example, the "national news" department).

The **publisher** is in overall charge of a newspaper and is usually

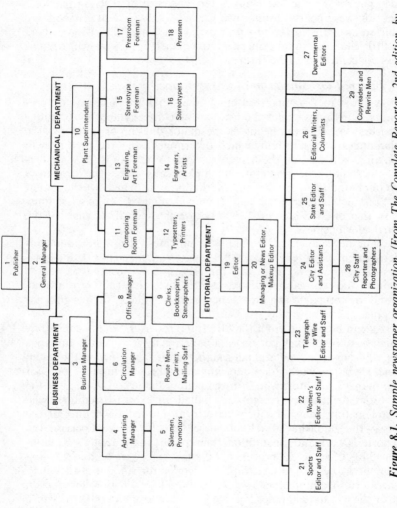

Figure 8.1. Sample newspaper organization. (From *The Complete Reporter, 2nd edition,* by Julian Harriss and Stanley Johnson. Reprinted with permission of Macmillan Publishing Co., Inc. Copyright © Macmillan Publishing Co., Inc. 1965)

responsible only to stockholders or other inactive owners if he or she does not own the paper outright. The publisher is generally not consulted on a regular basis about the editorial content of the paper, confining himself or herself to setting policy concerning broadscale definitions of emphasis or coverage. Exceptions usually arise only on matters of vital importance. For example, *Washington Post* publisher Kathryn Graham was occasionally consulted during some of the critical phases of the *Post's* Watergate investigation, and *New York Times'* publisher Arthur Ochs Sulzberger had to make the decision himself about whether to publish the Pentagon Papers.

The executive **editor,** or head of the editorial department, is responsible for carrying out the policy decisions of the publisher. He or she may take part in the editorial writing process, either directly or by close supervision. The editor may also occasionally be involved in refereeing disputes between departments or among personalities. As writer Gay Talese has pointed out, the *New York Times* Washington bureau is so prestigious that it often considers itself an independent fiefdom, reluctant to be ruled by the national political news department in New York.

The managing editor is in charge of the day-to-day operation of the paper. He or she "puts the paper to bed" every night, decides ultimately where stories are to appear or how they are to be featured, and is generally responsible for the "look" of a page. The managing editor also directly supervises the heads of the various news departments. These individuals are the immediate superiors of the reporters who gather and write (or rewrite) the stories that will appear in the paper. The department editor is also responsible for producing feature stories that go beyond daily news and may assign them to staff writers or he or she may write the features.

The internal structures of newsmagazines and opinion journals are similar. Newsmagazine departments lay more stress on feature writing, whereas journals generally are less rigidly divided into departments; however, functionally, the overall structure of newsmagazines and journals must be fairly similar.

The Mechanics of News Gathering

News that appears in the daily or weekly paper comes from a variety of sources. Prime among them is the **press release.** This is really an announcement by a newsworthy figure or entity that something has happened, is happening, or will happen. The release may come from an individual (a public official, a candidate for office, or a private or businessperson) or it may be put out by an organization (a government, or an agency thereof, or a private organization or business).

The press release may announce an accomplishment (or, more rarely, a failure), a policy, an event, or anything deemed worthy of public attention and appearance in the papers by the party presenting it. It serves two functions: an attempt to secure publicity for the announcer and a way to save time and shoe leather for the reporters. It is, at times, difficult to estimate whether the intention or effect of the press release is for information purposes or, because it is by definition one-sided, for propaganda. The art of public relations is largely the art of writing or determining the content of press releases.

Press conferences by public officials or private persons are essentially verbal press releases. Normally, the written handout accompanies the announcement made orally. Theoretically, a press conference is a dialogue between the questioner-reporter and the responder-announcer, thus making it more than simply an oral press release. It offers more of an opportunity for an official to find out what is on the mind of the public (or at least of its unofficial representatives) and for the public to get a more pointed explanation from the official. But this procedure can amount to a charade when the official is fully briefed on how to answer all expected questions, when he or she ducks or offers "no comment" to significant questions, or when questions are "planted" with accommodating reporters. Then a written press release would save everyone time and effort, although it would sacrifice the image of alert, responsive, and interested public servants.

Reporters are often given regular assignments or "beats" to cover, whether or not they expect anything of more than routine significance to happen. Nearly all the local news a paper publishes results from a dozen or so of these beats, which include city hall, police headquarters, the courthouse, and the local entertainment industry. The reporters assigned to these beats are the ones who attend press conferences and pick up press releases. They also provide on-the-spot coverage for breaking events that occur within their general area or jurisdiction. For example, the police reporter would cover a riot, the courthouse reporter would describe a major trial in progress, and the education reporter would report on a meeting of the local board of education. A larger paper would normally have some reporters available for varying assignments, depending on the flow of news from a particular area or areas.

Coverage of the nation's capital by a major paper is structured in much the same manner. A Washington bureau might have a White House correspondent, a congressional correspondent, a diplomatic or State Department correspondent, and a Pentagon correspondent, as well as reporters who cover the Supreme Court, the Justice Department and the FBI, the remainder of the executive branch, and other institutions. During an election year, in addition, certain reporters might be regularly assigned to cover particular major candidates, especially an incumbent president running for reelection.

The foregoing, brief list indicates the predominance of the administration, as head of the executive branch, as a newsmaking entity or source, with the consequent advantages in publicity. Because it is covered and reported on daily in its many facets, it makes news even when it is doing nothing. For example, the announcement by the Pentagon of the opening or closing of any army post can be held up until a "slow" day when nothing else is happening, even though the event occurred weeks ago or will not occur for another week or so. Press releases can be timed and coordinated (sometimes as a favor to reporters in order to give them something to report each day) so that a series of decisions made on the same day can be spaced out over the course of a week, both to give the appearance of constant activity and "busyness" and to avoid burying a favorable announcement that might win votes beneath an event of major significance.

As mentioned earlier, the wire services provide much of the national news for all but the largest papers. The Washington bureau of a wire service is organized similarly to those major papers that maintain their own bureaus. A wire service will have correspondents at the state houses of major states and in major cities. Capitals of smaller states and cities will have resident "stringers" whose reporting will appear on the national wire less frequently. Such reporters are usually available to cover breaking stories throughout the country and may be given specific assignments as well, such as covering a significant kidnapping in an area with no regular assignee.

Most papers print the wire service story directly as it appears on the wire and only occasionally rewrite it. The paper will use as many paragraphs of the story as it wants to make room for (or has room left for). Consequently, a wire service reporter must not only write as objectively as possible, but must take care to report the event as concisely and directly as possible. The most important aspect must be mentioned in the first paragraph, followed in the second paragraph by the next most important aspect, and so on, because some papers may have room for only one, two, or three paragraphs and will chop it off when they run out of space on the page, and different papers will run different lengths of the story. This leaves little room for interpretative reporting, which must be placed near the end of the wire story and often is not included in the article as it appears in the paper.

An important source of news is the **off-the-record remark** by an official or other newsmaker. The basis of this arrangement is an agreement between the reporter and the source that the reporter can use the information but cannot report from whom it came because the source does not want to be quoted or does not want it known (because it might damage him, his superior, or his position) that the information came from him. This arrangement benefits the reporter (who gets a story), the official (who is assured that the story or information gets out), and sometimes the public (which, thus, receives information).

When the remark is more than just an opinion or an overheard conversation, it is sometimes called a **leak.** No news leaks accidentally. The leak is intentional and may serve a variety of purposes. Information can be released covertly to generate support for policy or officials, to damage or defame an opponent, to undercut the factual basis of an opponent's position, to torpedo pending legislation or a policy change by focusing publicity on it prematurely, or to serve as a "trial balloon" to test public reaction before commitment.

When information is leaked, it may not even be important whether "insiders" can figure out who is the source, so long as there is no public record of the source. For example, just prior to the annual congressional consideration of the Defense Department's budget, the nation's press is overwhelmed by information about the (usually mammoth) size of Russia's armed forces and its newest missiles. The source of this ordinarily classified intelligence information is not revealed, even though everyone knows that it comes from the Pentagon. But, because the Administration and the armed forces are in favor of the budget request or want it increased, it is in their interest to reveal the information to convince Congress to act favorably on the budget.

On the other hand, when prosecution or dismissal of the offending source may be the result, it is vital that the source be kept hidden.

The leak of the secret Pentagon Papers was thought by the administration to be unfavorable and damaging. The alleged source, Daniel Ellsberg, was prosecuted (although not convicted), and the White House made an extensive effort to use "plumbers" to plug future leaks.

A more sophisticated and institutionalized type of leak is the *background press conference.* The name derives from its ostensible use to provide background or contextual information to reporters to aid them in describing events or a policy position. The key point about a "backgrounder" is that the source cannot be revealed and reporters are honor bound, as the price of admission to the conference, not to report the source directly. The purposes are the same as in other leaks. In addition, when a policy or position may offend another party (say, a foreign country), releasing information about it in a backgrounder serves to inform that other party while enabling the leaking official still to deal directly with the party.

For example, if the secretary of State wanted to declare a position toward another country and make it official policy, he might simply issue a press release or announce it in person. But if he wanted later to be able to back off from the position without losing face, he could hold a backgrounder. Then, rather than reporting, "The secretary of state said . . . ," the reporters would write something like "Informed sources high in the State Department said. . . ." Or, if the secretary wanted to be even more obscure as to source and still be able plausibly to deny that he said it, he could hold the conference on a "deep background" basis. Then, the attribution of source in the story might read, "Washington sources said . . ." On occasion, the official himself will state explicitly the extent to which he can be identified, such as "You may refer to me as 'an administration official.' "He may even add, as a postcript to a sensitive comment, "That's off the record" or "That's on background." Even the existence of the briefing is rarely mentioned.

Leaks and backgrounders have a number of pros and cons, from a reporter's or the public's point of view. Undeniably, information is released that would not ordinarily get out. It is "inside" information, sometimes advance information, or interesting "dirt" about public affairs and personalities. On the other hand, it is by definition one-sided, not objective, and often misleading. On such occasions, the reporter serves as a willing tool of someone who has an ax to grind or who is trying covertly to destroy an opponent or his or her position.

Another source of news is the result of investigative reporting. Here, a reporter digs out (sometimes with the help of leaked information) a story that exposes a situation damaging to the public interest. The result may be scandal, dismissal, or prosecution, sometimes even changing a policy. The sources may be secret or, as I. F. Stone used to report, may consist of obscure, but public, records.

Although investigative reporting performs a valuable public service, it has drawbacks for the reporter and his or her paper. It is tedious and expensive, often taking manpower away from more productive regular beats. It may not show any significant results. The investigative reporter's toughest job is often getting approval from his or her editor to spend so much time on the project. And, if the story is not thoroughly accurate or complete, it may never be used or, worse yet, may result in a black eye for the paper.

As in most other jobs, the pressures of the business largely determine the nature and quality of reporting. Reporters have deadlines to meet, determined by the times at which the paper must go to press. Even if the story is incomplete or unchecked, it must be ready to go by the deadline. If a reporter does not have a story ready, his or her superior may wonder whether the reporter is working at all. Consequently, the reporter is under pressure to produce something, even if it has little significance, even if in fact nothing at all has happened on his beat. (Thus arises the symbiotic reliance on well-timed press releases.)

Amid so much routine business, the unusual becomes newsworthy. Reporters are constantly on the alert for the "man-bites-dog" story, in which the unexpected occurs or where a new angle on an old story can be taken. Moreover, the reporter must be alert not to be "scooped," not to miss a major event, and not to omit reporting even something routine. Many a correspondent has been asked by his or her editor, "Why don't you have the same story as the AP wire?" To reply that it was not worth reporting is not often an acceptable excuse.

Legal Tangles. A number of reporters have lately been involved with the law. Often, in digging for a story about corruption or other illegal activity, a reporter will observe criminal conduct or use participants in a crime as his source. In recent years prosecutors have begun to require such reporters to give the particulars of the criminal conduct or to tell who was the source. Having no authority themselves to require the answers, they have called the reporters before a grand jury, which does have the authority. At that point, the reporter may be compelled, by the jury's power to imprison the reporter for failure to respond, to name his or her sources, or to testify about the conduct of persons whose confidence he or she gained.

In 1978 the Supreme Court held that prosecutors have the power physically to go into newsrooms without prior notice to the newspaper and to confiscate notes and materials relating to the reporting of alleged criminal conduct, provided only that the prosecutors first obtain a search warrant.

Journalists think this added pressure interferes with their ability to dig out stories involving criminal conduct because it makes information tougher to accumulate. No one, they claim, will do or say anything in front of a reporter who will subsequently be required to become a witness or whose notes may be confiscated. In defense of their profession, several reporters have gone to jail rather than betray a confidence.

Doing the Story.   What appears in a newspaper is not simply the result of a staff reporter writing an account of an event and the paper printing it. Often, a story is not even "written" by the reporter. He or she may telephone the paper with the story, only to have a **rewrite man** actually write it as the reporter is dictating it. The rewriting may be substantially different from the reporter's account. In any case, a copy editor must review the written material for errors, syntax, and so on, and the department, or news, editor must decide how much of it to use, whether it must be rearranged in any way, or whether it will be used at all. The managing editor or the **makeup man** must then decide, once again, if it is to be used and where to place the article in the paper, perhaps doing some additional editing as well. Someone also must decide how to headline the story (an art in itself). The reporter's original story may be barely recognizable by this time.

A wire service story must undergo the same process, although ordinarily the wire service itself will provide the needed rewriting and copy editing. The subscribing paper handles the other chores.

It is difficult not to deviate from purely "objective" reporting and publishing. Editorial judgments are by nature subjective ones. Placing a story on the front page will emphasize it; placing it on a back page will deemphasize it. The number of stories on a subject, as well as the headlines, will affect the reader's perception of the significance of the story. The decision to report or not to report an event is only the first step. There is plenty of room, beyond the reporter's own prejudices, for editorializing in and around the news story.

The opinions of those who run a paper are theoretically confined to the editorial page. This is the page where the editor (or publisher) expressly gives his views on public matters, views that are not strictly news. Editorials (which, labeled as such, may even appear on the front page) support or oppose candidates, pending legislation, or government policies, or comment on past and contemporary events. But in many ways management's views affect editorial judgments on the news pages, as when a paper is conducting a campaign against a particular public evil or when a publisher is doing all he can to influence an election. The theoretical standard of "objectivity" in reporting is not always attained or even made a goal.

The Electronic Media

History and Structure

Radio broadcasts began in the eastern United States early in the 1920s. By 1926 the Radio Corporation of America (RCA), a consortium formed by General Electric, Westinghouse, and Western Electric, had established a **network** of twenty-one stations called the National Broadcasting Company (NBC). Within a year, RCA had set up a second network: the two were called respectively the Red and the Blue networks. In February 1927 a rival network of sixteen stations, called the Columbia Broadcasting System (CBS), began operations. A third network the Mutual Broadcasting System, made a modest start with four stations in 1934.

Complaints from Mutual that Columbia and RCA were freezing it out of certain cities led to an FCC investigation. (For a discussion of the FCC, see Chapter 5, p. 181 and p. 285 of this chapter.) In 1943, the FCC ruled against NBC, forcing it to divest itself of the Blue network, which became an independent network, the American Broadcasting Company (ABC).

The number of stations and the number of radios increased steadily during the 1920s, fell off during the early 1930s, and began to rise again in the late 1930s. In 1928 there were 612 stations. After a dip to 591 in 1934, the number of stations rose to 1,867 in the late 1940s. At the same time, 94 per cent of America's homes had radios—about eighty million were in use. The networks had grown proportionately: in the late 1940s 519 stations were affiliated with Mutual; 272 with ABC; 179 with CBS; and 170 with NBC.

Radio reached its peak as a medium for entertainment and news in the late 1940s. Millions listened regularly to such favorites as Jack Benny and Fibber McGee and Molly, but also to speeches by political leaders and broadcasts of events such as political conventions. Beginning in the 1950s television took over many of radio's functions, especially entertainment and the live coverage of events. Nonetheless, the number of radio stations has continued to increase. Recent counts find over 4,500 commercial AM stations, and over 4,000 FM stations, including about 980 educational stations. In addition to the privately owned networks, National Public Radio connects a group of over 200 noncommercial stations. The number of radios in use has also grown to more than 320 million.

The networks began experimenting with television as early as 1927. Ten years later, RCA had established seventeen experimental stations. In July 1941 the FCC granted the first commercial TV license to an RCA station. World War II brought shortages of materials, curtailing TV's growth. Following the war, the development of television moved quickly. By 1948 there were a million home TV sets. More recent tabulations put the figure at more than eighty million. One estimate says that 97 per cent of the American public has access to television. The number of commercial stations grew to 746 in 1979; another 267 noncommercial stations were on the air, making the total of 1,013 stations.

While television grew, newspapers and radio declined. For most Americans television has become the major and most trusted source of news. In a recent survey 65 per cent identify television as an information source on which they depend a great deal. Fifty-two per cent refer to newspapers in this way, and another 39 per cent depend greatly on radio. Since 1966 the percentage of Americans having a "great deal of confidence" in the people who run television news has increased from 25 to 41.[1]

Both radio and television are organized around the local station, which broadcasts to a limited area on a fixed setting or channel. This pattern is not caused by technology, but by government policy. Increasing the transmitters' power would make it possible for a small

---

[1] Figures drawn from a 1973 Harris survey reported in U.S. Senate Subcommittee on Intergovernmental Relations, *Confidence and Concern: Citizens View American Government* (Cleveland, Ohio: Regal Books, 1974), p. 18.

number of stations to broadcast nationwide. In the 1930s a Cincinnati radio station with a powerful transmitter could be heard across the entire country.

The federal government's decision to limit broadcasting ranges was based on the idea that stations should be responsive to local interests and desires. However, the patterns of chain ownership and network domination of TV programming, make this a dubious proposition.

The four national radio networks own nineteen stations and have varying ties and contracts with hundreds of others. (The FCC limits network ownership of local outlets.) The influence of the networks has declined as many stations have turned to a "top 40" or "easy listening" format that relies on a disc jockey and records. In 1937 the networks collected nearly half of all the money made in radio; by 1967 the figure had dropped to 5 per cent. The local stations simply did not carry network programs. The days when families gathered around the radio to hear "The FBI in Peace and War" or "The Lone Ranger" had passed.

This does not mean that all radio stations are separated and independent businesses. Many commercial stations, approximately one third, are owned by chains and the number has increased steadily. (Bound together by common ownership, chains do not broadcast the same programs, although they may reflect the owner's political views.)

In television, networks are much more important. They accounted for about 40 per cent of all revenues. Network programming carried during prime time (7 to 11 P.M.) is estimated to be about 95 per cent of all programs played. These are the familiar weekly programs— "Archie Bunker's Place," "Mash," "Dallas," etc.

As in radio, chain ownership of stations has grown rapidly in television. No corporation may own more than seven stations, and few do, but many smaller chains exist. In 1967 nearly three quarters of commercial television outlets were controlled by chains. Further concentration of media ownership occurs when newspapers own radio and TV stations. This pattern is particularly common in big cities where 35 per cent of all TV stations are owned by newspapers.

Radio News

The average radio station requires a relatively small capital investment—in the neighborhood of $500,000—and a dozen staff people. A general manager, responsible to the owner, supervises a staff of engineers, disc jockeys, and announcers. The many stations of this size and the smaller stations usually have no news specialists or reporters.

When it is time for a newscast, the announcer or disc jockey simply takes the bulletins that have come in on the wire service teletype machine and reads them over the air.[2] To cover local news, the announcer reads stories from the local newspaper. This **rip-and-read** style of radio journalism applies to nearly all the smaller stations, and extends to the medium-sized ones as well.

Some of the latter may hire one or two news specialists and a stringer or two. Working under the direction of the general manager, these people will have time only to rewrite the wire services' bulletins and newspaper stories before reading them over the air. An occasional interview with a local figure, or a report from a stringer in a nearby city will be the main variations on this basic theme. Thus, most radio stations are simply rebroadcasting shorter versions of wire service and newspaper stories.

The largest radio stations have extensive staffs, including eight or nine people who specialize in the news. They usually work under the direction of one of the station's vice presidents, who is in charge of public affairs. Such a station will usually have extensive equipment with which to do on-the-spot reporting and interviews with public figures. With a staff of this size, the station is in a better position to do its own investigative and feature reporting, especially at the local level. Instead of presenting the hourly five-minute broadcasts as smaller stations do, the news staff may broadcast a nightly half-hour summary and a regular program on public affairs.

Most stations do some editorializing. General managers write and sometimes broadcast editorials for the smaller stations. In the larger operations there may be a commentator who editorializes regularly, a news director who writes and broadcasts occasionally, and a vice president who helps out more rarely.

In all these situations, the station's owner has ultimate authority over editorializing. The owner of a small station might supervise

---

[2] The wire services rewrite their news stories in a style suitable for radio and television broadcasts and transmit them over a special "broadcast wire." Stories are shortened and presented in a more conversational style.

closely or leave editorials to his general manager. On the medium-sized and larger stations that maintain separate news staffs, one would expect less owner control. However, some stations and chains are owned by people concerned with presenting a particular point of view. One prominent example was the late H. L. Hunt, an oil millionaire who owned a chain of western stations presenting a strongly right-wing point of view.

TV News

Most of the description of the structure and news gathering of local radio stations applies to local television stations equally well. Medium-sized and larger stations employ camera crews who travel with reporters to make film or videotape reports of local events, but with the exception of these technicians, the staff and the structure are similar.

The largest stations, especially those owned by the networks, often put on an hour's worth of national and local news before the network's national news broadcast. They may also do a half-hour late-night show and a morning program. Fifty or more people, including writers, reporters, cameramen, directors, and the "anchorman or woman"—those who read the reports before the cameras—work under the direction of a Vice President and a producer who makes assignments and chooses which stories will be put on the air and for how long. Figure 8.2 shows how these people work together.

Both the radio and television networks maintain extensive news organizations, including Washington bureaus and correspondents in foreign countries. Stations affiliated with the networks may draw on them for specific reports. The more important network contribution, however, is the half-hour nightly newscast of national and international news.

Those shows, known by the names of their anchormen—Dan Rather, Roger Mudd—are the major products of the network news organizations. A vice president directs the news staff and also supervises the people who produce specials and public affairs programs. On special occasions, such as political conventions, the network-President may supervise. As noted, TV broadcasts have become the most important source of news, both in terms of the number of people who depend on them and in terms of the trust that people place in them.

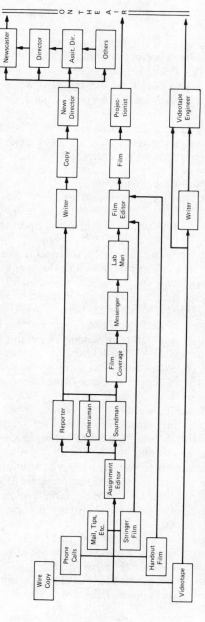

Figure 8.2. *The News Flow in a Large Television Station (From Television News, 2nd edition, by Dr. Irving Fang. Reprinted with permission of Hastings House, Publishers, Inc. Copyright © Hastings House, Inc. 1972)*

Network newscasts use the same sources as the national newspapers, and television reporters operate in much the same way as newspapermen. They depend on press releases, work regular beats, pursue leaks, and try to keep from getting scooped. There are, however, some important differences in emphasis and style that incluence content.

One major difference is that a television or radio report must be much shorter than a newspaper story. Thirty seconds is a long time on a four- or five-minute news program. On a half-hour show, ninety seconds is the average time devoted to a topic. In that time the anchorman or reporter can read only five or six paragraphs. There is little opportunity to give background, and even less to offer analysis, or to present more than one side of the issue. The result is that most broadcast stories are limited to the most important or most dramatic facts.

Another difference for a television reporter is the premium put on obtaining visually interesting material. Film of a candidate shaking hands in an old-age home may take precedence over a story on the candidate's economic program. How can economics be made visual? The consequence is that TV reporters become more concerned with a dramatic visual effect than with the substance of what is happening. Furthermore, the media are in danger of being manipulated by politicians and others who deliberately create dramatic events to get media attention. The virtue of electronic broadcasting is that it allows the audience a direct perception of an event. Viewers or listeners can judge the honesty and sincerity of a candidate, or the behavior of a protesting group.

They can only do this, however, if what they are shown is representative of the entire event. Take as an example a violent confrontation between demonstrators and police. If the networks broadcast a film segment showing six brawny policemen subduing one slender demonstrator, the viewer may get one impression. If the film shows the same demonstrator throwing rocks at the police, they may get another. The process of selecting and cutting film in a coherent fashion thus becomes crucial.

Because there is so little background, and because the reports are so short, the electronic media's presentations are almost bound to be fragmentary. They touch only the most important of the day's events and may not relate them to the ones that happened previously. In a newspaper account there is often space to give the context, to provide some details, and to offer the opinions of experts as to why an event occurred and whether it is a good thing. Even Walter Cronkite said, "We can't cover the news in a half-hour event evening. That's ridiculous."[3]

Occasionally the networks attempt in-depth reporting, but such efforts are risky. CBS did a famous special called "The Selling of the Pentagon," which described the military's extensive, tax-supported public relations campaigns. After a storm of controversy, including threats of investigations from hawkish senators, CBS seemed to turn away from this kind of program. However, in 1973 Walter Cronkite began to press for aggressive investigative reporting for the evening news program. He gave Stanhope Gould, a young producer, the assignment of finding out who had benefited from the Soviet-American grain deal. Gould produced a report shown in two segments, one eleven minutes long; the second, five minutes long. Devoting this much time to one story was a marked departure for the network news shows, but the immediate response seemed to confirm Cronkite's judgment. Even the *New York Times* called CBS to say that the programs had done a better job explaining the wheat deal than the *Times* itself.

Cronkite next assigned Gould to the Watergate story, which had just begun to surface after its initial dismissal as a "third-rate burglary." The first segment of the special report was shown on October 27, 1972, and ran for fourteen minutes, nearly half the program. The story's message was clear: political sabotage had been initiated by the White House. Again the story drew many favorable comments, but it also drew one unfavorable phone call. Charles Colson, President Nixon's special counsel—since convicted of crimes in connection with the trial of Daniel Ellsberg—called William S. Paley, the chairman of the board of directors of CBS. The second segment was cut from fifteen minutes to six.

These episodes illustrate two points. First, the contrast between these extended reports and the regular news programs shows the fragmented nature of most television reporting. Second, the vulnerability of the electronic media to government pressure is suggested. This subject is dealt with in more detail in the next section.

---

[3] Quoted by Timothy Crouse in *The Boys on the Bus* (New York: Bantam Books, 1972), p. 150.

The Pervasive Influence of Government

Although the news media comprise an institution that is not formally a part of government, government is not absent from its operation and behavior in a number of significant ways. In many countries the regime in power directly controls the content and structure of the news media. The control exercised by the American government is far more subtle, as well as less extensive and direct.

The First Amendment

The First Amendment to the United States Consitution provides that "Congress shall make no law . . . abridging . . . freedom of the press"; nor, according to the Supreme Court, may any state do so. But the extent of the freedom that may not be abridged, its content, and whether the electronic media are part of the "press" pose difficult problems that have not always been easily resolved.

The freedoms guaranteed by the Constitution have often been lumped together in the phrase, "the right to know"—that is, a political right belonging to the public that is the "press." Professor Edwin Emery has described this right as consisting of three main pillars: (1) to publish without official approval or license; (2) to criticize public officials without penalty; and (3) to report matters of public interest. But each of these pillars is limited to some extent and with respect to some of the news media, despite the constitutional guarantees.

Direct Regulation

No one is required to get a license to publish a newspaper or magazine. Early newspapers were largely political tracts and were accepted as such. Although the government on occasion has acted, most notably at the time of the Sedition Acts in the late 1790's, to prosecute newspaper publishers, no attempt has been made by the government to compel a publisher to obtain a government license in order to publish the paper. A newspaper must register and make public certain facts about its operation, such as its ownership, circulation, and key officials, but compliance with these regulations doesn't interfere with the exercise of either private or public rights. It might be best understood as an enlargement of the public's right to know more about the persons who run a significant political institution.

The electronic media are different. Radio and television stations must obtain a federal government license to broadcast, and must broadcast on an assigned frequency or channel. There are limits to the number of "outlets" an owner may operate. Furthermore, the license for each outlet is valid only for a specified number of years; if it is to be renewed, the station must have complied with the requirement that it operate in the public interest—a requirement that is defined (not too clearly) by the government and the courts. The government agency that exerts this control most directly is the Federal Communications Commission, one of Washington's most powerful independent regulatory agencies.

Thus, the government has a significant weapon that it can exercise against a news outlet it does not favor. Although license renewals have in the past been granted almost automatically and never denied for outright and apparent political reasons, the threat posed by this capability is an ever-present one.

Yet, the ostensible reasons for such control appear justifiable. Unlike newspapers, which respond to market forces, the nature of electronic transmission is such that there are a finite number of frequencies and channels for broadcasting purposes that can be received by listeners, and there always seem to be more entrepreneurs wanting stations than there are frequencies that can be utilized. Prior to the Federal Communications Act of 1934, stations often transmitted on frequencies so close to each other that interference with each other's signals was rampant. In practice this meant that small stations were overwhelmed by more powerful signal transmissions or, at best, reception was unclear. The result was chaotic. The government felt compelled, both in the service of the public and by the industry's clamor, to bring order to the chaos, and this meant regulation and licensing, guaranteeing clear and orderly broadcasting at the price of some freedom for just anyone to broadcast. The diffuse "public interest" standard became the guideline for deciding who would get official approval for the available channels.

Censorship

Since 1931 the Supreme Court has ruled that freedom of the press means that the government may not exercise "prior" censorship of what is published (or, presumably, broadcast). But that fundamental right has been watered down in a number of circumstances concerning two different problems. First, is there any subject matter over which *prior* censorship may be exercised; and second, even if a publisher is free to publish certain matters, is he subject to punishment *after* having published them?

There has been a lengthy history of litigation about the attempts by various arms of government to prevent (or censor) the publication of obscene material, for example. Although the Supreme Court has had enormous difficulty defining obscenity (usually in the context of books, magazines, or movies, and not newspapers or radio and television), it has seemed to conclude that material properly deemed obscene could be denied, by court injunction, the right to be published.

There has been a recurring conflict over whether the press has a right to report information concerning a current courtroom trial when the release of such information might prejudice a defendant. A defendant is constitutionally guaranteed a "public trial," but there is some question about whether that right belongs to the public (and exercised by its newsmen) or to the individual involved. Some divorce and many juvenile cases are ordinarily kept secret because of a perceived public interest in the privacy of the parties. Recently, in New York City, a judge enjoined the press from reporting any information about a trial before him in which a defendant with an Italian name had been alleged to have Mafia connections. The case was over before the reporters could get an appellate court decision on removing the "gag" order. This incident and others like it lend insight into the still unresolved "free-press-fair-trial" controversy over censorship.

If a paper, in the exercise of its freedom, falsely defames someone in a publication, it may be subject to a court judgment for libel and may have to pay damages to the person libeled. But, where public officials are defamed, the Supreme Court has severely restricted the circumstances in which the press may be held accountable. The apparent rationale is that the impossibility of thoroughly checking the accuracy of every story means that matters of public interest might never be reported if papers had to check each item before publishing and that public officials invite public attention.

The emerging law in areas where publication of certain information might damage national security or jeopardize a crucial national interest is still not fully developed. The news media sometimes impose censorship on themselves for "partriotic" or other reasons. There are situations in which they might in fact feel more comfortable with formal government censorship than with its absence.

Consider the prototypical case of the war correspondent. Two significant, newsworthy events occur, both of which concern soldiers in the field. Reporting the events may or may not jeopardize the soldiers' safety; the correspondent does not know. Consequently, he or she reports neither of them, because to do so might risk the soldiers' lives or harm the war effort and might lead the authorities to deny his or her accredited status, thereby barring him from the field. But one of the events may, in reality, be harmless. A regime of censorship on the battlefield would allow the report of that event to be sent back to his or her paper, holding back information only about the second event. Thus, the paradoxical result is achieved that censorship yields more information than pure freedom of the press.

Some Representative Struggles

The pull and tug of government influence on the behavior of the news media has already been illustrated in the earlier discussion of the use of grand juries to discover the identities of reporters' confidential sources. But several other events deserve mention.

There is evidence that, prior to the Bay of Pigs operation in 1961 (in which about 1,500 anti-Castro Cubans, under CIA direction, invaded Cuba and were captured and later ransomed, much to the embarrassment of President Kennedy and the United States), the *New York Times* had information that, if published, would have placed the operation in jeopardy and possibly caused its cancellation. At the request of the President, the *Times* censored itself, and the debacle ensued. In this case, the *Times* might have performed a significant public service had it exercised its freedom and satisfied the public's right to know by publishing the information.

If the *Times* felt guilty about holding back information in 1961, the guilt might have influenced its decision a decade later to publish the Pentagon Papers, a collection of Vietnam-related documents copied by a former government worker and delivered to the *Times*. As soon as the initial installments were published, the government secured a court injunction to prevent (that is, to censor) further publication on the ground that public and especially foreign knowledge of the contents of the documents would damage the nation's security.

In a significant but rather unclearly grounded decision, the Supreme Court vacated the injunction and permitted the *Times* to continue to publish the papers. Three justices held that the government could not *censor* a newspaper. Three more felt that it could do so when the subject of the censorship was information alleged by the government to jeopardize national security. The three swing justices voted to allow publication because the government had not shown any damage to national security, but left open how they would have voted had there been proof of damage or danger. Thus, the law on prior censorship in this area is hardly clear and the institutional role of the news media is less than fully defined.

The Effects on Political Choice

Most obviously, the media affects political campaigns and voting choices. These subjects will be taken up, but first we will discuss some other effects of the media's growth.

In the days before radio and television, politics provided entertainment and recreation for many people. Americans went to political rallies and followed candidates in much the same way that they now follow the careers of movie stars or go to football games. The growth of the media, of national sports, and of the entertainment industry have created competing systems of heroes and activities. With this in mind, one might say that the media has in these ways helped to divert people from politics and to cause the decline in participation. In the nineteenth century 80 per cent of the voters turned out for presidential elections. Now the turnout is about 65 per cent.

The media have helped to nationalize America as a society and, therefore, to nationalize our politics. When people across the country see the same entertainment and news programs, regional and ethnic cultures are weakened. To use a simplified example, people watched "The Waltons" instead of listening to their grandfather's stories. Seeing the President on the 7:00 P.M. news provides the entire country with the same experience and the same reference point.

Creating a national audience gives interest groups direct access to the rest of the nation. In the 1960s television coverage of civil rights demonstrations gave southern blacks a way to reach the entire country. Pictures of dogs and policemen brutalizing demonstrators stirred the people and created an atmosphere in which the Civil Rights Act of 1964 and the Voting Rights Act of 1965 became law. Had the television cameras been absent, most of the national public would never have known.

This is one example of how the media help to shape (some people would say create) an issue. By getting national attention, and arousing sympathy and support, these films helped to put civil rights on the national agenda. In similar fashion the 1973 televised hearings of the Senate Select Committee on Presidential Campaign Practices, the Ervin Committee, helped to make Watergate a national issue.

Presidents are in the best position to use the media to make an issue or to press for a policy. On most occasions the TV networks will give the president as much prime time as he desires for messages considered to be of public importance. They may extend an offer of equal time to spokespersons for the opposing party, if they consider the President's message to be partisan. The catch is that most people will not listen to the opponents, who lack the President's prestige and symbolic importance. Most Americans have never heard of the opposition spokepersons and don't want to listen to what they have to say.

Franklin Rossevelt, in his fireside radio chats, made the first extensive use of media to appeal for public support of a particular measure, or to raise an issue he thought important. Later Presidents have followed suit. Dwight Eisenhower's televised appeal for labor reform is widely thought to have helped to pass the Landrum-Griffin Bill. John F. Kennedy used a televised press conference to launch his fight against a steel price increase in 1962. Lyndon Johnson made a dramatic, late-night speech to gain support for the Gulf of Tonkin Resolution. Richard Nixon made frequent television speeches on behalf of his foreign and domestic policies. Gerald Ford used the media to attack congressional opposition to his energy proposals. Jimmy Carter also tried unsuccessfully to use television to mobilize support for his energy programs. Ronald Reagan began his campaign for budget reductions with a televised address to a joint session of Congress. His other speeches were very effective, as we described in Chapters 2 and 3.

This weapon, however, cuts in two directions. The same media that give the President the opportunity to shape public opinion, allow his opponents, sometimes those within his own party, to gain public recognition at his expense. This pattern is part of a larger one : By making possible direct appeals from individual candidates to the people, media have seriously weakened the political parties. The most dramatic example is a challenge to an incumbent President from within his own party. Thirty years ago, such a challenge was unthinkable. How could an unknown succeed against the president, who automatically is the leader of the national party as well as the country's best-known political leader? Yet, in 1968, Eugene McCarthy ran against Lyndon Johnson for the Democratic presidential nomination and did well enough in the early primary in New Hampshire to inspire Robert Kennedy to do the same, and to contribute to President Johnson's decision to retire. When he began, McCarthy was an obscure senator from Minnesota. In a few months, by media exposure, he had become a national figure: he was known around the country and many Democrats had decided that they liked him better than Johnson. It is difficult to imagine McCarthy's doing so well without the direct access provided by television.

Edmund Muskie's career in national politics shows the media's double edge: it first helped to put him in the lead for the Democratic presidential nomination in 1972 and then helped to defeat him. In 1968 Muskie ran as the vice presidential nominee with Hubert Humphrey. He campaigned well and, after the election, people began to talk of his running for President. By 1971 he was firmly established as the frontrunner for the nomination. One nationally televised speech was the major factor in this transformation. During the 1970 congressional elections, while Spiro Agnew and Richard Nixon campaigned shrilly for law and order, Muskie spoke for the Democrats. Seated in an armchair, before a fire, his dog at his feet, he presented a striking contrast to the arm-waving, shouting Republican leaders. His speech called for calm and national unity. All at once he was hailed as "Lincolnesque," a figure of great strength, sobriety, and wisdom. Over the next eighteen months, he gained the endorsements of many of the party leaders. By March, 1972, he was universally considered the certain winner of the Democratic nomination.

That month in the New Hahpshire primary, his downfall began. The media played a large role. First, on the basis of scant evidence and analysis, they established Muskie as the favorite to win by a landslide. After all, he came from Maine, a neighboring state, he was well known, he had the backing of the state party's most prominent leaders, and, like most of New Hampshire's registered Democrats, he was a Catholic. When he won only a slight majority, the media, on the basis of its own previous estimates, labeled the election a victory for George McGovern and a defeat for Muskie.

One episode inspired by a local newspaper and reported by the national press and networks severely damaged Muskie's reputation. The *Manchester* (New Hampshire) *Union Leader,* an aggressive right-wing newspaper, printed a letter accusing Muskie of having used the word "Canuck," a derogatory reference to French-Canadians, the largest ethnic group in New Hampshire's Democratic party. The paper also printed a story about Muskie's wife Jane's behavior on the campaign airplane, saying that she had sworn freely and suggested a session of dirty jokes. To defend himself and his wife, Muskie made a speech from a flatbed platform outside the *Union Leader's* offices. In the middle of the speech, he broke down and began to cry. The "crying" incident was widely reported; Muskie's image as a confident, mature leader was hurt badly. Many observers thought that Muskie had, by the end of the New Hampshire campaign, lost his chance for the nomination.

In his book *The Selling of the President,* Joe McGinnis describes a successful use of the media to create a favorable image for candidate Nixon in the 1968 presidential campaign. In television advertisements and appearances, Nixon's staff strove to present him as a "new man." The "new" Nixon was no longer the hard-fighting, aggressive prosecutor of Alger Hiss, or the tough in-fighter of the Helen Gahagan Douglas campaign. No longer was he the explosive sore loser who in 1962 told the press, "You won't have Nixon to kick around anymore." The new Nixon was a settled, philosophical man, free of the demons that had driven him in the past, successful in business, moderate in temperament. In short, he had grown to be a statesman instead of a power-hungry politician.

In congressional elections, the media give the incumbent a substantial advantage. To begin with, the incumbent senator or congressperson is considered newsworthy. His or her press releases and public appearances are reported the year round. Press releases which are often designed to glorify the congressperson, are simply repeated as news.[4] The incumbent becomes known and known favorably to his constituents. People who run campaigns refer to this as name recognition. If people don't recognize the candidate's name, they won't vote for him.

The incumbent's second major advantage consists of the $500,000 worth of studios built by the Congress for the Congress with tax money. A member of Congress can make films or tapes for use by local radio and television stations. Often these are treated as news, and simply broadcast without any notice to the audience that they were made by the incumbent and given free to the station.

[4] Ben Bagdikian, "Congress and the Media: Partners in Propaganda," *Columbia Journalism Review* (Jan./Feb. 1974).

Charges for these films and tapes to the congressperson or senator are minimal, and their use is heavy. Some members send local stations a monthly or even a weekly report, which may be played as part of a news program or as a separate program: "Your Congressman Reports."

Shaping Reality

One final point will bring the discussion back to its starting place. We have considered the effects of the media on politicians, interest groups, and institutions. We have discussed how groups and individuals use the media to their own ends. The most general issue—how the media provide the information that is the basis for people's perception of reality—is now discussed.

The media tries to influence people directly by editorializing. Many people who discount the media's influence argue that most people never read the editorial page or listen to televised commentaries. But this is not the only way the media can influence people; we would argue that it is not the most important. Here are some others:

The selection, position, and length of a story or series of stories may increase their importance or create a certain impression. In New York City, the *Post* gives front-page coverage, with photographs, to violent crime—murder, robbery, rape. It seems likely that this constant barrage has influenced the thinking of New Yorkers. Who can doubt that New York City is the most dangerous in the country? "Look at all the stories in the newspaper." In fact, New York's crime rate is lower than that of many other major cities. Simple repetition—the repeated coverage of a story—may serve to increase its importance. For over a year Walter Cronkite ended the CBS evening news by noting the continued detention of American hostages in Iran. It seems likely that this has helped to keep the issue prominent in people's minds.

Imaginative headlines also influence perceptions:

CAN RAPE BE PREVENTED IN THE CITY UNIVERSITY?

This headline implies that there is an epidemic of rape in progress and that there is little chance of stopping it.

A phrase or a term may have a similar slanting effect. In 1975 the national media gave prominent attention to New York City's fiscal crisis and the federal government's response. Anchormen and reporters referred over and over again to "bailing out New York City": "Will the federal government *bail out* New York City? Will the president agree to a *bail out?*" The phrase implies that New York City is a foundering ship. All by itself, through carelessness, the phrase implied New York City has gotten into trouble and must be rescued by the charity of the federal government and the rest of the country.

In fact, a good case could be made that the opposite is true; that New York City has been bailing out the rest of the United States for many years. Let us go through the argument. The city received millions of immigrants—Germans, Chinese, Jews, Poles, Irish—who came to the United States, educated them, and tried to give them basic services and a decent place to live. New York City began the process by which these refugees became part of American society. Often they became very productive citizens and moved to other parts of the country. In recent years New York City has been the host of a different sort of migration. People in the United States who could not find work or a decent life have come to New York City. Black farm laborers, displaced by the mechanization of southern agriculture, and eager to be free of southern racism, came to New York. Many Puerto Ricans, discouraged by lack of jobs or low wages, left their island for New York. Poor whites came from all over the country. Again, the city shouldered the burden and spent its tax money to educate, protect, and sometimes house and feed these disadvantaged people.

New York City took on the problems of other parts of the country. New York City "bailed out" Georgia, and Mississippi, and South Carolina. New York City took on the burden of caring for the people from those states. New York City took on the burden of solving national problems of unemployment and lack of opportunity. All this is glossed over and obscured when John Chancellor says: "The Senate voted today on a bill to bail out New York City."

In summary, whether or not the media cover certain stories, or parts of stories; the length and placement of the reports; and the words and phrases used in the report have an important impact on people's view of reality and, therefore, on their political choices.

GLOSSARY

Background press conference A press conference among an official and reporters with the understanding that the official will not be specifically identified or, in the case of a *deep* backgrounder, will be identified only in the most vague and general manner.

Editor An executive in a newspaper. Different editors supervise different departments and functions.

Investigative reporting Searching out a story, usually one that exposes a violation of the public interest.

Journal of opinion A periodical characterized by a particular editorial bias or point of view.

Leak Unauthorized release of information.

Makeup man A newspaper employee whose job is to determine the position and sometimes the length and style of a story.

National newspapers Newspapers that concentrate on news of national significance and that are widely read by important national figures, especially those in government.

Network A group of radio or television stations that broadcast the same programs, usually simultaneously, and are bound together by legal agreements.

Newsmagazines Weekly publications that summarize and report news of national significance.

Off-the-record remark A statement made to a reporter with the understanding that the reporter will not reveal the source.

Press release An announcement by a newsworthy figure or entity that something has happened, is happening, or will happen.

Publisher A person in a position of ultimate authority on a newspaper.

Rewrite man A newspaper employee whose job is to rewrite stores given him over the telephone by reporters.

Rip-and-read The name given to radio news reporting, which consists of ripping wire service reports off the teletype machine or stories out of the newspaper and reading them word for word over the air.

Stringer A person who sometimes supplies stories to a news organization but is not regularly employed by the organization.

Wire services Organizations that supply news reports to newspapers, radio and television stations, and magazines by sending the reports (over wires) to teletype machines (automatic electric typewriters) in the subscriber's building.

SUGGESTED READINGS

Bagdikian, Ben H. *The Information Machines*. New York: Harper & Row Publishing, Inc., 1971.

Barnouw, Eric. *The Image Empire: A History of Broadcasting in the United States. Vol. III, from 1953.* New York: Oxford University Press, Inc., 1970.

Cohen, Bernard. *The Press and Foreign Policy*. Princeton, N.J.: Princeton University Press, 1963.

Crouse, Timothy. *The Boys on the Bus*. New York: Bantam Books: 1972.

Epstein, Edward Jay. *News From Nowhere*. New York: Vintage, 1974.

Fang, Irving E. *Television News,* 2nd ed. New York: Hastings House, 1972.

Gans, Herbert. *Deciding What's News*. New York Pantheon 1979.

Gitlin, Todd. *The Whole World Is Watching*. Berkeley, Cal.: Univ. of Cal. Press, 1980.

Leroy, David J., and Christopher H. Sterling (Eds.). *Mass News*. Englewood Cliffs, N.J.: Prentice-Hall, Inc., 1973.

McGinniss, Joe, *The Selling of the President 1968*. New York: Pocket Books. 1970.

Rubin, Bernard. *Political Television*. Belmont, Cal.: Wadsworth Publishing Company, 1967.

Talese, Gay. *The Power and the Glory*. New York, World, 1969.

9 Policymaking

General Introduction

In previous chapters we have described American political institutions. In this chapter we present two case studies of these institutions in action. We hope to show how the structures operate and how specific circumstances and personalities influence results. The first case study deals with a domestic issue, and the second foccusses on a foreign policy issue.

Introduction to the First Case Study

This case study of the creation and short, precarious life of the Department of Education illustrates many of the points discussed previously in this book in general terms. Among these are the organization and actions of interest groups; the relations among interest groups, the President, the Congress, and agencies; the role of the presidency as an institution and the President as an individual, including relations to cabinet officials and the Congress; and the intricacy of congressional procedures and the resulting need for strong, knowledgeable leadership in legislative politics.

Background

Although most industrialized countries have a centralized education system run by one large bureaucracy, the United States, in part because of its federal system, and in part because of its traditions of liberalism and localism, does not. Instead, villages, towns, cities, counties, and states have run American public schools. Consequently, the Department of Education was not created until 1867. It was made a small, record-keeping bureau in the Interior Department soon after it was established.

Renamed the Office of Education, it was transferred in 1939 to the Federal Security Agency, which become the Department of Health, Education and Welfare (HEW) in 1953. Federal involvement in education expanded greatly after World War II. Many agencies such as the Veterans Administration and the Bureau of Indian Affairs ran their own education programs. During the 1960s federal involvement in education expanded further; for instance, the Great Society programs of President Lyndon Johnson provided aid for disadvantaged children through the Elementary and Secondary

Education Act. In 1972 the Congress established an Education Division within HEW. Headed by an assistant secretary, the division included the Office of Education and the new National Institute of Education. The Office of Education administered a variety of programs including occupational and adult education programs for the handicapped, and the programs for the disadvantaged mentioned previously. The institute encouraged research in education by giving grants and disseminating the results of that research.

During the 1976 presidential campaign, Jimmy Carter endorsed the idea of a separate department for education. Several studies had recommended this step as a way to better organize the many federal education programs. Besides this "good government" concern, Carter's action had a strongly political dimension. The powerful National Education Association (NEA)—a group of 1,470,000 teachers—wanted the separate department. The NEA felt that education in general and that the NEA in particular would get more attention from a separate department. Soon after Carter endorsed the idea of a separate department for education, the NEA endorsed him.

Opposition to the separate department of education came from the American Federation of Teachers (AFT), an organization that competed with the NEA to represent teachers. The AFT, which had about 400,000 members, had good ties to the existing Division of Education in HEW. They were joined by civil rights groups who feared that the new department would be weaker on racial issues, and by labor groups who feared that breaking up HEW would also break up the education/labor/civil rights coalition that had grown up around HEW's programs.

Early in 1978 the Congress began consideration of an Education Department bill supported by the Carter White House. The bill included the transfer of several important programs, such as Head Start, Indian education, and the child nutrition program, to the new department. Almost immediately the ranks of the administration divided. The secretary of Health, Education and Welfare, Joseph Califano, an experienced Washington insider, worked openly against the bill. Califano wanted, we may presume, to preserve his department's size and power, and, therefore, his own power. He may also have genuinely thought that a separate department was a bad idea. Often in politics, self-interest and ideology coincide. "Where you stand [on the issues], depends on where you sit [in which agency]," the late Professor Wallace Sayre used to say.

Whatever his reasons, Califano carried his fight against the new department to the Congress with energy and skill. Testifying on February 21, 1978, before a House subcommittee, Califano listed "candidates" for inclusion in the proposed Department of Education: The National Science Foundation, the Veteran's Administration's education programs, Head Start, and the Smithsonian Institution. Knowing that their leaders and supporters did not want these institutions to be included in the new department, Califano was deliberately arousing their opposition to the new department. He also sent a message to Congresspersons who feared the growth of another huge bureaucracy. The new department, he seemed to say, would develop into a monster, a gargantua.

You might ask how Califano could openly oppose the President's wishes. The episode should call to mind the discussion in Chapter 2 of the natural opposition between the President and his cabinet secretaries. Califano himself denied that there was an open conflict between him and the President. The President, he said, had not made his position, "explicit." Therefore, other members of the administration were free to state their own views. Of course, this was only a convenient rationalization. The President's stand on the new department was clear to everyone. Nonetheless, neither Carter nor his White House staff had moved quickly or decisively enough to prevent Califano's defection. Such clumsiness and disunity were frequent throughout Carter's four years in office and greatly damaged his administration.

Despite these difficulties the bill emerged from committee in both the House and Senate. The full Senate passed its version of the bill, which omitted the transfers of Head Start, Indian education, and school lunch programs. However, when the House bill moved to the floor, a parliamentary tangle defeated it. Because it was scheduled for a final vote near the end of the session, the bill was vulnerable to delaying tactics. Opponents of the bill took the opportunity and offered many amendments and carried out other delaying tactics to extend the debate. Fearing that other, more important business would be neglected, the leadership of the House withdrew the bill, effectively killing it.

The Second Try—1979

The White House. Several important factors shifted in 1979. First, the White House organized early and effectively. Having suffered several important legislative defeats, the President and his advisors badly wanted a victory. They also wanted, we may assume, to repay the political debt owed the NEA and thus to enlist their support in 1980. A task force was created to coordinate the executive branch's activities. Since Secretary Califano had been forced to resign the previous summer, one major internal opponent had been removed. An HEW spokesperson noted that the creation of the new department was a "heightened priority for the President and we'll all be working on it."

President Carter personally lobbied members of the House and Senate. He invited some to the White House and talked to others on the telephone. He also made a special effort to impress Democratic congressional leaders with the importance of the issues.

Interest Groups. Both sides intensified their efforts in 1979 by building broader coalitions. About a hundred groups formed a supporting coalition, modeled on the National Coalition to Save Public Education, a group founded in 1978 to block tax credits for private school students. The new coalition aimed to change the idea that the bill was strictly an NEA project. They wanted the Congress to know that many other educational groups, including some community colleges, supported the new department.

The opposition also added to its coalition. As noted, the major civil rights groups, the AFL-CIO, and the AFT opposed the bill. In April 1979, these groups joined with others including representatives of some higher education institutions to form the Committee Against a Separate Department of Education. The heads of some important private universities, such as Harvard, Stanford, and Columbia, as well as some major public institutions, such as the Universities of Illinois, California, and Michigan, joined the committee. Two months earlier, the Association of American Colleges, representing four-year liberal arts colleges, had announced its opposition to the new department. A Harvard spokesperson objected to the creation of a monolithic education agency and expressed a preference for a pluralistic system with many agencies dispensing grants.

Special interest groups such as those representing veterans and Indians continued to oppose the transfer of their education programs to the new department.

Congressional Action

The Senate. The pattern in the Senate followed that of 1978. The Government Operations Committee, after dropping some of the controversial transfers such as Head Start, Indian education, and school lunches, reported the measure with only one dissenting vote. In response to concerns over federal control of education, the committee added a stipulation that the new department would not increase federal power over local school systems.

On the floor of the Senate opponents tried to weaken the bill by adding amendments that would alienate liberal supporters. For instance, Jesse Helms, the conservative republican from North Carolina, succeeded briefly in amending the bill to permit voluntary prayer in the public schools. The Senate majority leader, Robert Byrd, came to the rescue. First, he recessed the Senate to gain time to gather his forces and frame a strategy. When the Senate reconvened Byrd moved to attach Helms' amendment to a different, unimportant bill. After the switch, Byrd moved successfully to kill the second bill and the amendment. Other controversial amendments went down to simpler defeats. On April 30, 1979, the bill, numbered S210, passed, 72–21.

The House. Passage through the House Government Operations Committee proved difficult. Some members expressed fear of bureaucratic expansion; others warned about increased federal power. In response to such concerns, the committee added amendments limiting the number of employees in the new department and prohibiting it from increasing federal power. Opposition groups, including colleges, did some lobbying, but committee members expressed surprise at the relative absence of pressure. Caldwell Butler, a Republican from Virginia, heard so little about the bill that he wrote to all the school administrators in his district asking for their opinions.

With the committee divided, intervention by the President and the NEA-led coalition produced a majority. Carter personally lobbied the undecided committee members and two out of three were won over. On May 2, 1979, the committee reported HR 2444 favorably by one vote, 20–19. The chairman, Jack Brooks of Texas, succeeded in passing an amendment shifting Indian education programs to the new department. Previously the NEA had abandoned this effort in the face of the Indians' opposition.

After another narrow squeak through the House Rules Committee, the bill reached the House floor in June. After two days of debate and growing uncertainty, the decisive vote took place on June 13. David Obey, a Wisconsin Democrat, moved to strike the bill's enacting clause, which would have killed the bill. With the motion given a fair chance to pass, Speaker Thomas P. ("Tip") O'Neill, Jr., made one of his rare speeches. "Are we being fair to ourselves?" he asked. "Are we being fair to the President of the United States who has sent this message to Congress?" O'Neill's dramatic appeal carried the day. Obey's motion lost decisively, 146–266.

Following this vote, however, opponents of the bill succeeded in attaching three controversial amendments that were designed to undermine liberal support. One repeated the Helms provision's mandate for public school prayer. Another prohibited the department from requiring school districts receiving federal aid to bus students to achieve racial balance. The third said that no student should be denied access to education by racial or sexual quotas. These amendments did alienate some liberals. The Congressional Black Caucus—the association of all the black members of the House—which had been neutral on the bill, said they would wait to see whether or not the amendments survived the conference. The plain implication was that if the amendments survived, the Caucus would oppose, and probably defeat, the bill.

On July 11, 1979, just before the formal floor vote, two amendments restricting abortions were passed. Then the bill itself passed narrowly, 210–206.

Conference. Supporters and opponents of the bill both knew that the conference would be decisive. If any of the controversial amendments on race or abortion survived, the compromise bill would almost certainly be defeated on the House floor. To enhance the chances for passage, the House leadership departed cleverly from the usual procedures. Instead of waiting for the Senate to ask for a conference as would have occurred normally, Speaker O'Neill had the House ask for a conference. This meant that the Senate would vote first on the compromise and that the House, voting second, would be in a take-it or leave-it position. Therefore, the House would be more likely to vote yes for the sake of getting something.

In the conference the House members, appointed by the Speaker, allowed all the provocative amendments to be deleted or diluted. Despite objections from conservative opponents the compromise version of the bill passed the Senate, by 69 to 22 on September 24, and then passed the House Rules Committee. On September 27, the bill as amended passed the full House, by a vote of 215 to 201. On September 29, the NEA praised Carter and said that it would back him in 1980. On October 17, the President signed the bill into law.

Later in the year Carter nominated and the Senate approved Shirley Hufstedler to be the first secretary of Education. A former federal judge, Ms. Hufstedler took charge of a department with about seventeen thousand employees and a budget of about $14 billion.

Some Points to Notice

This brief narrative indicates the complexity of American politics. Consider first the interest groups involved. Instead of there being one interest group to represent teachers, there are two, and they are bitter rivals. Institutions of higher education were also divided on this issue: some stayed neutral, many opposed the bill, and a few supported it. Although civil rights groups opposed the bill, the Congressional Black Caucus remained neutral.

In regard to specific institutions, the study is also revealing. The difference between 1978 and 1979 indicates that the powers of the President and the presidency must be exercized skillfully if they are to be effective. In 1978 Jimmy Carter did very little and his aides did not unify the executive branch in support of his proposal. In this situation, a cabinet secretary publicly opposed the President. A year later, Carter gave the issue considerable personal attention and his special task force mobilized and unified the executive branch.

Responding to a clear signal and effective leadership, the congressional leadership used parliamentary maneuvers and personal appeals in support of the President's proposal. They did their utmost to mobilize the congressional parties and to protect the bill from the many pitfalls in the legislative process. The slim margin of victory in the House of Representatives testifies to the importance of their efforts.

Postscript: Presidential Politics—Again

Less than a year after the creation of the Department of Education, it was once again an issue in a presidential campaign. The Republican party platform called for the department's abolition, as being unnecessary and a threat to local autonomy. Candidate Ronald Reagan said on September 8, 1980, that the Department of Education planned to limit and restrict private schools. Shortly after Reagan's election, his chief advisor, Edwin Meese, said that Reagan would consider abolishing the department, but the new administration's stance changed quickly. President Reagan announced that he would appoint a new secretary because the department did have some legitimate functions. Later announcements indicated that the effort to abolish the department would not be pressed in the near future. Nonetheless, the Department of Education remained a target for conservatives and Reagan himself proposed to reduce substantially the budgets for education programs. Therefore, the department's future remains uncertain.

Institutional Conflict: The Taiwan Treaty

On December 15, 1979, the Supreme Court ordered a civil action filed in U.S. District Court in Washington, D.C., to be dismissed. By this routine procedure, the Court apparently laid to rest a dramatic and emotion-laden conflict arising out of the early cold war years that involved virtually all of our governmental institutions. The conflict primarily pitted the Congress against the President in another round of a never-ending power struggle. The outcome of the struggle is not yet determined and, many argue, can never be ultimately resolved without leading to the control of the government (and the country) by one political organ.

The Background

From no later than mid-1937 to 1949, a civil war was fought in China between the Nationalist government and the Communist party. The war was intermittent, as both sides from time to time had to contend with the Japanese invasion that did not end until 1945. The Nationalist government, headed by Generalissimo Chiang Kai-shek, saw itself as heir to the revolution that overthrew the dynasty in 1912, having overcome the havoc of the "warlord" years in the 1920s and instituted a comparatively stable, more or less Westernized form of government. The Communists, under Mao Tse-tung, having once been characterized as "agrarian reformers," had a radically different concept of the government they sought to implant in China.

The U.S.S.R., under Joseph Stalin, did not commit itself fully to the Communists until World War II was ending, having flirted with Chiang off and on since the 1920s, prior to the establishment in 1927 of the Chinese Communist party. United States policy was also ambiguous until, with the end of the "hot" war and the beginning of the "cold" war, we commenced vigorous support of the Nationalists in opposition to the Soviets.

The civil war went badly for Chiang in the 1940s. Finally he removed his government to the offshore island of Formosa (the Japanese name), which had recently been regained from Japan, and on October 1, 1949, Mao proclaimed the People's Republic of China.

Concurrently, postwar economic difficulties in the United States and the perception of Soviet aggression in Europe and elsewhere had led to a revival of intense anticommunism in this country. This was evidenced by such various measures as the Marshall Plan, the Truman Doctrine (and its theoretical underpinning, the "containment" doctrine), loyalty oaths, and the dismissal from the State Department of alleged supporters of communism. Although discussion of these and similar events is beyond the scope of this book, they illustrate the temper of the times.

When North Korea invaded South Korea in 1950, the appearance of Communist aggression, together with Mao's expressed desire to invade Formosa and put a cap on the Communist victory in China, led President Truman to order the U.S. Seventh Fleet to install itself in the Straits of Formosa to prevent any invasion. The United States maintained its position that Chiang's government was the official government of China and continued its efforts to protect the Nationalists. These efforts culminated in the signing on December 2, 1954, of a Mutual Defense Treaty between the United States and the Nationalist government (known as the Republic of China). The treaty was ratified by the Senate shortly thereafter and provided that, in the event of attack on Taiwan, each signatory "would act to meet the common danger in accordance with its constitutional processes," which was widely viewed as committing the United States to the defense of Taiwan (the Chinese name for Formosa) if the Communists attacked. The treaty was to remain in force "indefinitely" and provided that either country "may terminate it one year after notice has been given to the other."

The treaty found widespread favor both in Congress and across the country. Virtually all of our political institutions supported both the treaty and its expression of opposition to the Communists: the executive branch negotiated it and the legislative branch approved it; both political parties gave their support (the Democrats perhaps less enthusiastically than the Republicans); the press lauded it and the bureaucracy had been purged of open opposition; interest groups, especially those of a conservative orientation, rallied around the treaty.

A loosely knit and not well-defined coalition of groups became known as the "China Lobby." Composed of politicians, writers and editors, businessmen, and others, the China Lobby acted, after the fashion of ad-hoc interest groups (see Chapter 6), to influence the political process at as many significant points as possible to continue support for Chiang's government and to oppose the Communists.

With the passage of time, however, the Chinese Communist position was perceived as less threatening to many Americans. The China Lobby began to lose influence. Diplomats began to view China as a potential obstacle to Russian aggression. Businessmen began to see economic opportunities in China. Writers began to see Chiang as a dictatorial warlord. Anti-Communist fervor began to diminish. President Nixon, a former stalwart of the China Lobby, even visited Communist China in 1972 and conversed with its leaders. He agreed to the incorporation in a joint communiqué of a statement that full diplomatic recognition of the People's Republic (pronounced as an objective) was preconditioned on, among other things, termination of the 1954 Mutual Defense Treaty. This step met with substantial opposition in Congress and among the still-active China Lobby, and Nixon did not pursue it. President Carter, however, did.

The Issues: Political and Legal

It was evident that the United States was moving slowly toward "normalization" of relations with the People's Republic of China throughout the 1970s. Because the issue was still controversial and powerful groups and institutions were arrayed on both sides, progress was uncertain. Members of Congress, as representatives of the people, had a special interest and concern that movement toward normalization be made with the concurrence of Congress and not over its opposition. Congress further saw that its influence as a political institution might be weakened if the President could take drastic steps without its agreement, particularly as such steps could further erode its already diminished position in foreign affairs. As a result Congress passed the International Security Assistance Act of 1978, one provision of which declared

> the sense of the Congress that there should be prior consultation between the Congress and the executive branch on any proposed policy changes affecting the continuation in force of the Mutual Defense Treaty of 1954.

The Act had numerous other provisions and Carter signed it in September 1978.

In spite of this Act, Carter on December 15, 1978, unilaterally announced diplomatic recognition of the People's Republic as the sole legitimate government of China and that the 1954 treaty would be terminated. Eight days later, the State Department formally notified the Republic of China that the treaty would terminate on January 1, 1980, pursuant to the terms of the treaty that one year's notice of termination be given. Defying Congress's expression of its "sense" that he had approved three months earlier, Carter in effect challenged Congress to do what it could to prevent termination.

The issues were clearly drawn. Politically, the battle was between those individuals and groups who supported the Nationalists and those who sought accommodation with the Communists. Additionally many in and out of Congress (even among those who favored the administration's position) reacted hostilely to the President's acts and foresaw a diminution of Congress's role, especially the Senate's, as a political institution if the President were allowed to take this step on his own. An ideologically diverse array of forces regarded this issue as a crucial one for the political process in this country.

Legally, the issues were also fairly clear, although the outcome was less so. Did the President have the power, within the limits of the Constitution and the terms of the treaty, unilaterally to terminate the treaty? Did anyone have the right to challenge the President's action in a judicial setting? Would the Courts decide it, if called upon to do so?

The First Shots

Congress reacted immediately to the President's actions by considering several resolutions in appropriate committees and by passing a statute that provided in part that Congress "approves the continuation in force of all treaties [with Taiwan] * * * in force between them on December 31, 1978, unless and until terminated in accordance with law." The President signed it into law, possibly because it ducked the issue of what action was "in accordance with law."

The Senate voted to consider a resolution:

That it is the sense of the Senate that approval of the United States Senate is required to terminate any mutual defense treaty between the United States and another nation.

But, after voting to consider the resolution and debating it, the Senate took no final vote.

On December 22, 1978, several members of Congress, led by Senator Barry Goldwater, instituted a suit in the federal District Court in Washington, D.C., alleging that the President had exceeded his powers and had violated his duty to uphold the laws (including the treaties) of the United States, that he had no unilateral power under the Constitution to terminate a treaty ratified by the Senate, and that he should be enjoined from terminating the treaty without senatorial or congressional consent. The lawsuit thus focused the battle in the courts. This step, similar to those taken in other disputes in which Congress has won some victories, arguably admitted the weakness of Congress's institutional position, but it also stood to gain recognition of its institutional power.

As noted in Chapter 4, however, the courts do not like being cast into the position of having to resolve a conflict between the President and Congress. On June 6, 1979, the District Court threw out the suit. The court said that, since several possible resolutions were then before the Congress for action, Congress apparently still had its remedies and the issue was not "ripe" for judicial intervention and resolution.

After Congress had further debated and taken no action, Senator Goldwater and his colleagues reinstituted their suit on the grounds that the District Court now had before it a justiciable controversy that was "ripe" for decision.

A Surprising Victory

On October 17, 1979, Judge Oliver Gasch of the District Court sustained Senator Goldwater's position and addressed all three legal issues raised by the matter.

The judge held first that, if it were true that the President had exceeded his powers, then the members of Congress had been denied their right to be consulted and to vote on termination of the treaty. This meant that they were "injured in fact" by the President's unilateral action, that there was a real "case or controversy," and that they had standing to sue for redress.

Second, he held that a question of the constitutional allocation of power between institutions was a proper one for judicial resolution. This case did not require the court to evaluate the wisdom of a political decision or to make one but "simply to determine whether the treaty termination was effectuated by constitutionally permissible means." It was, therefore, justiciable.

Finally, he ruled on the merits of the dispute that the President had exceeded his powers. He stated that, although the Constitution requires senatorial approval in creating treaties, it is silent as to their termination. The judge examined the more than fifty instances of treaty termination in American history and noted that, although treaties had been terminated in any number of ways, few had been terminated by the President acting alone and none of those involved a mutual defense treaty. He reviewed the language and purpose of the Constitution and the numerous reported cases involving the President's powers in foreign affairs and concluded that the "termination of a treaty is not a single act entrusted by the Constitution to one or the other of our political branches." Accordingly, the judge declared that the notice of termination must be approved either by two thirds of the Senate or by a majority of both houses of Congress.

Although many had written that the decision reached by Judge Fasch on the merits was the "right" one, the result that Senator Goldwater could overcome the procedural obstacles of standing and justiciability was not widely anticipated. The Congressmen were jubilant and, although appeal by the government was expected, they and their supporters felt that a constitutional imbalance had been corrected.

Defeat on Appeal

Their celebration, however, was short lived. Only one month later, on November 30, 1979, the U.S. Court of Appeals reversed the District Court on the merits. Five of the seven judges agreed that the members of Congress had standing to raise the issue in court because the President's action had nullified their opportunity to act themselves. All seven agreed that it was "the duty of the court to confront and decide that issue."

On the merits, four of the seven judges (one dissenting; two not reaching the merits because of their view that the members of Congress lacked standing) cited ten reasons that, taken together, supported the President's position. These included the President's sole power to give diplomatic recognition to a government, the lack of a constitutional provision giving the Senate any role in treaty termination, the variety of means used historically to terminate treaties, and the treaty termination provision itself that failed to require congressional approval for termination.

The Court then vacated the District Court's judgment and directed that the suit be dismissed.

Senator Goldwater immediately petitioned the Supreme Court, on an expedited basis, for a writ of certiorari, the effect of which would be to order the case brought before the Supreme Court for its ruling. On December 13, 1979, nineteen days before the treaty termination was to be effective, the Supreme Court acted.

Technically, what the Court did was to grant certiorari, to vacate the judgment of the Court of Appeals without a hearing, and to remand (or send back) the case to the Court of Appeals with directions to dismiss the complaint. But it so ordered in a somewhat confusing manner so that only the conclusion was clear: the Senators and Representatives had lost.

All but Justice Brennan concurred in the Supreme Court's action. The Court gave no opinion and offered no reasons for its determination. Justice Marshall merely stated that he concurred in the result. Justice Powell agreed with the result but filed a statement that he believed that the case was "not ripe for judicial review" primarily because Congress (by not actually voting) had chosen not to confront the President, and he saw no reason why the Court should do so. Justice Powell expressly disagreed with Justice Rehnquist's view. Justice Rehnquist filed a statement, joined by the Chief Justice and Justices Stewart and Stevens, concurring in the judgment but stating that he believed the case was "political" and therefore nonjusticiable because the issue should be decided between the two branches concerned. Justices Blackman and White agreed that the writ of certiorari should have been granted but stated that the Court should have heard argument on the case. Justice Brennan was the only Justice who argued that the Court should not vacate the judgment of the Court of Appeals but should leave it as good law.

Thus, the Supreme Court threw out the complaint although it had four (possibly five) different reasons, none of which commanded a majority. Both lower court opinions that analyzed the law were discarded. By refusing to decide the case, the Supreme Court left the antagonists right back where they had begun.

Conclusion

After the Supreme Court's decision, the issue simply died. The treaty is apparently no longer in effect; Congress never voted to continue it. The United States maintains a bewildering variety of "unofficial" relations with Taiwan, short of recognition. No one knows (or cares to think about) what would happen if the Communists invaded Taiwan, although they have said they would not do so. President Reagan could, if he wished, reverse Carter's recognition of the People's Republic, although he has given no indication that he has that objective. But this installment of the ongoing institutional conflict between the President and Congress is over and, except as to this single case, it is not clear whether the presidency emerged with an accretion of power.

As with many other historical political conflicts in the United States, the courts were called upon to referee the dispute. A century and a half ago, a foreigner journeying in this country, Alexis de Toqueville, noted the penchant of Americans for taking their political disputes to court for resolution. We appear to have changed very little in the intervening years in this respect.

Many times, even in recent years, the Supreme Court has become the battleground of conflicts that, in other nations, would never get to court. When President Truman seized the steel industry during the Korean War, the Supreme Court rebuffed him. When the news media published the "Pentagon Papers" in 1971, the Court prevented the government from intervening. When President Nixon sought to impound funds appropriated by Congress, the Court sustained Congress's position. In each of these instances, the political issues were transformed into legal ones. The conflict between or among institutions was resolved by resort to the courts.

In many cases, as here, the issues are resolved in ambiguous fashion. Because the Supreme Court spoke not with one voice, no one knows what the law is with respect to the President's power to terminate treaties unilaterally. Similarly, in the steel seizure case, the Court wrote seven different opinions, offering six different rationales why the President could not take over the steel industry. In the Pentagon Papers case, there were three opinions, none of which commanded a majority.

In the case of the Taiwan treaty, virtually all of our political institutions, constitutional as well as extraconstitutional, were involved at one time or another in a political conflict. It boiled down to two sides, one represented by Congress, the other by the presidency, although some components of both sides were uncomfortable with their allies. Both sides agreed to slug it out in the judicial arena. The result of the Court's action was perhaps less to resolve the conflict than simply to defuse it.

Not every political issue can be disposed of in this manner (as can be seen by the first half of this chapter). Institutional conflicts go on endlessly and, perhaps because institutions like the courts can and do resolve some of them but not others, such conflicts show no signs of abating.

10 American Politics in the 1980s

Introduction

In this book we have tried to describe and explain the patterns of American national politics. We have noted the complexities, the built-in conflicts, and the styles and goals of different groups and institutions.

Although the next decade may bring shifts in political alliances and voter allegiances and introduce a substantial number of new issues into the political ferment, it can safely be predicted that the recurring institutional conflicts we have described will persist. The politics of the 1980s will focus on the questions of which groups, individuals, and institutions will gain the power to make decisions on the key issues. Who will formulate policy on energy and on the economy? Who will make foreign policy? In general, who will determine America's priorities for this decade?

The 1980 Elections

On December 15, 1980, electors gathered in all fifty states and the District of Columbia and cast 489 votes for Ronald Reagan and 49 votes for Jimmy Carter for President. The same number of votes was cast for George Bush and Walter Mondale for Vice President. All of the electors had been pledged to the candidate they voted for and none cast an "independent" vote.

Unlike the 1976 election, in which Carter beat Gerald Ford by an electoral count of 297–241, and where a shift of eight thousand votes in Ohio and Hawaii would have given the election to Ford, no minor shift would have transformed Carter into a winner in 1980. Reagan simply won too many states (44) and, under the winner-take-all system (see Chapter 7), this produced an electoral vote landslide for Reagan.

The electoral vote count, of course, did not proportionally reflect the popular vote. Of the 86,513,296 votes cast, Reagan won 50.7 per cent (43,901,812) and Carter 41.0 per cent (35,483,820), giving Reagan a plurality of 9.7 per cent or 8,417,992 votes. Thus, the popular vote was considerably closer than the electoral vote, although a plurality of almost 10 per cent ranks as quite a substantial margin.

Neither the popular nor electoral results were widely anticipated. Up until the last week preceding the election, almost all of the polls had the candidates running neck-and-neck. A few polls released just prior to the election began to show a widening Reagan lead. And many of the polls taken during the last week but not tallied or released until after the election confirmed the last-minute shift.

The most widely held explanation for the supposedly close race turning into a runaway for Reagan was that voters who had made up their minds early (predominantly ideologically committed or straight party-line voters) were about evenly split between the candidates but that the undecided voters, who made up their minds in the last week and who had contributed about a quarter of all probable voters, had decided ultimately for Reagan. The two factors considered most significant in motivating the shift were the gradually worsening economy that Carter appeared helpless to overcome and the generally favorable impression made by Reagan in the televised debate during the last week before the election. Although the Carter people tended to blame the Iranian hostage situation for their loss of support, it does not appear to have been more than an incidental factor.

Carter received a share of the popular vote that was about ten percentage points less than his 51 per cent of 1976. Although for many years the "two-term" president was thought to be the norm, barring exceptional circumstances, Carter became the fourth consecutive President who failed for political reasons to serve his maximum term. It may well be that the 1980 election confirmed the trend toward one-term Presidents, although President Reagan's survival of the assassination attempt in March 1981 may make him politically unassailable if he should choose to run again in 1984.

Another distinguishing factor of the 1980 elections was that third-party candidates received more than 8 per cent of the presidential vote, about eight times as much as the vote in 1976 for nonmajor party candidates. But this figure does not seem so great when it is recalled that John Anderson, a Republican who ran an Independent campaign, received the support of more than 15 per cent of the voters in the polls taken in March and April of 1980. The course of the campaign cost Anderson about 60 per cent of his support (much of it apparently going to Reagan). Had Anderson been able to solidify his early support or even to increase it, not only might the election have turned out differently, but the American political scene might have witnessed the birth of a new movement and perhaps a significant change in the two-party system.

The Democrats lost thirty-one seats from their majority in the House of Representatives as a result of the 1980 elections. Although they now have a plurality of about fifty, the Democrats lost four of their committee chairmen, including Al Ullman of the powerful Ways and Means committee.

In the Senate the results were even worse for the Democrats. The Republicans gained twelve seats and took control of the Senate by the count of 53–47, the first time since the first Eisenhower election that the Republicans have controlled either House of Congress.

American government has had very little experience with this sort of alignment, in which the President and one House are of one party and the other House is run by the other party. The politics of administering the government and passing laws will require different patterns of give-and-take which may take some time to work out.

On the other hand there may not be much time to work it out. It is quite conceivable that this pattern is only transitory. Which way it will go in 1982 or 1984 is a vital question. Will the Republicans win the House and control the entire government, or will the Democrats reassert their prior numerical supremacy?

Some writers have described President Reagan's victory, together with his party's enormous gains in the Senate, as a "mandate" for Reagan's policies. Others have noted that Reagan won barely 50 per cent of the vote against one of the most unpopular Presidents in modern times. The fact is that, whatever the analysis, Reagan, the Republicans, and the conservatives won a lot of votes. It is difficult to say in 1981 whether this election can be characterized as a "critical" election, marking a realignment of the coalitions that comprise our political parties and foreshadowing the politics of the future, or whether 1980 is merely an aberration on the political scene, characterized by unique events and indicating no more than the swing of the pendulum within a stable, Democratic-dominated party structure.

One has only to recall the premature comment back in 1969 of then-Attorney General John Mitchell ("This country is going so far to the right you won't recognize it.") to voice skepticism concerning any permanent changes in the political makeup of the country. Yet there is no doubt that Republicans and conservatives are well organized, well financed, and increasingly popular. Whether the decade of the 1980s inaugurates a new party system (our sixth—see Chapter 7) probably depends less on the existence of overriding forces directing the system than on how the individuals and groups work things out in the next few years. For example, can Reagan convince the country that he can deal with inflation-recession? If so, there is lilely to be irresistible pressure toward majority status for the Republicans. If not, the Democrats will probably get another chance. The politics of the short-term future, particularly whether the Democrats can stem the rising conservative tide, are therefore crucial to the long-term outlooks for both parties.

The Loyal Opposition, 1981 and After

The 1980 elections put the congressional Democrats in an unfamiliar position. They had some experience of being in opposition to a Republican President, having done so from 1969–1977. The difference in 1981 was that the Democrats had also lost their majority in the Senate. Thus, the Republicans could claim a mandate based not only on the presidential race but also on the Senate races.

Furthermore, the Democrats were much weakened in terms of institutional politics. There was no chance that they could pass bills over the President's veto as they had occasionally done in 1969–1977. Their best chance was to modify presidential proposals, to force compromises that would protect the most important Democratic constituencies and principles. To do this would require careful, thorough organizing of the remaining congressional Democrats.

In the Senate the former majority leader Robert Byrd, now the minority leader, seemed stunned by the election results. After losing an early battle over the appointment of former general and Nixon aide Alexander Haig as secretary of State, Byrd seemed to retreat into pessimism. Without strong leadership, Senate Democrats found no effective way to oppose or modify the Reagan budget. A few Senators such as Howard Metzenbaum of Ohio and Edward Kennedy of Massachusetts denounced the reductions in government spending on social programs as "cruel" and "inhuman," but many made only minor criticisms. Attempts by Democratic members of the Budget Committee to soften or shift the cuts were consistently defeated, usually by the Republican majority, sometimes by a coalition of conservative Democrats and Republicans. In the final Budget Committee vote all the Democratic members joined the Republicans, saying that they favored the cuts in general but opposed some specifics. Plainly, the Senate Democrats feared that failure to support the President might cost them seats in the next election.

The Democrats in the House of Representatives had retained their majority, although by a reduced margin. Their leader, Speaker

"Tip" O'Neill, moved quickly after the election to strengthen his party. Several important leaders including Al Ullman, the chairperson of the Ways and Means Committee, and John Brademas, the party whip and third-ranking Democratic leader behind O'Neill and Jim Wright, the majority leader, had been defeated. Ordinarily, Dan Rostenkowski, a regular Democrat from Chicago would have taken Brademas' place as whip. Since O'Neill was expected to retire in 1982, Rostenkowski could count on moving up to Majority Leader at that time when Wright succeeded O'Neill. Thus, in two years Rostenkowski would be the number two Democrat with a good chance of becoming Speaker one day.

However, Rostenkowski also stood next in line to succeed Ullman as chairman of Ways and Means. O'Neill appealed to him to take the committee job and to leave the whip's job to Thomas Foley of Washington. O'Neill had several reasons for asking, all related to party unity and effectiveness in opposition. First, O'Neill considered Rostenkowski a more loyal, reliable party man than Sam Gibbons of Florida who was next in line for Ways and Means. Gibbons was a bit of a maverick, independent and impulsive. Since taxes would obviously be a major issue, O'Neill wanted a cooperative party man to unify and lead the committee's Democrats in developing alternatives to the Republican proposals.

O'Neill also viewed Rostenkowski as a more able leader than the abrasive Gibbons. Rostenkowski got along well with everyone and had the old-line politician's knack for promoting compromise and avoiding divisions. These qualities would be particularly important in leading House Democrats into conference committee battles with the Republican-controlled Senate.

Besides providing strong leadership for the Democratic Party against the Republicans, Rostenkowski might also help to prevent the development of a bipartisan conservative coalition that could take power away from the Democrats. During the 1950s a coalition of conservative Southern Democrats and Republicans had often dominated the House. To avoid a similar situation in the 1980s O'Neill sought to keep control of Ways and Means in the hands of the moderate-to-liberal segment of the Democratic party.

After some soul searching, Rostenkowski, who described himself as a "party man," agreed to take the chairmanship of Ways and Means. In March 1981, O'Neill's strategy seemed to be working as Rostenkowski announced that Democrats would propose substantial changes in the Reagan tax proposals. Other House Democratic leaders, including Jim Wright and James R. Jones of Oklahoma, the chairperson of the Budget Committee, argued against cuts in domestic spending that they said would only increase unemployment and swell the welfare rolls.

Then a combination of events created a wave of support for the President. His attempted assassination and dramatic return in a televised speech before a tumultuous joint session of Congress created an atmosphere in Washington and in the country that the White House exploited brilliantly. Appeals to the grass roots brought large numbers of letters and phone calls to Congresspersons. Administration lobbyists reminded representatives of the several standing ovations the President had received from Democrats and Republicans alike and traded favors for votes. The President himself met with many Congressmen, individually and in groups, and proved an effective persuader. Curiously, the Democratic leadership did little in response. Over the Easter recess, when the White House was making its strongest efforts, O'Neill and Rostenkowski went on vacation to New Zealand. Many wavering Democrats received several calls from the White House, but none from the Democratic leadership. When O'Neill returned to Washington, he disappointed liberal Democrats by conceding victory to the President, thus eliminating any chance to convert liberal Republicans or to hold conservative Democrats. After a coalition of conservative Democrats and Republicans passed the President's budget guidelines in May, some Democrats complained about their party's leadership.

Stung by the criticism and by the President's apparent refusal to compromise, O'Neill and the other Democratic leaders tried to rally their forces for a fight on the second stage of the budget process— the vote on the detailed budgets for specific programs produced by the Democratically controlled House committees. Again Reagan and his aides organized a strong campaign using the media, grass roots pressure, personal lobbying by the President, and old fashioned wheeling and dealing. Again the President won, as a similar coalition of Southern, conservative Democrats and Republicans voted for his substitute budget. The only remaining opportunity for a major Democratic victory was the issue of taxes.

The President had proposed a three year, twenty-five per cent tax reduction. Led by Rostenkowski, the Democrats on the Ways and Means Committee developed a tax reduction plan which they claimed was more prudent because it made a third year's tax reductions contingent on the state of the economy. They also said the President's plan favored the rich, whereas their plan gave more relief to the average American family. The President replied in a nationally televised address two days before the crucial House vote. He said that his three year proposal contained the only true tax cut and accused the Democrats of playing politics on the issue of economic recovery. His supporters organized further media efforts including full page ads in national newspapers. This combination generated hundreds of letters and phone calls to Democratic Congressmen. In one case the President added a phone call to a radio talk show in a wavering Democrat's district. That Congressman voted with the President. To pressure another Democrat the White House arranged to have his major campaign contributors telephone their support for the President's bill. He also voted with the President.

In addition to ideological appeals, both sides played old fashioned log-rolling politics. As he met individually with dozens of Representatives in the days before the vote, President Reagan would ask, "What can I do to help you make up your mind?" For one Oklahoma Congressman, a hand written note from the President pledging to veto any bill putting special taxes on gas producers seemed to make a difference. For others a promise to review the third year of the tax cut or to keep a minimum social security benefit proved decisive.

Of course, some of the same issues could be turned in the opposite direction. A promise to limit peanut imports, a matter of some concern for Georgia's Congressmen, carried at least by implication the threat to allow *more* foreign peanuts into the country. The Democratic leadership responded with threats and promises of its own, but had less to offer and was in no position to match the well financed, well organized Republican campaign coordinated from the White House.

The result was another triumph for the President. Some forty-eight Democrats crossed over to vote for his plan, whereas only one Republican defected. The critical vote was 238 to 195, the largest margin of victory of any of the three major domestic issues of 1981. The size of the margin and the scope and power of the President's (and the presidency's) efforts indicated that the White House would retain control of Congress on economic issues. Whether or not his power would extend to social issues such as school prayer and abortion remained to be seen.

In summary, the President used his electoral victory, the popular sympathy that followed the attempt on his life, extensive lobbying in Washington and at the grass roots, personal persuasion, horsetrading, and televised speeches to dominate Congress. In opposition, the Democrats lacked the resources and the skills to fight back effectively. Whether or not they can develop the necessary organization and leadership, and attract the necessary support are open questions.

Prospects

Several factors in the immediate future make the outlook for the Democratic party rather bleak. Many more Democratic Senators than Republicans are up for reelection in 1982. Thus, it is unlikely the Democrats can regain control of the Senate.

Second, the Republicans and associated interest groups such as the National Conservative Political Action Committee have organized very effective fund raising, candidate selection, and targeting operations. The last means that the Republicans can select congressional and state legislative districts where they have the best chance of winning. This is done by using computers to analyze data about social, economic, and political characteristics among the people of a particular area. Based on this analysis the Republican party can concentrate on districts that are relatively easy to win, thus maximizing the efficient use of its resources. A further, and perhaps even more important application of this practice, is in the process of **reapportionment**. As explained in Chapter 3, seats in the House of Representatives are apportioned to states according to population. Every ten years the Census provides the data for reapportionment. After reapportionment the state legislatures must redraw the lines for congressional districts in their state to take account of additions and subtractions. The computer analysis is particularly helpful in creating districts that give the party the maximum number of good chances to win. Experts in the field say that the Democrats lack the capacity to do this kind of analysis and that they are not likely to develop it. The necessary programs and data bases are expensive. Consequently, the Democrats are likely to lose House seats in 1982. They may well lose control of the House itself.

None of this means that the Democrats are doomed, of course. In 1974, after Watergate and the disastrous Congressional elections, the Republicans' prospects looked equally bad. Their remarkable recovery indicates that the issues of the day—inflation, economic growth, and energy will determine the parties' fates in the 1980s. If one party can satisfy a majority of voters on these issues, it will be the majority party for the last third of the twentieth century. Should the Reagan policies be "successful" in this sense, we will look back to 1980 as a critical election.

If neither party can satisfy a majority of the voters on these issues, then neither party will dominate, and voters will switch from one party to the other, as they switched from the Democrats to the Republicans in 1980, hoping that change will produce improvement. Eventually, voters may shift to a third party or become so discouraged that they will stop voting entirely.

Whatever the long term brings, the next two or three years are likely to be very important, perhaps even crucial in setting the trend. We hope this book has provided some of the information necessary to understand these years and to endure the mixed blessings of "interesting times."

GLOSSARY

Reapportionment The process, required by the Constitution, by which Congressional seats are alloted among the states, in proportion to population as determined by the census.

SUGGESTIONS FOR FURTHER READING

Pomper, Gerald. *The Election of 1980*. Chatham, N.J.: Chatham House, 1980.

Constitution of the United States

We the people of the United States, in order to form a more perfect union, establish justice, insure domestic tranquillity, provide for the common defense, promote the general welfare, and secure the blessings of liberty to ourselves and our posterity, do ordain and establish this Constitution for the United States of America.

Article 1

Section 1

All legislative powers herein granted shall be vested in a Congress of the United States, which shall consist of a Senate and House of Representatives.

Section 2

1. The House of Representatives shall be composed of members chosen every second year by the people of the several States, and the electors in each State shall have the qualifications requisite for electors of the most numerous branch of the State legislature.

2. No person shall be a representative who shall not have attained to the age of twenty-five years, and been seven years a citizen of the United States, and who shall not, when elected, be an inhabitant of that State in which he shall be chosen.

3. Representatives and direct taxes[1] shall be apportioned among the several States which may be included within this Union, according to their respective numbers, which shall be determined by adding to the whole number of free persons, including those bound to service for a term of years, and excluding Indians not taxed, three-fifths of all other persons.[2] The actual enumeration shall be made within three years after the first meeting of the Congress of the United States, and within every subsequent term of ten years, in such manner as they shall by law direct. The number of representatives shall not exceed one for every thirty thousand, but each State shall have at least one representative; and until such enumeration shall be made, the State of New Hampshire shall be entitled to choose three, Massachusetts eight, Rhode Island and Providence Plantations one, Connecticut five, New York, six, New Jersey four, Pennsylvania eight, Delaware one, Maryland six, Virginia ten, North Carolina five, South Carolina five, and Georgia three.

4. When vacancies happen in the representation from any State, the executive authority thereof shall issue writs of election to fill such vacancies.

5. The House of Representatives shall choose their speaker and other officers; and shall have the sole power of impeachment.

Section 3

1. The Senate of the United States shall be composed of two senators from each State, chosen by the legislature thereof,[3] for six years; and each senator shall have one vote.

2. Immediately after they shall be assembled in consequence of the first election, they shall be divided as equally as may be into three classes. The seats of the senators of the first class shall be vacated at the expiration of the second year, of the second class at the expiration of the fourth year, and of the third class at the expiration of the sixth year, so that one-third may be chosen every second year; and if vacancies happen by resignation, or otherwise, during the recess of the legislature of any State, the executive thereof may make temporary appointments until the next meeting of the legislature, which shall then fill such vacancies.[4]

---

[1] See the Sixteenth Amendment.
[2] Partly superseded by the Fourteenth Amendment.
[3] See the Seventeenth Amendment.
[4] See the Seventeenth Amendment.

3. No person shall be a senator who shall not have attained to the age of thirty years, and been nine years a citizen of the United States, and who shall not, when elected, be an inhabitant of that State for which he shall be chosen.

4. The Vice-President of the United States shall be President of the Senate, but shall have no vote, unless they be equally divided.

5. The Senate shall choose their other officers, and also a president *pro tempore,* in the absence of the Vice-President, or when he shall exercise the office of President of the United States.

6. The Senate shall have the sole power to try all impeachments. When sitting for that purpose, they shall be on oath or affirmation. When the President of the United States is tried, the chief justice shall preside: and no person shall be convicted without the concurrence of two-thirds of the members present.

7. Judgment in cases of impeachment shall not extend further than to removal from office, and disqualifications to hold and enjoy any office of honor, trust or profit under the United States: but the party convicted shall nevertheless be liable and subject to indictment, trial, judgment and punishment, according to law.

Section 4

1. The times, places, and manner of holding elections for senators and representatives, shall be prescribed in each State by the legislature thereof; but the Congress may at any time by law make or alter such regulations, except as to the places of choosing senators.

2. The Congress shall assemble at least once in every year, and such meeting shall be on the first Monday in December, unless they shall by law appoint a different day.

Section 5

1. Each House shall be the judge of the elections, returns and qualifications of its own members and majority of each shall constitute a quorum to do business; but a smaller number may adjourn from day to day, and may be authorized to compel the attendance of absent members, in such manner and under such penalties as each House may provide.

2. Each House may determine the rules of its proceedings, punish its members for disorderly behavior, and, with the concurrence of two-thirds, expel a member.

3. Each House shall keep a journal of its proceedings, and from time to time publish the same, excepting such parts as may in their

judgment require secrecy; and the yeas and nays of the members of either House on any question shall, at the desire of one-fifth of those present, be entered on the journal.

4. Neither House, during the session of Congress, shall, without the consent of the other, adjourn for more than three days, nor to any other place than that in which the two Houses shall be sitting.

Section 6

1. The senators and representatives shall receive a compensation for their services, to be ascertained by law, and paid out of the Treasury of the United States. They shall in all cases, except treason, felony and breach of the peace, be privileged from arrest during their attendance at the session of their respective Houses, and in going to and returning from the same; and for any speech or debate in either House, they shall not be questioned in any other place.

2. No senator or representative shall, during the time for which he was elected, be appointed to any civil office under the authority of the United States, which shall have been created, or the emoluments whereof shall have been increased during such time, and no person holding any office under the United States shall be a member of either House during his continuance in office.

Section 7

1. All bills for raising revenue shall originate in the House of Representatives; but the Senate may propose or concur with amendments as on other bills.

2. Every bill which shall have passed the House of Representatives and the Senate, shall, before it become a law, be presented to the President of the United States; if he approve he shall sign it, but if not he shall return it, with his objections to that House in which it shall have originated, who shall enter the objections at large on their journal, and proceed to reconsider it. If after such reconsideration two-thirds of that House shall agree to pass the bill, it shall be sent, together with the objections, to the other House, by which it shall likewise be reconsidered, and if approved by two thirds of that House, it shall become a law. But in all such cases the votes of both Houses shall be determined by yeas and nays, and the names of the persons voting for and against the bill shall be entered on the journal of each House respectively. If any bill shall not be returned by the President within ten days (Sundays excepted) after it shall have been

presented to him, the same shall be a law, in like manner as if he had signed it, unless the Congress by their adjournment prevent its return, in which case it shall not be a law.

3. Every order, resolution, or vote to which the concurrence of the Senate and House of Representatives may be necessary (except on a question of adjournment) shall be presented to the President of the United States; and before the same shall take effect, shall be approved by him, or being disapproved by him, shall be repassed by two thirds of the Senate and House of Representatives, according to the rules and limitations prescribed in the case of a bill.

Section 8

1. The Congress shall have the power to lay and collect taxes, duties, imposts, and excises, to pay the debts and provide for the common defense and general welfare of the United States; but all duties, imposts, and excises shall be uniform throughout the United States;

2. To borrow money on the credit of the United States;

3. To regulate commerce with foreign nations, and among the several States, and with the Indian tribes;

4. To establish an uniform rule of naturalization, and uniform laws on the subject of bankruptcies throughout the United States;

5. To coin money, regulate the value thereof, and of foreign coin, and fix the standard of weights and measures;

6. To provide for the punishment of counterfeiting the securities and current coin of the United States;

7. To establish post offices and post roads;

8. To promote the progress of science and useful arts, by securing for limited times to authors and inventors the exclusive right to their respective writings and discoveries;

9. To constitute tribunals inferior to the Supreme Court;

10. To define and punish piracies and felonies committed on the high seas, and offenses against the laws of nations;

11. To declare war, grant letters of marque and reprisal, and make rules concerning captures on land and water;

12. To raise and support armies, but no appropriation of money to that use shall be for a longer term than two years;

13. To provide and maintain a navy;

14. To make rules for the government and regulation of the land and naval forces;

15. To provide for calling forth the militia to execute the laws of the Union, suppress insurrections and repel invasions;

16. To provide for organizing, arming, and disciplining the militia, and for governing such part of them as may be employed in the service of the United States, reserving to the States respectively the appointment of the officers, and the authority of training the militia according to the discipline prescribed by Congress;

17. To exercise exclusive legislation in all cases whatsoever, over such district (not exceeding ten miles square) as may, by cession of particular States, and the acceptance of Congress, become the seat of the government of the United States, and to exercise like authority over all places purchased by the consent of the legislature of the State in which the same shall be, for the erection of forts, magazines, dockyards, and other needful buildings; and

18. To make all laws which shall be necessary and proper for carrying into execution the foregoing powers, and all other powers vested by this Constitution in the government of the United States, or in any department or officer thereof.

Section 9

1. The migration or importation of such persons as any of the States now existing shall think proper to admit, shall not be prohibited by the Congress prior to the year one thousand eight hundred and eight, but a tax or duty may be imposed on such importation, not exceeding ten dollars for each person.

2. The privilege of the writ of *habeas corpus* shall not be suspended, unless when in cases of rebellion or invasion the public safety may require it.

3. No bill of attainder or *ex post facto* law shall be passed.

4. No capitation, or other direct, tax shall be laid, unless in proportion to the census or enumeration hereinbefore directed to be taken.[5]

5. No tax or duty shall be laid on articles exported from any State.

6. No preference shall be given by any regulation of commerce or revenue to the ports of one State over those of another: nor shall vessels bound to, or from, one State be obliged to enter, clear, or pay duties in another.

[5] See the Sixteenth Amendment.

7. No money shall be drawn from the treasury, but in consequence of appropriations, made by law; and a regular statement and account of the receipts and expenditures of all public money shall be published from time to time.

8. No title of nobility shall be granted by the United States: and no person holding any office or profit or trust under them, shall, without the consent of the Congress, accept of any present, emolument, office, or title, of any kind whatever, from any king, prince, or foreign State.

Section 10

1. No State shall enter into any treaty, alliance, or confederation; grant letters of marque and reprisal; coin money; emit bills of credit; make anything but gold and silver coin a tender in payment of debts; pass any bill of attainder, *ex post facto* law, or law impairing the obligation of contracts, or grant any title of nobility.

2. No State shall, without the consent of the Congress, lay any imposts or duties on imports or exports, except what may be absolutely necessary for executing its inspection laws: and the net produce of all duties and imposts laid by any State on imports or exports, shall be of the use of the treasury of the United States; and all such laws shall be subject to the revision and control of the Congress.

3. No State shall, without the consent of Congress, lay any duty of tonnage, keep troops, or ships of war in time of peace, enter into any agreement or compact with another State, or with a foreign power, or engage in war, unless actually invaded, or in such imminent danger as will not admit of delay.

Article 2

Section 1

1. The executive power shall be vested in a President of the United States of America. He shall hold his office during the term of four years, and, together with the Vice-President, chosen for the same term, be elected, as follows:[6]

---

[6] See the Twenty-second Amendment.

2. Each State shall appoint, in such manner as the legislature thereof may direct, a number of electors, equal to the whole number of senators and representatives to which the State may be entitled in the Congress: but no senator or representative, or person holding an office of trust or profit under the United States, shall be appointed an elector.

The electors shall meet in their respective States, and vote by ballot for two persons, of whom one at least shall not be an inhabitant of the same State with themselves. And they shall make a list of all the persons voted for, and of the number of votes for each; which list they shall sign and certify, and transmit sealed to the seat of the government of the United States, directed to the president of the Senate. The president of the Senate shall, in the presence of the Senate and House of Representatives, open all certificates, and the votes shall then be counted. The person having the greatest number of votes shall be the President, if such number be a majority of the whole number of electors appointed; and if there be more than one who have such majority, and have an equal number of votes, then the House of Representatives shall immediately choose by ballot one of them for President; and if no person have a majority, then from the five highest on the list the said House shall in like manner choose the President. But in choosing the President, the votes shall be taken by States, the representation from each State having one vote; a quorum for this purpose shall consist of a member or members from two-thirds of the States, and a majority of all the States shall be necessary to a choice. In every case, after the choice of the President, the person having the greatest number of votes of the electors shall be the Vice-President. But if there should remain two or more who have equal votes, the Senate shall choose from them by ballot the Vice-President.[7]

3. The Congress may determine the time of choosing the electors, and the day on which they shall give their votes; which day shall be the same throughout the United States.

4. No person except a natural born citizen, or a citizen of the United States, at the time of the adoption of this Constitution, shall be eligible to the office of President; neither shall any person be eligible to that office who shall not have attained to the age of thirty-

[7] Superseded by the Twelfth Amendment.

five years, and been fourteen years a resident within the United States.

5. In case of the removal of the President from office, or of his death, resignation, or inability to discharge the powers and duties of the said office, the same shall devolve on the Vice-President, and the Congress may by law provide for the case of removal, death, resignation, or inability, both of the President and Vice-President, declaring what officer shall then act as President, and such officer shall act accordingly, until the disability be removed, or a President shall be elected.[8]

6. The President shall, at stated times, receive for his services a compensation, which shall neither be increased nor diminished during the period for which he shall have been elected, and he shall not receive within that period any other emolument from the United States, or any of them.

7. Before he enter on the execution of his office, he shall take the following oath or affirmation:—"I do solemnly swear (or affirm) that I will faithfully execute the office of President of the United States, and will to the best of my ability, preserve, protect and defend the Constitution of the United States."

Section 2

1. The President shall be commander in chief of the army and navy of the United States, and of the militia of the several States, when called into the actual service of the United States; he may require the opinion, in writing, of the principal officer in each of the executive departments, upon any subject relating to the duties of their respective offices, and he shall have power to grant reprieves and pardons for offenses against the United States, except in cases of impeachment.

2. He shall have power, by and with the advice and consent of the Senate, to make treaties, provided two thirds of the senators present concur; and he shall nominate, and by and with the advice and consent of the Senate, shall appoint ambassadors, other public ministers and consuls, judges of the Supreme Court, and all other officers of the United States, whose appointments are not herein otherwise provided for, and which shall be established by law; but the

[8] See the Twentieth Amendment and the Twenty-fifth Amendment.

Congress may by law vest the appointment of such inferior officers, as they think proper, in the President alone, in the courts of law, or in the heads of departments.

3. The President shall have power to fill up all vacancies that may happen during the recess of the Senate, by granting commissions which shall expire at the end of their next session.

Section 3

1. He shall from time to time give to the Congress information of the state of the Union, and recommend to their consideration such measures as he shall judge necessary and expedient; he may, on extraordinary occasions, convene both Houses, or either of them, and in case of disagreement between them with respect to the time of adjournment, he may adjourn them to such time as he shall think proper; he shall receive ambassadors and other public ministers; he shall take care that the laws be faithfully executed, and shall commission all the officers of the United States.

Section 4

The President, Vice-President, and all civil officers of the United States, shall be removed from office on impeachment for, and conviction of, treason, bribery, or other high crimes and misdemeanors.

Article 3

Section 1

The Judicial power of the United States shall be vested in one Supreme Court, and in such inferior courts as the Congress may from time to time ordain and establish. The judges, both of the Supreme and inferior courts, shall hold their offices during good behavior, and shall, at stated times, receive for their services, a compensation, which shall not be diminished during their continuance in office.

Section 2

1. The Judicial power shall extend to all cases, in law and equity, arising under this Constitution, the laws of the United States, and treaties made, or which shall be made, under their authority;—to all cases affecting ambassadors, other public ministers and consuls;—to

all cases of admiralty and maritime jurisdiction;—to controversies to which the United States shall be a party;—to controversies between two or more States;—between a state and citizens of another State;[9]—between citizens of different States,—between citizens of the same State claiming lands under grants of different States, and between a State, or the citizens thereof, and foreign States, citizens or subjects.

2. In all cases affecting ambassadors, other public ministers and consuls, and those in which a State shall be party, the Supreme Court shall have original jurisdiction. In all the other cases before mentioned, the Supreme Court shall have appellate jurisdiction, both as to law and to fact, with such exceptions, and under such regulations as the Congress shall make.

3. The trial of all crimes, except in cases of impeachment, shall be by jury; and such trial shall be held in the State where the said crimes shall have been committed; but when not committed within any State, the trial shall at such place or places as the Congress may by law have directed.

Section 3

1. Treason against the United States shall consist only in levying war against them, or in adhering to their enemies, giving them aid and comfort. No person shall be convicted of treason unless on the testimony of two witnesses to the same overt act, or on confession in open court.

2. The Congress shall have power to declare the punishment of treason, but no attainder of treason shall work corruption of blood, or forfeiture except during the life of the person attained.

Article 4

Section 1

Full faith and credit shall be given in each State to the public acts, records, and judicial proceedings of every other State. And the Congress may by general laws prescribe the manner in which acts, records and proceedings shall be proved, and the effect thereof.

---

[9] See the Eleventh Amendment.

Section 2

1. The citizens of each State shall be entitled to all privileges and immunities of citizens in the several States.

2. A person charged in any State with treason, felony, or other crime, who shall flee from justice, and be found in another State, shall on demand of the executive authority of the State from which he fled, be delivered up, to be removed to the State having jurisdiction of the crime.

3. No person held to service or labor in one State under the laws thereof, escaping into another, shall, in consequence of any law or regulation therein, be discharged from such service or labor, but shall be delivered up on claim of the party to whom such service or labor may be due.

Section 3

1. New States may be admitted by the Congress into this Union; but no new State shall be formed or erected within the jurisdiction of any other State; nor any State be formed by the junction of two or more States, or parts of States, without the consent of the legislatures of the States concerned as well as of the Congress.

2. The Congress shall have power to dispose of and make all needful rules and regulations respecting the territory or other property belonging to the United States; and nothing in this Constitution shall be so construed as to prejudice any claims of the United States, or of any particular State.

Section 4

The United States shall guarantee to every State in this Union a republican form of government, and shall protect each of them against invasion; and on application of the legislature, or of the executive (when the legislature cannot be convened) against domestic violence.

Article 5

The Congress, whenever two-thirds of both Houses shall deem it necessary, shall propose amendments to this Constitution, or, on the application of the legislatures of two-thirds of the several States, shall call a convention for proposing amendments, which, in either case, shall be valid to all intents and purposes, as part of this Constitution when ratified by the legislatures of three-fourths of the several States, or by conventions in three-fourths thereof, as the one or the other mode of ratification may be proposed by the Congress; Provided that no amendment which may be made prior to the year one thousand eight hundred and eight shall in any manner affect the first and fourth clauses in the ninth section of the first article; and that no State, without its consent, shall be deprived of its equal suffrage in the Senate.

Article 6

1. All debts contracted, and engagements entered into, before the adoption of this Constitution, shall be as valid against the United States under this Constitution, as under the Confederation.

2. This Constitution, and the laws of the United States which shall be made in pursuance thereof; and all treaties made, or which shall be made, under the authority of the United States, shall be the supreme law of the land; and the Judges in every State shall be bound thereby, anything in the Constitution or laws of any State to the contrary notwithstanding.

3. The senators and representatives before mentioned, and the members of the several State legislatures, and all executive and judicial officers, both of the United States and of the several States, shall be bound by oath or affirmation to support this Constitution; but no religious test shall ever be required as a qualification to any office or public trust under the United States.

Article 7

The ratification of the conventions of nine States shall be sufficient for the establishment of this Constitution between the States so ratifying the same.

Done in Convention by the unanimous consent of the States present the seventeenth day of September in the year of our Lord one thousand seven hundred and eighty-seven, and of the independence of the United States of America the twelfth. In witness whereof we have hereunto subscribed our names.

[Names omitted]

ARTICLES IN ADDITION TO, AND AMENDMENT OF, THE CONSTITU-
TION OF THE UNITED STATES OF AMERICA, PROPOSED BY CONGRESS,
AND RATIFIED BY THE LEGISLATURES OF THE SEVERAL STATES, PUR-
SUANT TO THE FIFTH ARTICLE OF THE ORIGINAL CONSTITUTION.*

*(The first 10 Amendments were ratified December 15, 1791, and form
what is known as the "Bill of Rights")*

Amendment 1

Congress shall make no law respecting an establishment of religion, or prohibiting the free exercise thereof; or abridging the freedom of speech, or of the press; or the right of the people peaceably
to assemble, and to petition the Government for a redress of
grievances.

Amendment 2

A well regulated Militia, being necessary to the security of a free
State, the right of the people to keep and bear Arms, shall not be
infringed.

Amendment 3

No Soldier shall, in time of peace be quartered in any house, without the consent of the Owner, nor in time of war, but in a manner to
be prescribed by law.

Amendment 4

The right of the people to be secure in their persons, houses,
papers, and effects, against unreasonable searches and seizures, shall
not be violated, and no Warrants shall issue, but upon probable

---

* Amendment 21 was not ratified by state legislatures, but by state conventions
summoned by Congress.

cause, supported by Oath or affirmation, and particularly describing the place to be searched, and the persons or things to be seized.

Amendment 5

No person shall be held to answer for a capital, or otherwise infamous crime, unless on a presentment or indictment of a Grand Jury, except in cases arising in the land or naval forces, or in the Militia, when in actual service in time of War or public danger; nor shall any person be subject for the same offence to be twice put in jeopardy of life or limb; nor shall be compelled in any criminal case to be a witness against himself, nor be deprived of life, liberty, or property, without due process of law; nor shall private property be taken for public use, without just compensation.

Amendment 6

In all criminal prosecutions, the accused shall enjoy the right to a speedy and public trial, by an impartial jury of the State and district wherein the crime shall have been committed, which district shall have been previously ascertained by law, and to be informed of the nature and cause of the accusation; to be confronted with the witnesses against him; to have compulsory process for obtaining witnesses in his favor, and to have the Assistance of Counsel for his defence.

Amendment 7

In suits at common law, where the value in controversy shall exceed twenty dollars, the right of trial by jury shall be preserved, and no fact tried by a jury, shall be otherwise reexamined in any Court of the United States, than according to the rules of the common law.

Amendment 8

Excessive bail shall not be required, nor excessive fines imposed, nor cruel and unusual punishments inflicted.

Amendment 9

The enumeration in the Constitution, of certain rights, shall not be construed to deny or disparage others retained by the people.

Amendment 10

The powers not delegated to the United States by the Constitution, nor prohibited by it to the States, are reserved to the States respectively, or to the people.

Amendment 11

(Ratified February 7, 1795)

The Judicial power of the United States shall not be construed to extend to any suit in law or equity, commenced or prosecuted against one of the United States by Citizens of another State, or by Citizens or Subjects of any Foreign State.

Amendment 12

(Ratified July 27, 1804)

The Electors shall meet in their respective states and vote by ballot for President and Vice-President, one of whom, at least, shall not be an inhabitant of the same state with themselves; they shall name in their ballots the person voted for as President, and in distinct ballots the person voted for as Vice-President, and they shall make distinct lists of all persons voted for as President, and of all persons voted for as Vice-President, and of the number of votes for each, which lists they shall sign and certify, and transmit sealed to the seat of the government of the United States, directed to the President of the Senate;—The President of the Senate shall, in presence of the Senate and House of Representatives, open all the certificates and the votes shall then be counted;—The person having the greatest number of votes for President, shall be the President, if such number be a majority of the whole number of Electors appointed; and if no person have such majority, then from the persons having the highest numbers not exceeding three on the list of those voted for as President, the House of Representatives shall choose immediately, by ballot, the President. But in choosing the President, the votes shall be taken by states, the representation from each state having one vote; a quorum for this purpose shall consist of a member or members from two-thirds of the states, and a majority of all the states shall be necessary to a choice. [And if the House of Representatives shall not choose a President whenever the right of choice shall devolve upon them, before the fourth day of March next following, then the Vice-President shall act as President, as in the case of the death or other constitutional disability of the President.—]* The person having the greatest number of votes as Vice-President, shall be the Vice-President, if such number be a majority of the whole number of Electors appointed, and if no person have a majority, then from the two highest numbers on the list, the Senate shall choose the Vice-President; a quorum for the purpose shall consist of two-thirds of the whole number of Senators, and a majority of the whole number shall be necessary to a choice. But no person constitutionally ineligible to the office of President shall be eligible to that of Vice-President of the United States.

Amendment 13

(Ratified December 6, 1865)

Section 1

Neither slavery nor involuntary servitude, except as a punishment for crime whereof the party shall have been duly convicted, shall exist within the United States, or any place subject to their jurisdiction.

Section 2

Congress shall have power to enforce this article by appropriate legislation.

* Superseded by section 3 of the twentieth amendment.

Amendment 14

(Ratified July 9, 1868)

Section 1

All persons born or naturalized in the United States, and subject to the jurisdiction thereof, are citizens of the United States and of the State wherein they reside. No State shall make or enforce any law which shall abridge the privileges or immunities of citizens of the United States; nor shall any State deprive any person of life, liberty, or property, without due process of law; nor deny to any person within its jurisdiction the equal protection of the laws.

Section 2

Representatives shall be apportioned among the several States according to their respective numbers, counting the whole number of persons in each State, excluding Indians not taxed. But when the right to vote at any election for the choice of electors for President and Vice-President of the United States, Representatives in Congress, the Executive and Judicial officers of a State, or the members of the Legislature thereof, is denied to any of the male inhabitants of such State, being twenty-one years of age,* and citizens of the United States, or in any way abridged, except for participation in rebellion, or other crime, the basis of representation therein shall be reduced in the proportion which the number of such male citizens shall bear to the whole number of male citizens twenty-one years of age in such State.

Section 3

No person shall be a Senator or Representative in Congress, or elector of President and Vice-President, or hold any office, civil or military, under the United States, or under any State, who, having previously taken an oath, as a member of Congress, or as an officer of the United States, or as a member of any State legislature, or as an executive or judicial officer of any State, to support the Constitution of the United States, shall have engaged in insurrection or rebellion against the same, or given aid or comfort to the enemies

---

* Changed by section 1 of the twenty-sixth amendment.

thereof. But Congress may by a vote of two-thirds of each House, remove such disability.

Section 4

The validity of the public debt of the United States, authorized by law, including debts incurred for payment of pensions and bounties for services in suppressing insurrection or rebellion, shall not be questioned. But neither the United States nor any State shall assume or pay any debt or obligation incurred in aid of insurrection or rebellion against the United States, or any claim for the loss or emancipation of any slave; but all such debts, obligations and claims shall be held illegal and void.

Section 5

The Congress shall have power to enforce, by appropriate legislation, the provisions of this article.

Amendment 15

(Ratified February 3, 1870)

Section 1

The right of citizens of the United States to vote shall not be denied or abridged by the United States or by any State on account of race, color, or previous condition of servitude—

Section 2

The Congress shall have power to enforce this article by appropriate legislation.

Amendment 16

(Ratified February 3, 1913)

The Congress shall have power to lay and collect taxes on incomes, from whatever source derived, without apportionment among the several States, and without regard to any census or enumeration.

Amendment 17

(Ratified April 8, 1913)

The Senate of the United States shall be composed of two Senators from each State, elected by the people thereof, for six years; and each Senator shall have one vote. The electors in each State shall have the qualifications requisite for electors of the most numerous branch of the State legislatures.

When vacancies happen in the representation of any State in the Senate, the executive authority of such State shall issue writs of election to fill such vacancies: *Provided,* That the legislature of any State may empower the executive thereof to make temporary appointments until the people fill the vacancies by election as the legislature may direct.

This amendment shall not be so construed as to affect the election or term of any Senator chosen before it becomes valid as part of the Constitution.

Amendment 18

(Ratified January 16, 1919)

Section 1

After one year from the ratification of this article the manufacture, sale, or transportation of intoxicating liquors within, the importation thereof into, or the exportation thereof from the United States and all territory subject to the jurisdiction thereof for beverage purposes is hereby prohibited.

Section 2

The Congress and the several States shall have concurrent power to enforce this article by appropriate legislation.

Section 3

This article shall be inoperative unless it shall have been ratified as an amendment to the Constitution by the legislatures of the several States as provided in the Constitution, within seven years from the date of the submission hereof to the States by the Congress.*

Amendment 19

(Ratified August 18, 1920)

The right of citizens of the United States to vote shall not be denied or abridged by the United States or by any State on account of sex.

Congress shall have power to enforce this article by appropriate legislation.

Amendment 20

(Ratified January 23, 1933)

Section 1

The terms of the President and Vice-President shall end at noon on the 20th day of January, and the terms of Senators and Representatives at noon on the 3d day of January, of the years in which such terms would have ended if this article had not been ratified; and the terms of their successors shall then begin.

Section 2

The Congress shall assemble at least once in every year, and such meeting shall begin at noon on the 3d day of January, unless they shall by law appoint a different day.

Section 3

If, at the time fixed for the beginning of the term of the President, the President elect shall have died, the Vice-President elect shall become President. If a President shall not have been chosen before the time fixed for the beginning of his term, or if the President elect

---

* Repealed by section 1 of the twenty-first amendment.

shall have failed to qualify, then the Vice-President elect shall act as President until a President shall have qualified; and the Congress may by law provide for the case wherein neither a President elect nor a Vice-President elect shall have qualified, declaring who shall then act as President, or the manner in which one who is to act shall be selected, and such person shall act accordingly until a President or Vice-President shall have qualified.

Section 4

The Congress may by law provide for the case of the death of any of the persons from whom the House of Representatives may choose a President whenever the right of choice shall have devolved upon them, and for the case of the death of any of the persons from whom the Senate may choose a Vice-President whenever the right of choice shall have devolved upon them.

Section 5

Sections 1 and 2 shall take effect on the 15th day of October following the ratification of this article.

Section 6

This article shall be inoperative unless it shall have been ratified as an amendment to the Constitution by the legislatures of three-fourths of the several States within seven years from the date of its submission.

Amendment 21

(Ratified December 5, 1933)

Section 1

The eighteenth article of amendment to the Constitution of the United States is hereby repealed.

Section 2

The transportation or importation into any State, Territory, or possession of the United States for delivery or use therein of intoxicating liquors, in violation of the laws thereof, is hereby prohibited.

Section 3

This article shall be inoperative unless it shall have been ratified as an amendment to the Constitution by conventions in the several States, as provided in the Constitution, within seven years from the date of the submission hereof to the States by the Congress.

Amendment 22

(Ratified February 27, 1951)

Section 1

No person shall be elected to the office of the President more than twice, and no person who has held the office of President, or acted as President, for more than two years of a term to which some other person was elected President shall be elected to the office of the President more than once. But this Article shall not apply to any person holding the office of President when this Article was proposed by the Congress, and shall not prevent any person who may be holding the office of President, or acting as President, during the term within which this Article becomes operative from holding the office of President or acting as President during the remainder of such term.

Section 2

This article shall be inoperative unless it shall have been ratified as an amendment to the Constitution by the legislatures of three-fourths of the several States within seven years from the data of its submission to the States by the Congress.

Amendment 23

(Ratified March 29, 1961)

Section 1

The District constituting the seat of Government of the United States shall appoint in such manner as the Congress may direct:

A number of electors of President and Vice-President equal to the whole number of Senators and Representatives in Congress to which the District would be entitled if it were a State, but in no event more than the least populous State; they shall be in addition to those appointed by the States, but they shall be considered, for the purposes of the election of President and Vice-President, to be electors appointed by a State; and they shall meet in the District and perform such duties as provided by the twelfth article of amendment.

Section 2

The Congress shall have power to enforce this article by appropriate legislation.

Amendment 24

(Ratified January 23, 1964)

Section 1

The right of citizens of the United States to vote in any primary or other election for President or Vice-President, for electors for President or Vice-President, or for Senator or Representative in Congress, shall not be denied or abridged by the United States or any State by reason of failure to pay any poll tax or other tax.

Section 2

The Congress shall have power to enforce this article by appropriate legislation.

Amendment 25

(Ratified February 10, 1967)

Section 1

In case of the removal of the President from office or of his death or resignation, the Vice-President shall become President.

Section 2

Whenever there is a vacancy in the office of the Vice-President, the President shall nominate a Vice-President who shall take office upon confirmation by a majority vote of both Houses of Congress.

Section 3

Whenever the President transmits to the President pro tempore of the Senate and the Speaker of the House of Representatives his written declaration that he is unable to discharge the powers and duties of his office, and until he transmits to them a written declaration to the contrary, such powers and duties shall be discharged by the Vice-President as Acting President.

Section 4

Whenever the Vice-President and a majority of either the principal officers of the executive departments or of such other body as Congress may by law provide, transmit to the President pro tempore of the Senate and the Speaker of the House of Representatives their written declaration that the President is unable to discharge the powers and duties of his office, the Vice-President shall immediately assume the powers and duties of the office as Acting President.

Thereafter, when the President transmits to the President pro tempore of the Senate and the Speaker of the House of Representatives his written declaration that no inability exists, he shall resume the powers and duties of his office unless the Vice-President and a majority of either the principal officers of the executive department or of such other body as Congress may by law provide, transmit within four days to the President pro tempore of the Senate and the Speaker of the House of Representatives their written declaration that the President is unable to discharge the powers and duties of his office. Thereupon Congress shall decide the issue, assembling within forty-eight hours for that purpose if not in session. If the Congress, within twenty-one days after receipt of the latter written declaration, or, if Congress is not in session, within twenty-one days after Congress is required to assemble, determines by two-thirds vote of both Houses that the President is unable to discharge the powers and duties of his office, the Vice-President shall continue to discharge the same as Acting President; otherwise, the President shall resume the powers and duties of his office.

Amendment 26

(Ratified July 1, 1971)

Section 1
The right of citizens of the United States, who are eighteen years of age or older, to vote shall not be denied or abridged by the United States or by any State on account of age.

Section 2
The Congress shall have power to enforce this article by appropriate legislation.

Proposed Amendment 27

(Proposed March 22, 1972)

Section 1
Equality of rights under the law shall not be denied or abridged by the United States or by any State on account of sex.

Section 2
The Congress shall have power to enforce, by appropriate legislation, the provisions of this article.

Section 3
This amendment shall take effect two years after date of ratification.

Index